Danger, Duty,
and Disillusion

Danger, Duty, and Disillusion

The Worldview of
Los Angeles Police Officers

Joan C. Barker
Santa Monica College

WAVELAND
PRESS, INC.
Prospect Heights, Illinois

For information about this book, write or call:
Waveland Press, Inc.
P.O. Box 400
Prospect Heights, Illinois 60070
(847) 634-0081

All text photos and cover (lower-left and right) by Gene Blevins
except pages 1, 63, and cover (upper-left) by David Butow.

Contents

Acknowledgments

This is always the part of the book when authors thank numerous other folk and say that "of course any errors are mine alone . . ."—now I know why. I have benefitted mightily from the input of many persons; this book, and the earlier study from which it draws heavily, would not be possible without the sometimes wary, sometimes gracious, occasionally uplifting, often sad—always engaging—help of many, many officers with the Los Angeles Police Department. For obvious reasons and following the conventions of the discipline they will remain anonymous. Fortunately they know who they are and, I hope, know how thankful I am for their trust, words and friendship. In addition to the folks in blue, my dear friends and colleagues Jan Austin and Karin Costello were a constant source of support and comfort. In addition to their overall support, Jan brought her keen analytical mind and skills as an anthropologist to our lunch-table discussions, while Karin, master of the language, probing questioner and reader extraordinare made many insightful, useful suggestions—many of which saved me from public embarrassment. The book-project would never have taken place had it not been for the early support of Mari Womack, and my thanks to her are deep and heartfelt. This work has also been processed through two extremely thoughtful students, Terri Butow and Suzanne Pelka, both of whom took time from their very full calendars to read versions and share their responses and suggestions. The editors at Waveland made the process as painless as possible— Tom Curtin who encouraged me to submit a manuscript and then waited patiently for me to do so, giving good advice and support each step of the way. Jeni Ogilvie, without whom I can honestly say this work would never have seen the light of day, is a dream-editor. Her gentle guidance, knowledge of the field and keen eye have greatly improved the presentation in numerous ways. To all of you my thanks are boundless. Yet even having said that, I must reserve the greatest measure of thanks for my husband, David, who has always believed in me and my work and has, in so many ways, made this all possible.

Preface

This study of street officers working for the Los Angeles Police Department was conducted over a period of many years, beginning in 1976, coinciding with various times when the department was in a state of disruption. This book presents an insider's perspective on the police, how *they* see the job of policing, not a critical analysis of what they do. The focus of this study is on street officers and the five phases of occupational socialization which normatively mold their experiences and perceptions. This is the job as Los Angeles Police patrol officers experience and describe it. Direct quotes from taped interviews of officers are used as much as possible, and some of these are fairly lengthy to provide relevant human and situational context. Any emphasis indicated in the quotes reflect the sentiment of the officer, not the ethnographer.

As officers learn the job and become occupationally socialized, their views of the job and the concerns they express change. With an analysis of the five phases of the career of a police officer we find that these changes are consistent and predictable. As is true of many of us, officers often fail to see patterns, and shifts of patterns, in their lives. They often believe themselves to be quite atypical, even unique, in their feelings, fears and concerns. Of course not every officer in the department goes through all of the phases, but the vast majority of officers do. It is too soon to tell whether the career trajectories and the phases of the careers will continue to reflect the same patterns. Time, and further research, will tell.

Chapter one provides an overview of the structure of the Los Angeles Police Department, its setting, history and organization, and provides insight into being a police officer.

Chapter two discusses the way the research was conducted and the significant difficulties and successes in conducting the study. Police are noted for being difficult subjects to study, and they have the ability and inclination to say "no" to such invasions of their well-guarded privacy. Issues of access, insider/outsider perspectives and rapport are addressed.

Chapter three presents the officers' views of the structure of the job, the world of policing and the attendant issues of the danger inherent in the job, and the duties they perform.

Chapter four presents the *first phase,* "Hitting the Streets," of occupational socialization: the first three years of the job. This phase covers officers' introduction to policing the streets and is subdivided into three stages: (1) their training at the academy; (2) an early stage of initiation into the department and the working watch where they get a taste of the streets, meet the requirements of the department, and satisfy the official period of probation; and (3) the last stage, when they prove themselves as they absorb the informal, as well as formal, teachings of their colleagues and begin to learn the realities of the street and how to do the job.

In chapter five, "Hitting Their Stride," officers enter the *second phase* of career development. This is roughly a five-year phase in which the officers gain confidence and, within certain perimeters, develop their own work rhythm and style of policing. Their lives continue to be drawn into conformity with police perceptions and practices. In this phase officers not only develop competence, but also begin to express feelings of discontent regarding some unavoidable aspects of the job.

The sixth chapter examines the *third phase,* "Hitting the Wall," when officers begin to question many aspects of the job and become disillusioned with many essential components of urban policing. This is a time, lasting roughly four years, when they recognize and acknowledge the nature and extent of their adversity/distress and set about finding ways of coping with their disillusion.

The *fourth phase,* "Regrouping," is covered in the seventh chapter. It focuses on the ways officers deal with or resolve the issues raised during the tumult of the third phase. They re-evaluate their careers and choices and determine a course of action and strategy for finishing the career. Often they make major changes in their lives, personal and professional. This can also be a time of mellowing. This fourth phase lasts until the time when they are permitted to retire, although they may not exercise this option.

Chapter eight covers the *fifth phase,* "Deciding to Retire." While police officers have the opportunity to retire at a fairly early age, many factors enter into the decision to do so. It is rarely an easy decision. Retiring from the police force is fraught with a constellation of considerations unique, perhaps, to this profession.

The ninth chapter, "Reflections of a Traditional Officer," is, to me, the single most important chapter of this work on many levels. "Fred," my informant, is extremely articulate and very willing to share his story, which provides the kind of raw material from which we can glean data to explore and understand human actions and interactions. This chapter provides the "fleshing out" of the academic abstraction of "police officer" into the human. At the same time, I would be reluctant to have anyone read the selection without the matrix of the book to provide essential information for processing the account. Together the analysis and the human who has lived the job provide an opportunity for understanding, which is seldom available.

The final chapter, "Making a Difference," focuses on some of the recent developments in the Los Angeles Police Department which may have implications for the future of the city, for the department, and for other research possibilities. Some of the issues and problems that have become intensified in recent years are briefly addressed. But it is racial polarization—perhaps always a subtext—that has taken center stage in police, government and community concerns and has played a major role in the "institutional" and "personal" life of the L.A.P.D. While there continue to be problems (this work is to some extent problem-oriented because that is what emerges from the data), the job of an officer is such an important one that the need to understand and deal with any of its aspects over which we have control is crucial.

It is important for us to realize that even in the midst of their criticisms and disillusion, officers are proud of the work they do, and value this complex and demanding career.

1

The L.A.P.D.

The Los Angeles Police Department serves a city of 4.5 million people and has a police force of approximately eleven thousand: over eight thousand sworn officers and more than three thousand civilian employees. Statistically, the L.A.P.D. is one of the smallest in the nation in terms of numbers of officers per population and is responsible for a very large geographical area. The 4.5 million population figure is somewhat misleading, since the city of Los Angeles is part of a continuous metropolitan area with a population of 14.5 million. This urban patchwork complicates the job of policing because, while suspects can move freely across city boundaries, it is more difficult for police to do so. Jurisdictional differences can impede investigations, increase paperwork and make it more difficult for police to spot crime patterns quickly.

The department was established in 1869 and has undergone many changes. From 1950 to 1966, Police Chief William Parker transformed the L.A.P.D. from an agency with a reputation for corruption into one that has had, in law enforcement circles, one of the best reputations in terms of honesty and integrity, and in setting law enforcement standards and practices. The department has not enjoyed the same glowing reputation in all circles. While white middle-class inhabitants of the city have often felt the department was providing good service, the minority community has not shared these views. The relationship between the African-American community and the police has been particularly problematic. Until fairly recently the tensions between the police and minority communities had not permeated the consciousness of the general public, and nationally the L.A.P.D. has enjoyed a good reputation.

This positive reputation has been important to the agency and its administrators, but is even more important to the officers themselves. It is both a source of pride and also a vehicle for mobility when officers decide to seek work in another law enforcement agency or consider a career independent of policing. The department's reputation is now in decline—some might say it has hit rock bottom—and many officers feel the agency has been coasting on its past performance. While acknowledging problems in the department, virtually all officers feel that the agency has been victimized by excessive and unfair criticism, especially in the

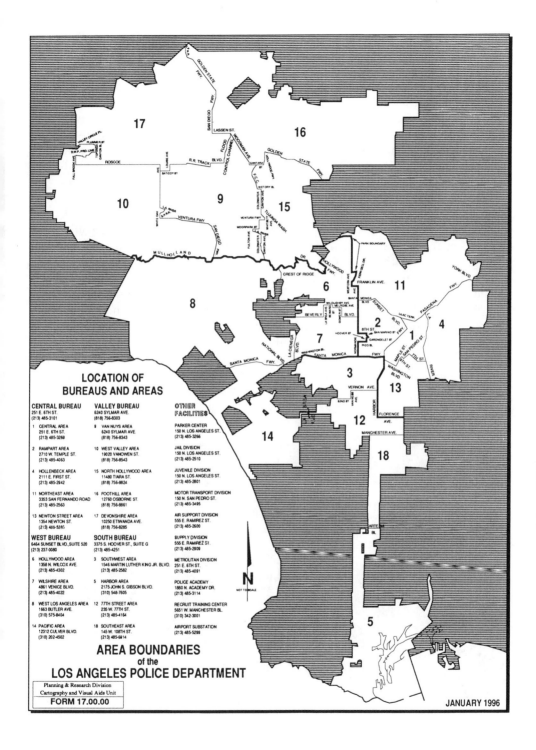

LOCATION OF BUREAUS AND AREAS

CENTRAL BUREAU
251 E. 6TH ST.
(213) 485-3101

1 CENTRAL AREA
251 E. 6TH ST.
(213) 485-3269

2 RAMPART AREA
2710 W. TEMPLE ST.
(213) 485-4063

4 HOLLENBECK AREA
2111 E. FIRST ST.
(213) 485-2942

11 NORTHEAST AREA
3353 SAN FERNANDO ROAD
(213) 485-2563

13 NEWTON STREET AREA
1354 NEWTON ST.
(213) 485-5285

WEST BUREAU
6464 SUNSET BLVD., SUITE 520
(213) 237-0080

6 HOLLYWOOD AREA
1358 N. WILCOX AVE.
(213) 485-4302

7 WILSHIRE AREA
4861 VENICE BLVD.
(213) 485-4022

8 WEST LOS ANGELES AREA
1663 BUTLER AVE.
(310) 575-8404

14 PACIFIC AREA
12312 CULVER BLVD.
(310) 202-4502

VALLEY BUREAU
6240 SYLMAR AVE.
(818) 756-8303

9 VAN NUYS AREA
6240 SYLMAR AVE.
(818) 756-8343

10 WEST VALLEY AREA
19020 VANOWEN ST.
(818) 756-8543

15 NORTH HOLLYWOOD AREA
11480 TIARA ST.
(818) 756-8824

16 FOOTHILL AREA
12760 OSBORNE ST.
(818) 756-8861

17 DEVONSHIRE AREA
10250 ETIWANDA AVE.
(818) 756-8285

SOUTH BUREAU
3375 S. HOOVER ST., SUITE G
(213) 485-4251

3 SOUTHWEST AREA
1546 MARTIN LUTHER KING JR. BLVD.
(213) 485-2582

5 HARBOR AREA
2175 JOHN S. GIBSON BLVD.
(310) 548-7605

12 77TH STREET AREA
235 W. 77TH ST.
(213) 485-4164

18 SOUTHEAST AREA
145 W. 108TH ST.
(213) 485-6914

OTHER FACILITIES

PARKER CENTER
150 N. LOS ANGELES ST.
(213) 485-3266

JAIL DIVISION
150 N. LOS ANGELES ST.
(213) 485-2510

JUVENILE DIVISION
150 N. LOS ANGELES ST.
(213) 485-2801

MOTOR TRANSPORT DIVISION
150 N. SAN PEDRO ST.
(213) 485-3495

AIR SUPPORT DIVISION
555 E. RAMIREZ ST.
(213) 485-2600

SUPPLY DIVISION
555 E. RAMIREZ ST.
(213) 485-2909

METROLITAN DIVISION
251 E. 6TH ST.
(213) 485-4091

POLICE ACADEMY
1880 N. ACADEMY DR.
(213) 485-3114

RECRUIT TRAINING CENTER
5651 W. MANCHESTER BL.
(310) 342-3001

AIRPORT SUBSTATION
(213) 485-5299

N
NOT TO SCALE

AREA BOUNDARIES
of the
LOS ANGELES POLICE DEPARTMENT

Planning & Research Division
Cartography and Visual Aids Unit
FORM 17.00.00

JANUARY 1996

3

media. Although many are hopeful that the positive aspects of the department will receive renewed attention, many more are convinced that will never happen.

The perceived erosion of the department's reputation in the view of veteran officers, and even some newer recruits, has influenced many of their career decisions. Veteran officers may decide to retire as soon as possible; newer officers may stay on the job just long enough to establish themselves as competent officers so they can apply for jobs in other agencies and have a head start on promotion.

Traditionally, other agencies have been eager to hire officers with experience on the L.A.P.D. In five years with the department, these officers see more than police in smaller departments may see in their entire careers. In addition to dealing with natural disasters—earthquakes, fires, floods and mudslides—the human element also provides officers with many varied experiences. This is largely due to the cosmopolitan nature of Los Angeles and environs. The extreme economic diversity and heterogeneity of the population is a fertile ground for conflicts and for acting out statements on every sort of political and social issue.

L.A. police officers have faced a wide variety of demonstrations— from peaceful protests to assassinations of international political figures. Presidential visits are common, and chief executive officers and film per-

sonalities must be protected during their public appearances. In addition, the department is responsible for policing the Los Angeles International Airport, with all its potential for crises. There are approximately two thousand calls for service throughout the city in a twenty-four-hour period.

While technically the department has always had an open recruitment policy—the first African-American officer was hired in 1886, the first woman officer in 1903—the department was predominantly a white male domain until 1980 when affirmative action policies were implemented. These policies required the department to increase the number of female officers to 20 percent and the numbers of African-American and Latino(a) officers to correspond to their percentage of the metropolitan workforce. Prior to this "affirmative action" mandate, numbers of women in the department were low and female officers were generally restricted to cases involving home and hearth: abused and neglected children; truancy; and interviewing female victims of physical abuse, rape and incest. Women were not assigned to patrol duty, regarded by most traditional officers as real police work, nor were they assigned to domestic disputes, since these were viewed as being too dangerous.

ORGANIZATION

As is true with police departments in general, the L.A.P.D. is paramilitary in nature and is a bureaucracy, divided into special divisions and units run by a hierarchical chain of command. The department is advised and administered by the police commission and the chief of police. Of far greater importance to officers is the division of the department into the headquarters, Parker Center, and four operations bureaus.

Parker Center contains many of the more specialized units and support systems for the entire department. It is the home office for traffic coordination, crime laboratories and tactical planning. In addition, there is also an extensive bureaucracy for dealing with employee relations, the press, special events coordination, administrative services, support services, fiscal support, training, and other special services.

The four operations bureaus represent geographical and administrative districts, each of which is further broken down into individual precincts, or divisions. Each bureau contains four or five geographically based divisions and a traffic division deployed within the area covered by the entire operations bureau. While these divisions are not autonomous or self-contained, they do have different personalities that reflect the policing demands of the particular region of the city they serve. Some divisions are located in inner-city or other high-crime, high-poverty areas;

others, located in affluent regions of the city, are known as "silk stocking" divisions. Though these differences may affect rates of certain types of crimes, as many officers say, "There's no King's X," meaning that all types of crimes occur in every part of the city. A police cliché is that "you'll see it all in twenty years."

TRADITIONAL AND NEW POLICE

Initially the police career was twenty years, the length of time required for an officer to become eligible to retire with a pension. Many officers stay on the job longer and many do not make it to twenty years, but the twenty-year mark is both an administrative milestone and a symbolic goal. Leaving the department with less than twenty years means either that the officer has been fired or has resigned—in which case there is no pension—or that the officer has become injured to such an extent that he/she cannot continue the job of policing. "Doing twenty" is commonly regarded as having completed the police career, although many officers stay longer.

Officers consciously use years on the job to evaluate another officer and to set the tone for interaction with that officer. Thus, among colleagues, a twenty-year officer may well have more status than other officers of higher rank in the department. It is, of course, a different kind of rank, signifying degree of socialization into police culture and experience. Years on the job may be the only necessary information for the assessment of another officer's actions or stance on an issue. This point is frequently stressed to officers viewed as not having enough "time on" to know what they're talking about.

Years on the job also create generational differences that often generate communication problems found in many social groups, and, in spite of their emphasis on solidarity, police are no exception to this rule. However, for police, generational conflict has been accentuated by changes in hiring, training, and promotional policies accompanying implementation of affirmative action guidelines in the 1980s.

These abrupt policy changes have produced essentially two distinct categories of police: traditional and new. Traditional police are those hired during the period when the force was made up primarily of white males— before 1979, the year a cluster of lawsuits was filed against the department resulting in dramatic changes in hiring practices. New police refers to those officers hired after 1979 and includes significantly larger numbers of women and minorities, making up a force that is more racially, ethnically and sexually diverse. It would be simple to view differences between the two groups based on the differences in diversity between the old order and the new. While such simplicity would avoid some of the tougher questions and appear more balanced, it would be a distortion.

The diversity built into the new police, and relative lack of it in traditional police, has highlighted and exacerbated processes that not only emphasize differences found between the two groups, but also hinder the development of solidarity within the department in general and even among the ranks of the new police. Thus, it is much easier to find and document patterns and consensus among traditional police. For this reason in those chapters focusing on the phases of the career (chapters 4–8), the traditional view is well represented while new police perceptions are not as often specifically cited. This should not be construed to be an endorsement of the traditional view. Views shared by both simply will be cited as "police" views; when there appears to be a difference in the perceptions of the two groups, whenever possible both views will be cited. Rather than stretch the data to make for the appearance of balance, this work will reflect what is known.

At this time, a brief comparison of the views of traditional and new police is appropriate in the following discussion of recruitment, retention, recreation, attitude toward the job and proactive policing. Knowledge of these important components of policing in Los Angeles will provide the necessary groundwork for the rest of the book.

Recruitment

Both traditional and new police include male and female officers from various ethnic backgrounds. However, as previously mentioned, there are significantly greater numbers of women and minorities among new police. Traditionally, recruits on the L.A.P.D. were predominantly white males, with military experience, from lower to lower-middle socioeconomic strata. Recruits must be at least twenty years and six months (therefore they will be twenty-one by the time they hit the streets) and not older than thirty-five years of age. They must have a U.S. high school diploma or GED equivalent and be a U.S. citizen, or have applied for citizenship, with no felony convictions. Recruits must pass an entrance exam that tests their basic literacy, general knowledge, problem-solving skills and attitudinal/psychological profile. The exam is followed by interviews, sometimes a visit to a department psychologist, and a background check.

Traditional police cite varying combinations of four principal motivations for becoming police: (1) they had relatives or friends on the job who had encouraged them to join; (2) they were just out of the military and felt that policing would be something familiar that they understood, could do, and would be "a step up"; (3) they felt that the job of policing was honorable and that the kind of work and situations they would encounter would be exciting; or (4) they were idealistic and felt they could "make a difference," or "make a change for the positive." Almost all of the traditional officers cited idealism as a primary reason for joining, along with one or more other factors. Financial considerations were well represented, but rarely mentioned as either primary or even secondary motivations. Pre-1979 recruits were also motivated by the relatively high pay for unskilled workers without college degrees.

Affirmative action policies implemented in 1979 mandated that each academy class contain 50 percent minority representation, made up of a minimum of 25 percent women. Male minority recruits tend to be African American and Latino, predominately from lower socioeconomic groups, with a small number of individuals from lower-middle socioeconomic groups. Female recruits tend to be from upper-middle socioeconomic backgrounds if white, predominately lower to lower-middle socioeconomic backgrounds if African American or Latina. There are very few female Asian-American recruits; male Asian-American recruits generally come from upper-middle-class backgrounds.

Virtually all new police lack military experience. They tend to be motivated to join the department by economic considerations, as well as by the image of the job as exciting, and to some degree powerful. Almost all of the new officers mentioned economic motivations, the benefits as well as starting pay, which is over $40,000, as their primary reason for joining. The potential excitement of the job was often linked with idealism as additional motivation.

Both new and traditional police cite a desire to make a contribution and serve society. This is consistent with results of research conducted by John Stratton among Los Angeles County Sheriff recruits:

> In exploring the motives that lead young people into law enforcement, studies have shown that the desire to serve society is very high on the list. In a study of over 800 cadets, 50 percent listed service to society, helping and working with people, as their foremost reason for wanting to be police officers. (1984:32)

I suspect this 50 percent figure is low for traditional officers on the L.A.P.D. Traditional officers often speak about the job in very ideal terms. They comment about using the job as a way to "do good," "make it better," to "stand for something clean and good," and to "make a difference."

One traditional officer joined the department on the advice of a much-admired friend:

> I didn't know what I was getting into at the time I decided to join. I hadn't made up my mind, but I was at the point where I had to get going with a job or had to go back to school and use my G.I. Bill to finish my B.S. My friend is a copper in Newton and he told me about the job. He said he thought I should check it out, and he thought I'd make a good cop. I truly respected him and figured if he was [a cop]

being a cop might be a way to do something. It sounds stupid, but I thought I could do something for the good, to help people, to save people. . . . The rest of it seemed pretty good, too. I didn't have my college finished, and I wasn't trained in anything in particular. I mean the skills I had weren't exactly in demand, and I could live on what they [the department] paid. Real secure—and the job sounded like I could do a good job, make decent money, work that I could be proud of, and not get bored.

Another officer considered himself lucky to be selected for what he had considered an elite job:

I didn't plan to be a police officer. It never occurred to me until a friend told me they were taking applications. I don't know how I thought people became officers. I just didn't think that they advertised, and just took people off the street to do the job. I was surprised. I DID NOT think that they'd select me for a job like that. Wow. I was so impressed. [I] got fingerprinted, and carried my forms, sure all the time that they'd tell me that it was all a mistake, that they couldn't possibly take me. I figured it was too important a job for a guy like me.

New police focus much less on the idealistic components of policing and tend not to consider themselves committed to the job for twenty years. Instead they emphasize economic benefits, job security, using the job as a stepping stone to another career, and the excitement of the job. One new female officer describes her attitude toward the job:

My theory in life is, everything you do in life leads to the next thing . . . I was working down at the county jail. It was when the big push came on for women, and I used to talk with all the deputies, and they were looking to hire—the Sheriff's Department as well as the P.D., and I got to thinking, working a patrol car . . . you'd never know what you were going to get. Every day would be different, and I need little spurts of adrenaline and excitement during the day. . . . I don't really fit the image of what the department wants . . . I mean I know these people who just *live* for the department, twenty-four hours a day, and I guess it's really good to be loyal to that extent, but I don't think that it's healthy. You need a balanced life. You need your off time to go off and travel and vacation and have fun, see your friends, and do all that other stuff . . . one reason I left Mental Health was an eight-thousand-dollar increase. Even though I had my master's degree, working with the Department of Mental Health, I went into the academy as an idiot recruit and I still made eight-thousand dollars more. I won't get rich on it, but I get enough so I can pay my bills, and go out and have fun vacations, and buy neat toys—and have job security.

At the time of the interview, this officer had been on the job for only two years; nevertheless, she was a respected officer. This probably had to do with the fact that she was not a small woman (5' 6"). She was strong and mature at 32 and, above all, she was street smart. She already knew how to read situations on the streets because of her experience with working with psychiatric emergency intervention teams.

There have also been changes in standards for recruits' background searches, a procedure aimed at uncovering anything in applicants' lives that would indicate they are unacceptable as police officers. A police academy instructor provides one example:

> With "background," when we came on the job, illegal drug use was a disqualifier. Now it's within a certain range. Now an applicant can come in and say, "Yes, I smoked marijuana, or did pills so many times," and, if they're within the acceptable range, it's okay. We will accept that candidate. It's not disqualifying anymore, but that just reflects what's gone on in this society. It's dealing with reality. When we came on the job, there were lots of people who had never tried marijuana, never did any drugs, but that just isn't true anymore.

The instructor suggests that relaxed standards in background searches are due to hiring needs:

> We have about a five-hundred-officer attrition rate per year; that's just from officers pensioning off, or retiring, or leaving for whatever reason. For the last three years, we've been trying to boost our numbers, so we have been trying to hire an extra one-thousand officers each year. That means we interview forty to fifty thousand applicants to come up with one thousand who get into the academy. If we're talking written examination, we probably give close to one hundred thousand of those just to get down to the forty to fifty thousand we interview. If we said "never, ever, had any illegal drug use," we would never fill those positions. If we did, the person might be socially retarded. So now we're going with a range that we think will not exclude what you might call "normal" exposure to illegal drug use. Says something, doesn't it?

Traditional police often view new police with disdain because of what the former views as lowered standards in hiring. This is particularly true of the hiring of smaller officers who are often considered to be a liability rather than an asset in a physical confrontation. It is a widely held perception of officers that shorter officers cannot provide appropriate physical back-up, and worse yet, might even require extra protection. There are other issues that involve the height of officers. For example, traditionally the officer with more time on the job had the choice of driving or keeping the log. This choice has been a sign of status and respect for seniority. However, due to the wide variation in officers' height, senior officers no longer have this choice. The vast majority of police cars have bench seats, requiring that the taller officer (usually the senior) be the driver; if the bench seat is brought forward to accommodate the shorter officer, the taller person cannot ride comfortably. While not having the choice between driving and riding may sound like a petty concern, it is tied to critical elements in the police officers' worldview.

Some dissatisfaction on the part of traditional police also comes from their perception that new police have no real commitment to police work, beyond the paycheck. Partially this is due to the differing ways in which traditional and new police value the idealistic and economic aspects of the job.

Early in their careers, traditional police more often stated idealistic reasons for joining the department than did new police, although this may be tied to societal shifts rather than characteristic of differing police populations. Traditional police are less idealistic than they like to think of themselves, and new police are more idealistic than they like to admit. Both reflect cultural values of their place and time.

Retention

Prior to implementation of affirmative action policies, screening out candidates during police academy training was common. According to one training officer:

> Most of the time [before the late 1970s], if you saw someone, and you knew that person just wasn't going to make it on the streets, you'd tell him to resign. Then in several cases, where someone re-signed "under duress," he would file a case. The court would some-times take three or four years to find that this person should have his job back. So then the city was ordered to give him back pay. Po-liceman's pay for three or four years of nothing. Then, on top of that, you had someone who really wasn't suited to do police work on the job. It didn't take too many of those before the city made it real dif-ficult to fire them.

The training officer is referring to several successful lawsuits filed against the city in the 1980s claiming recruits had been washed out due to racial or sexual bias on the part of the instructors. In the latter part of that decade, there was a marked turnover of faculty at the academy, largely because training officers quit over loss of their discretionary power to eliminate those they perceived as problem officers:

> The staff used to have more latitude about the trainees. Now what with case law and labor laws and employment laws, we don't have the discretion we used to have, because you really can spot someone who just doesn't fit in. You used to set a run, and you'd watch and there would be one guy lagging behind, usually the same guy, and

you'd ride him. Partly, just to see how he'll respond—does he blame something else, does he whine, is it excuse this, and excuse that? And then there's attitude. Sometimes they weren't really failing anything, they were just a shithead. You'd pull out the resignation of position sheet and have them sign it. You knew they weren't going to work out.

The training officer notes that attitude, which is closely associated with collegiality, is important on the job:

> You'll hear hundreds of horror stories. Quite often with unsavory cadets, it's attitude. If they're a loner, or argumentative, belligerent, the staff will try to let them know. If nothing else, the job, being a police officer, requires being able to operate and function in a group of people. If you are not accepted by the peer group you cannot function. But we don't have the latitude with attitude we used to have.

Recreation

Recreational events are a focal point of exchange of information and testing as well as providing a setting for further reinforcement of occupational values and can be a powerful agent of solidarity. Officers who spend time together in off-duty activities such as listening to music, playing sports, dining, going to bars, and attending lectures, come to see each other in fuller measure than officers who do not have shared experiences. This seems fairly self-evident. Virtually any shared activity fosters group unity, some more so than others. Sporting events are legendary in their ability to create solidarity.

Tests of any sort are revealing. This is particularly true of the kind of testing that takes place in recreational sport activities of police officers. Among these are tests of physical abilities and willingness to take risks, the ability to evaluate unnecessary risks and to demonstrate resourcefulness, reliability, and a sense of humor and proportion. Participants pay attention to who is willing to play hurt, who can avoid getting hurt, people who consistently assign blame to anyone or thing other than themselves, good sports, poor sports—all important information.

Following the recreational activity, or as a part of it, traditional officers usually relax, eat and converse together. Depending on the context of the activity, often not only the officers but also their families are involved, fostering even greater interaction and embeddedness within the police community. The majority of new officers, on the other hand, do not seem to be interested in socializing with other police off duty; this is often viewed by traditional police as a lack of commitment.

Attitudes

Traditional officers are concerned because they perceive that new police not only lack commitment to the job, but even more importantly, they don't care about fellow officers. A traditional African-American female officer was especially critical of new women police:

> The females are just here to find husbands. I wouldn't want to work with them. They're not here to do police work. The other day [a male officer] was working with [a female officer], and he was struggling with this suspect. His partner didn't come to his aid; she just stood there. She didn't do anything. Finally some citizen helped [him]. When it was all over she just called it in. No discussion. [He] was so mad. [Gesturing around the restaurant where the interview took place.] Now I ask you, you see these waitresses and folks around here, if someone came in here and started pounding on one of them, don't you think they would come to the aid of their co-worker? And they're just waitresses. They're not cops. I swear. I won't work with any of them.

Traditional officers also feel that new police are not disciplined for misconduct because the department wants to "keep up the numbers," as they put it, to retain enough of the "A.A." (Affirmative Action) officers to satisfy the "brass" (the upper management of the police department) and ultimately the courts. One example that illustrates this concerned a new, female police officer who left the city to participate in a sporting event, ignoring a subpoena to appear in court on a felony arrest. Instead, her partner, a traditional male officer who had been injured on duty (I.O.D.) and was off work with a back injury, was required to go to court to testify.

For the injured officer, finally getting the suspects into court was rewarding, but not at the expense of his long-term recovery from the injury. The injured officer could not sit, stand, or walk without extreme pain. After testifying, he was taken to the emergency room. His injury was exacerbated by the activity; he was hospitalized and was off work for nearly two months. Other officers, traditional and new, expressed great sympathy for the injured officer. When the able-bodied officer returned to the job, "she was talked to . . . [but] didn't get days [wasn't required to work without pay, she was] just 'talked' to."

The female new officer acknowledged that she ignored the subpoena but also said she did not realize the extent of her partner's injuries or that his presence in court would exact such a high physical price. She believed that if he were "really hurting" he should have contacted her. She felt that missing the athletic event, in which she was a team member representing the division, would be "wussing out and letting everybody down."

Most officers, traditional and new, considered her punishment to be light in terms of her offense. Police simply do not ignore subpoenas. Traditionally, police who miss court for whatever reason have been punished by "getting days." Many officers felt that the officer got away with inappropriate behavior and that the sanctions were lenient because the officer was female.

Traditional officers are likely to label this type of unacceptable behavior as A.A., female, or new police behavior, in which case it ceases to be viewed as an individual case—a personal lapse—and is generalized to the entire group. To be categorized as an officer who disregards the well-being of comrades makes future interaction with fellow officers problematic. Eventually, getting this kind of reputation is destructive to one's career. Lack of collegiality is a serious problem in an occupation that requires prolonged, intensive interaction among its members.

Another disadvantage faced by officers hired after the late 1970s is that traditional officers are less likely to offer advice unless they feel the new officer is serious about the job. Being out of the loop deprives the new officer of valuable information that may make the job easier and safer. Traditional police tend to be extremely critical of the new officers, often interpreting lack of experience as lack of interest or as having a bad attitude. As one officer put it:

> There's no point in trying to tell them anything. They know it all, or they don't know anything, and they don't care. Most of 'em are just about useless. All they want is the paycheck, and then they're not even going to last. They'll quit—God knows, no one has the balls to fire them—or they'll lateral [transfer to a different police department]. They're not here to be police.

Another complained, "They're all pissed off because they all want to be gunfighters and most of this job is paperwork." This was interesting to me because I have heard the same criticism leveled at traditional police in the first two phases of their careers.

Proactive Policing

Though traditional police supply endless anecdotal examples of the deficiencies of the new police—focusing on their abuse of the system, lack of competence, and general lack of civility—there do not appear to be significant increases in rates of injuries, altercations, shootings, or citizen complaints generated by the new police. Still, many traditional police maintain that the department is in decline *because* of a combination of influx of new police and management decisions.

One of the biggest criticisms of the way the new police perform the job really has nothing to do with these officers; rather, it has to do with a shift in departmental policies that has quite by chance coincided with the heavy influx of new officers. This is due in part to a decrease in what Albert J. Reiss, Jr. (1971) has described as *proactive policing*. Reiss describes this as "pursuing matters through investigative activities, preventive patrol, and direct intervention in the lives of citizens (including the techniques of stopping, frisking, searching, and questioning)" (1971:64). This proactive approach was developed and became policy for the L.A.P.D. during the 1950s. This approach is linked to the "broken windows" theory that if a window in a building is broken and is left in disrepair, people will soon come along and break the other windows. This theory assumes that, if ignored, small acts of lawlessness lead directly to larger transgressions, and it is crucial to deal with transgressions swiftly. Thus if windows aren't repaired and "window breakers" are not apprehended and punished, a breakdown in community controls occurs and escalates, deteriorating the community further (Wilson and Kelling, 1982). The proactive approach to policing is one of maintaining order so that "windows are not broken."

Proactive policing was a strategy for policing the city with fewer than five thousand officers. At the time, being proactive meant officers were constantly active—stopping people, patrolling, being highly visible—it seemed as though they were everywhere: the desired effect. Because officers were supposed to suppress crime—stop it before it started—officers stopped people for "probable cause," often because they "looked out of place." This approach is the major reason the department gained its reputation for its aggressive, and sometimes abusive, enforcement style. Citizens, especially minority citizens, were rightfully outraged at some of the assumptions made regarding where they were deemed "out of place," and by the wider implication that they should literally know and stay in their place.

Further at the core of the proactive approach is an emphasis on authority and control in encounters with citizens. The traditional officers were trained in using the proactive approach, while the new police have been trained differently. One traditional officer took a philosophical stance:

> Change is perceived as going to "hell in a handbasket" or "down the toilet fast," by some of the officers. After all, most of us have been hired basically to keep the status quo. In the fifties and sixties, we were all proactive. Now they are telling us they don't want that. The city has been very clear on that issue. Be reactive—wait until something happens, then respond. They want us to be more passive. I think it's just change, and change is hard on some people. If they, the police officers didn't care, they'd just say, "fine," and kick back. These guys do care, and they want the job done right, and they don't understand the changes. It will all come around, because it is going to change whether people are happy with that or not.

"STREET COPS"

As we have seen, to officers, the distinctions among themselves are readily apparent and significant. In addition to the distinctions marked by "traditional" and "new," others (which are discussed in more detail in chapter 3) are based on the structure of the job and include: the kinds of duty performed, the watch or shift, and the official rank within the department.

The terms street cop and management cop are used in the literature on police (Reuss-Ianni, 1983), and the police themselves refer to patrol officers as cops, coppers, or uniforms. They do not use these terms to describe officers who work indoors or hold management positions. Street cops refer to management cops as suits, pencil pushers or brass. My study focuses on street cops—officers who normally work on patrol. It is these officers with whom the public primarily interacts. The study also includes patrol officers working special duty assignments (specialized crime units such as narcotics, gangs, and major crime task force) and sergeants.

Sergeants inhabit a kind of no-man's land between the street officers and management. They are considered to be management but are included in this study as street officers, because they are officers who have been promoted from the streets and continue to work the streets with patrol officers in a supervisory capacity and because their rank as sergeant is significant in the analysis of police careers. With the possible exception of some sergeants who prefer to stay indoors, insulated from the streets, and manage to do so, most sergeants expect to be out and about during the course of their watch. They interface with the public as they spend most of their working watch on the streets.

Virtually all officers begin their careers on patrol, but officers who continue to work the streets generally do so because that is where they believe they should be. They view real police work as patrolling the streets and, more specifically, as "putting the bad guys in jail." In their view, the kind of supervisory work done by upper management (sergeants who prefer to work indoors, lieutenants, and captains) is not real police work. In Los Angeles, "patrol" is made up of new officers, experienced officers who choose to be there and some officers who stay on patrol biding their time until retirement: the gung ho, the extremely competent, and the burnouts.

Patrol officers are critical of officers who occupy the higher ranks of the police hierarchy. As mentioned previously, their respect for the policing abilities of other officers is often in inverse proportion to rank. Though management officers have a higher rank, earn higher salaries, and occupy higher-stratus positions in the hierarchy—having the ability to set policy and give directives—officers who have directed their careers toward promotion and advancement (management cops) are not viewed by street officers as being part of the same brotherhood. They may be police officers, but they are not doing real police work and are not cops. Their careers, concerns, experiences, and aspirations are entirely different from those of street officers.

Before embarking on our closer examination of the world of policing in the L.A.P.D., we will learn in chapter 2 how this study was conducted, given that police officers do not welcome such attention. Chapter 3 explores the police worldview, which defines the world as dangerous and draws a sharp line between police and outsiders, and the social context of policing. The next five chapters focus specifically on the five phases of the police career. While the phases of the police career are interesting and may have application in altered form to other occupations, my primary interest is in examining the phases to discover the core identity of the officers themselves and their perceptions. Chapter 9, "Reflections of a Traditional Officer," gives readers the opportunity to apply what they have learned in the previous chapters as they read an officer's personal account as an L.A.P.D. police officer. The book concludes with a brief summary and an interpretation of what being a police officer in the L.A.P.D. might be like in the future.

Methodology

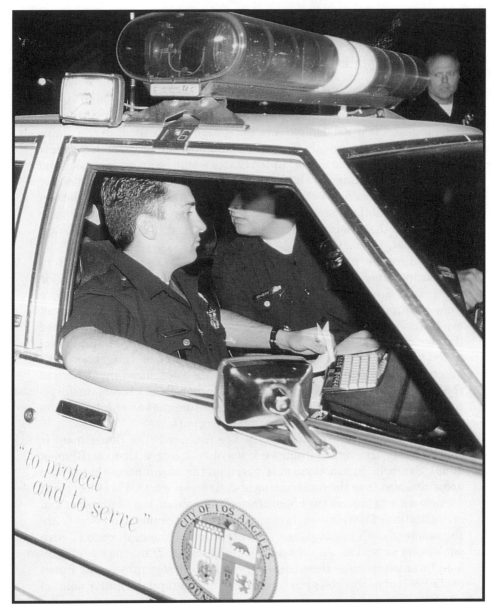

THE THEORETICAL APPROACH

We know that culture is a set of shared beliefs, attitudes and values and includes ways of thinking and behaving. The notion that cultural meanings are learned, shared and integrated places them in the mainstream of anthropological interpretation. Understanding the worldview of people born or living in the United States would be an easier task if the model of the "melting pot" had validity. However, rather than a melting pot we have the salad bowl. It is through ethnographic study that we can discover the subtle or sharp variations within our own culture and come to recognize that there are "strangers" living next door (Bohannan and van der Elst, 1998).

The routine experiences of police officers are as far removed from the routine experiences of most urban North Americans as those from far more exotic climes. In this study I came to realize that, as much as people from a distant tribal society, police officers inhabit a world different from my own. Police officers' behavior and attitudes are best understood through an approach that emphasizes knowledge as a dynamic and negotiated process and pays special attention to interaction. Interaction with others (outsiders) tempers to some degree the specialized input born of the police experience, and interaction with other police officers (insiders) provides a tremendously compelling yet shifting means of interpreting these experiences (including the non-police input).

My approach to the study of the Los Angeles Police Department is shaped by the theoretical framework of symbolic interactionism (Blumer, 1969). Symbolic interactionism is based on the assumption that people are active agents in the construction of their social world. This theoretical framework emphasizes the importance of interaction, the negotiation and renegotiation of worldviews. Meanings of persons, actions and events are the result of each participant's interpretation of them, in concert with one's peers as well as with outside, empirical facts. Thus, the use of symbolic interactionism as theoretical approach to ethnography is well suited to the goals of anthropological research: to understand the native point of view.

In an effort to understand the worldview of patrol officers, this work follows officers from their induction into the police academy, where they are trained in an entirely different set of meanings from those ascribed to the world prior to their training. When they hit the streets they quickly learn that, while the meanings they have learned in their formal training at the academy are helpful, they are also incomplete. They have embarked upon a critical and dynamic process that will set them apart from those who do not share these interpretations so common to police. Even within the police community they will be divided into subgroups on the basis of shifts of meaning and interpretation.

James Spradley suggests symbolic interactionism as a particularly useful approach to the study of culture. Spradley indicates that there are features of culture about which members of a culture have knowledge that is explicit (exist on a conscious level) and easily articulated. There will be other aspects that do not exist on a conscious level, although they are still a formative part of the culture; they are implicit, or tacit.

> Every ethnographer employs this same process of inference to go beyond what is seen and heard to find out what people know. Making inferences involves reasoning from evidence (what we perceive) or from premise (what we assume). (Spradley, 1980:10)

In conducting my fieldwork, the concept of explicit and implicit culture was particularly useful. During the early stages of research many aspects of the police officers' lives were not available, thus rendering inferences from those behaviors, artifacts and statements impossible. In addition, there were cases of conscious withholding of information that might have helped in inference building. Most significantly, there are many aspects of the tacit culture of police officers that play a significant role in the way they perform their duties as police officers and live their lives as individuals. The officers are not necessarily consciously aware of some of these features that influence their lives. They act in response to the meanings they share, but they are not necessarily always able to articulate these meanings.

Police officers are consciously aware of their role as active participants in the creation and interpretation of their social world. They are aware of a perceived necessity for adherence to their construction of reality in order to perform their job. They believe that their ordering of reality is essential for social survival and also for literal survival. Adherence to the police version of the world confers actual, literal, survival value in the performance of a job that has extraordinary risks and deals with high levels of uncertainty and danger.

Most police researchers using firsthand information on police and focusing on police officers—rather than on particular police-related issues or management styles—obtained their data through two major sources: either they arranged to do department-sanctioned "ride alongs" or they went through the training to become reserve police officers, usually for less than a year. In neither case would these researchers be likely to have access to the kind of data that comes only with prolonged intensive interaction within the police community. The strengths of their studies come from the keen analysis of short periods of intensive study of primarily on-duty activities.

Thus, while some scholars have studied the police "from within," data dealing with the off-duty lives of officers are scarce. They have not concerned themselves with the lives of the persons filling the role of police officer beyond the policing role. With this omission the dynamic that reintroduces human beings into the formula is lost. Human beings, as opposed to our conceptions of the roles they may fill, reveal the motivations, strategies and interpretations they bring to the job of policing. This revelation clarifies their endeavors for those of us who do not experience them firsthand. While many popular images of police officers, such as those offered by former L.A.P.D. officer, Joseph Wambaugh (1970, 1972, 1973), present protagonists who are emotionally and often morally bankrupt, common sense might suggest that there are well-adjusted police officers, happy police marriages, and police who gain satisfaction and even pleasure in the compassionate and even-handed performance of their jobs. One would think there must be some middle ground, or positive aspects to the police career; otherwise how, and why, would people undertake a job with such obvious negative elements?

THE HOOK

When one of my students invited me to a cop bar, I had no intention of conducting a study of police, especially not one that would stretch over two decades, but as I looked around, I was paying attention and beginning to pose questions in the privacy of my own mind. These were not necessarily anthropological questions, although there were some of those as well. These questions went unasked partially because I was consciously keeping a low profile and also because I am, to the great disbelief of my students, almost pathologically shy. Most of the time I listened—not at all a bad strategy for anyone wishing to learn about others. I did not feel compelled to try to make any comprehensive sense out of the things I was observing.

From the first contact with these officers I was hooked. They were interesting, their stories were fascinating and much of what I learned was totally unexpected and new to me. I also had to confront my own frailties, erroneous assumptions, and biases based on my past experiences with the police. As a child I had been raised in a family in which the "policeman" was a friend. I was told that if I ever needed help, I should look for a police officer. I was, however, a child of the sixties and years of anti-war and civil rights activism had on occasion placed me in (at least structural) opposition to police. They frightened me. I had been arrested. I had not been mistreated, unless one considers being teargassed—I had, after all "failed to disperse"—as being mistreated. I wore my arrests and confrontations as a kind of generational badge of honor; however, I had no desire to spend any time with police officers. Thus, I was fascinated almost as much by the realization of the depth of my own prejudices as by my insight into the police officers' world. I felt that despite my bias I would be able to apply the tools of the discipline to observe and investigate at least some peripheral issues of policing in an unbiased way.

The twenty-one years of fieldwork upon which this book is based has gone through many stages. I will elaborate on them in the next section of this chapter because they will make more sense once a few critical bits are revealed. From this very nondirected and somewhat inauspicious introduction to the field, my research progressed through passive participation, characterized by getting my bearings and shifting into the earliest forms of the moderate participation style of research (Spradley, 1980). I then switched into higher gear that included participant observation, formal taped interviews as well as less formal data gathering to obtain the materials on which I based my doctoral dissertation. After the completion of my Ph.D., I returned to the field to conduct formal interviews, primarily with female and minority officers, and more data gathering (see Womack and Marti, 1993).

I have never been totally out of the field. After five years of studying police and deciding that no one would want anyone about whom he or she really cared to have this job, I had a date with one of my informants. This, of course, is strictly taboo in anthropology. There are good reasons for the prohibition—it complicates matters, can compromise your work, can create new problems in the field—and so on. Nevertheless, I did it. I assure the reader that I am not unique in having broken this taboo, but it is still a transgression in anthropology. Three months later we were married. It is unclear whether or not this makes the infraction of the "no fraternization" rule better or worse.

Most of the possible negatives suggested above never materialized. Some did, but in terms of the research, I think there were many more advantages than disadvantages. The major disadvantage was that my work could become a more likely candidate for charges of loss of scientific detachment and objectivity. The major advantage was my diminished outsider standing and my having free access to an entirely new universe of understanding the lives of these officers, giving me insider status.

THE PROBLEM OF OBJECTIVITY/NEUTRALITY

One of the issues that must be addressed for any researcher is the concern over objectivity—the problem of remaining a neutral observer. In traditional sociocultural anthropology we are admonished to remain neutral observers. The "prime directive" has been to go, to observe, but not to interfere, intervene or be swayed from our scientific detachment. Central among the values that guide sociocultural inquiry is the awareness that cultural relativity is the key to understanding how a reasonable person, who appears to be like yourself, could do things that you would never do. Being aware of ethnocentrism—using our cultural values, structures and experiences as a yardstick by which we measure all others—keeps us from falling into its trap. When we fall back on what seems reasonable and even "natural" to us, our naive assessment of reality may, in fact, be quite an aberration to someone else.

Another approach to doing fieldwork is used by applied anthropologists who feel it is not necessary or desirable to maintain their distance from informants and their concerns. Indeed, applied anthropologists are often committed to using anthropology to direct cultural change. When we study segments of cultures within our own society, such as the police, we may already be sensitized to certain issues and share concerns with our informants. Yet, in all contexts the goal remains the same: to understand other lives, perceptions, issues and strategies of others.

Part of being as objective as possible involves acknowledging our biases to the degree that we are aware of them and being vigilant that they do not insinuate themselves into the process. Because of my marriage, I am more open to a charge of being biased—supposedly having lost my (presumed) objectivity. However, it is my contention that far from obscuring the process of studying the police, being married to a police officer has helped me to understand—beyond the intellectual to the visceral—the nature of the job of policing and the role it plays in the lives of police officers. The initial five years of research is complemented by the years spent as a researcher/participant in the culture of the Los Angeles Police Department.

Being both an anthropologist and a part of the police community has enabled me to apply analytical tools of the discipline to insider knowledge of the job and the officers who perform it. Combining formal interviews with prolonged interaction proved to be productive. Data gathered from formal interviews provided information that was often unknown to me and unlikely to emerge in normal interaction. Conversely, information gathered through prolonged involvement and interaction often provided insight into more formally collected data. The two acted as checks and balances to help keep a sense of perspective.

Few researchers, and few people in general, are neutral when it comes to the topic of police. I am not neutral on the subject of police, but I am aware of the need to be as objective as possible in the presentation and analysis of the data. This has been, at times, a struggle for me. It is so easy to be selective, especially when anticipating that my study might evoke negative reactions. Thus, I have made a concerted effort to sidestep the danger of skewed data by interviewing a large number of officers at different points in their careers and by including a representative sample of responses. Ultimately, I believe the only bias in these materials is the one which emerges from the worldview of the officers from whom this study is drawn.

As mentioned previously, the entire study was conducted over a period of twenty-one years and, predictably, under differing circumstances. Rarely did it receive my full attention for long expanses of time. I was concurrently involved in other activities as well: teaching anthropology, conducting other research projects, doing fieldwork in West Africa, teaching in Cambridge, England, in addition to other professional and personal activities.

The research is divided into the following four periods: "I: Entering the Field" took place from 1976 through 1977 and consists of informally establishing rapport and first impressions. "II: Gaining Rapport . . ." was the first attempt at a more formal study and began in 1977 while I was in graduate school. It continued through 1980. "III: Taking the Vow" began in 1981 with my marriage to a police officer and continued through 1990. "IV: As Easy as It Gets" includes research conducted after I completed my Ph.D. This last stage of research (1991–1997) was necessary because of the dramatic changes affecting the department, and to round out some of the data. I wanted to increase input from officers hired in the 1990s, and this book reflects the addition of that data. However, more research is necessary to focus specifically on those newer officers. Because their time on the job is somewhat limited, it is not yet possible to determine whether or not they will follow the same career phases in the job, which are illuminated in this book. So far the data suggest that change is in the air, but the particulars of the change remain to be seen.

I: ENTERING THE FIELD

I owe a great debt to the officer who first exposed me to the police community. For a long time I did not know enough to appreciate how important it was that such a highly respected officer provided my initial introduction to the community. By so doing, he was vouching for my good behavior and making the public statement that I was okay at a time when he may not have been completely certain that was the case, given his knowledge of my anti-police bias. The fact that he was so highly regarded by the other officers, and was a training officer, meant that he was also one of the human hubs of interaction. Physical proximity, simply sitting at the same table with him, put me into the thick of things.

During the initial three months I spent approximately five hours a night, three or four nights a week, with the officers, either at the police bar or at one of the local coffee shops. I also attended various recreational events. During this period of research I believed it was normal for most police officers to disperse from the local station to the local bar catering to the police.

Initially I did not realize that the officers who frequented the bar, especially those who visited it on their off-duty days, were not representative of most police. I was aware there were some selective factors at work, but I did not know what those factors were. With time, exposure and a more complete understanding of the patterns of police behavior, it became clear that most of the officers who frequented the bar on off-duty days were new (either new to the job or recently transferred from another division), recently divorced or, rarer still, retired. They were there for the same reason I was—to tap into the most readily available essence of the police community.

People who were non-police, but involved in some way in the police community, were also there. These people were those who were well-known to the police and who formed a core socializing unit. They were citizen employees of the police department, relatives of police officers, even former wives, and the others consisted of friends, girlfriends, athletic team colleagues and police groupies. Occupationally, nurses and firemen predominated. There were of course other people in the bar, but the fact that it was a cop bar was no secret, and people who were not comfortable with that fact did not stay long or soon return.

During the time they were in the bar there appeared to be a great deal of camaraderie. Upon entering the bar, almost every person was acknowledged by greetings of varying heartiness. There was usually a great deal of joking, and plans were made for other social activities. The mood, predictably, changed from night to night and even from table to table. Officers appeared to select their tables almost as much by mood as by personnel.

An additional function of these interactions was to reveal to each other some of the individual features less easily accessible in the course of normal working interaction: areas of vulnerability, interpersonal skills, abilities and coping mechanisms. Recreational drinking often involved a fair amount of testing, taunting and kidding—with the added element of alcohol. In some respects the alcohol was a blueprint for disaster, but it was also viewed as yet another test of how well people could conduct and control themselves, even while drinking.

Usually conversation flowed as easily and plentifully as did the drinks. Most of the conversation was dominated by shop talk. Recounting events that occurred during the evening shift, if in fact there was anything worthy of comment, frequently resulted in the recounting of other similar events, counterexperiences, and variations on a theme. Sometimes it appeared as though this storytelling was purely entertainment. Sometimes the recounting of an event was extremely meticulous in detail, precise, and clearly very carefully expressed. At other times descriptions of events resembled some sort of burlesque comedy routine, often involving the input of several officers. Frequently these stories seemed to serve a didactic purpose. Officers new to the job or the division learned a wide array of these stories. The lore of particular persons, places and divisions became well known to officers within the first year on the job.

It is in the social context of the bar scene where officers, by telling stories, disseminate information they deem important and convey and reaffirm "appropriate" attitudes, perceptions and responses to each other and to the situations they are likely to encounter. This is also an important way in which officers process and detoxify some of the less pleasant events of their watch—the events officers do not want to take home with them.

These early impressions were important because they stimulated some of the questions I began to formulate about the police and their lives. The officers seemed to spend a great deal of their off-duty time with each other. Why? How much? Doing what? They seemed to play long and hard and frequently their play was risky: skydiving, motorcycle racing and running rapids. It is the norm for officers to engage in several of these sports—especially in the beginning of their careers. I learned that their participation in potentially dangerous sports provided them with more information about each other which they consider, if not vital, then at least useful. The kind of information gleaned gives greater depth to how people respond to stress, competition, fair play and risk taking and demonstrates how they focus and perform.

Neophyte officers tended to be quite idealistic; the older ones tended to be cynical, but some of the officers who had been on the job the longest seemed to be much less judgmental than the others. I wondered about these transformations. Eventually it became necessary to ask questions, and that was when I learned the limitations of my access to much of the critical data.

Erroneous Assumptions

From the time of my first contact with the group, I began to collect data, albeit informally and somewhat naively. I made several erroneous assumptions. The first was that since the police officers I had encountered were from my culture, there would be minimal room for misunderstanding or for cultural misses. Another incorrect assumption, made after I decided on a more formal study of police, was that the police would realize that I was not a threat to them and would be cooperative, particularly because they seemed to spend so much time being on the job and talking about the job and each other. It became clear over time that when they were talking about the job, it was for their purposes, for their agenda, for themselves. I was peripheral to those concerns. My original assumptions proved false, but holding them did no real harm. In fact, it resulted in a fairly long period of becoming a familiar part of the police community that, over time, proved to be a great asset.

I regard the first two years of data gathering as time required to get my bearings and establish rapport with the police officers. Although during this period I was less effective in gathering the kind of data I was seeking, it was a good opportunity to learn how differently the police see themselves, how closed their group is, and the extent to which any outsider, even a friendly one, can be perceived as a threat. This time was prolonged partly because there were limits on the amount of time available for interaction with the officers and partly due to their cynicism, suspicion and "clannishness."

Data Gathering Techniques

Ultimately, throughout much of this stage of research, I was reduced to attempting to understand the world of the patrol officers and the role of police solidarity simply through listening in a nondirected way. I was there, but I did not ask questions. I shamelessly eavesdropped on neighboring conversations. This was easy to do when there were several audible conversations within easy range. This somewhat dubious but very effective tactic was facilitated by the fact that most of my early contacts took place either at the police bar or at sporting events or parties, all of which tended to be well attended. They also provided a context in which I could move from conversation to conversation, sampling many different interactions. This yielded a great deal of information, and I did not have to hold up my end of the conversation, so that I could devote my full attention to the exchange. This also meant that these discussions were directed by the officers' concerns, rather than mine, and reflected information they deemed important.

II: GAINING RAPPORT . . . AGAIN,
AND AGAIN, AND . . .

After the introductory stage, and after committing to do the study for my doctoral research, I decided to begin a more orderly and directed study of the police aimed at a more formal and manageable accumulation of data. The first formal stage of the study began late in 1977 and continued until 1981, when I began spending time with the police community, police officers and the support personnel in a wider variety of contexts. During this phase I expanded my base of operations from the cop bar, the local cafes and the occasional recreational activities to encompass more of the sporting events, social events (parties, picnics, weddings) and funerals.

Once I decided to investigate police as my dissertation topic, I focused on the nature and extent of their homogeneity: physical as well as attitudinal. Both their physical conformity and their behavioral, attitudinal clannishness may be viewed as expressions of police solidarity. The physical homogeneity on duty was fairly easy to see and explain—of course the uniform conveys authority—but beyond the clothing there are other elements that cannot necessarily be removed at the end of the watch. Male officers' haircuts, sideburns and mustaches (if they have them) are regulated. Female officers must cut thier hair short or wear it pinned up. Part of the conformity derives from historic patterns of hiring, which at one time basically limited the pool of candidates to relatively tall white males; some of it comes from wearing clothing that will conceal the gun, as well as walking and sitting in such a way as to accommodate the gun and sore muscles.

I wondered whether or not the job itself attracted certain individuals who already possessed characteristics that would lend themselves to this persona. I learned that, to a degree, these characteristics are selected for during the application process, but virtually everyone who does the job for any prolonged period soon acquires the characteristic look, attitudes, values and behaviors associated with the job—at least as part of their working persona. I felt it was important to understand officers' formal training at the police academy to fully appreciate this aspect of the process of creating and/or reinforcing their apparent conformity. I investigated the selection process involved in choosing recruits and the academy training they received by asking officers about it and by visiting the police academy.

As I focused on the working persona I found myself thinking of the officers somewhat as robots and began to worry about losing the people in the patterns. I feared glossing over individual variation, strategies, manipulations, motivations (all those factors that make us individuals even as we fit into and become parts of groups) while focusing on the patterns found in the roles, rule and structure of the job. This early orientation has proved a necessary link to a fuller understanding of the wide variation that one finds in police lives, while providing a framework for discussion and analysis. With the luxury of this perspective, it is now easier to see which aspects of the job are negotiable and which are not.

The problem of obscured individuality is hardly unique to my study. The same issues arise whenever we generalize the structure, forgetting that individual people—hunters and gatherers, promised wives, people at their initiation ceremonies, folks in all kinds of culturally predictable situations—can act the same way for different reasons. Many do the thing expected of them wholeheartedly, others do it but feel conflicted. Many, in fact, do not do the expected thing. For the cultural anthropologist, people's motivations and intentions, how they see the situation, is of critical importance.

For many reasons individuals in the group of police officers that made up my sample was shifted—officers changed divisions, watches, marital status, their minds, their patterns. They left the job. They retired. Some died. The result was that the number of contacts might remain fairly constant, but the individuals changed. It is partially this feature of the job of policing that first alerted me to the pronounced difference in behavior and attitudes among police officers with varying years on the job.

At roughly this point in my fieldwork, I was seized with a false sense of accomplishment. I felt, optimistically, that I had achieved the necessary rapport to enable me to become more directive in my data gathering. I never made any attempt to hide the fact that I was an anthropologist and interested in police, but this was interpreted by some as standard police-groupie behavior, rather than a research interest.

In the early stages of my research I did not come into contact with any women who were on the job. They existed, but their numbers were small and they did not socialize with the male officers. In 1980 women comprised only about 2.5 percent of the police force in Los Angeles. They were usually restricted to duties other than general patrol and they were not often included in the off-duty recreational patterns of the male officers. The first female officers in my sample were from police families and viewed their exclusion as part of the way the game was played. This view was not shared by the female officers who came on the job in the 1980s.

Initially, information appeared to be easily accessible, and I was eager to set out an interview schedule and launch into a full-fledged study of the police. I thought that if so much valuable information was so easily available in the bar and at other events, it surely could not be too difficult to get officers to go into greater depth, under more controlled conditions. I had not realized that this information was easily accessible because it was essential to the officers that it be available to other officers, but not, certainly, for research purposes. It was also difficult for me to differentiate between straight answers, "put ons" or the antiseptically ideal responses generally reserved for outsiders. I now know that some of the data I faithfully transcribed and marveled over was more fiction than fact.

Formal Interviews

While I had informed the police of my intent to do a study of them, many officers did not take me seriously on this issue. Once I began to act more like a researcher, it became more disquieting for them. I started trying to gather data formally, with scheduled interviews and by openly taking notes. This was unsuccessful. They did not want to be on the record in any way, shape, or form. They indirectly, but very effectively, resisted my attempts at formal data gathering. They would agree to interviews and not show up. We would reschedule. They would not show up. Police officers always had a ready excuse for anything they did not want to do: they worked overtime; they had court; training days coincided, at the last minute, with scheduled interviews. All of these explanations were available in addition to the normal arsenal of excuses people use when they do not want to do something. Their lists of excuses were inexhaustible and effective. After many repeated attempts, it became clear that following the agenda and schedule of my informants was more productive than imposing my schedule on them. However, I was still concerned about rigor in my methodology. I temporarily abandoned my attempts at formal interviews and tried to hone my skills at gleaning data in less formal means.

One technique that yielded some of the most interesting and easily obtained attitudinal data was informal discussions of mass media presentations of police. I used this device during the early portion of my fieldwork, when it was still difficult to get straight answers, and continued to use it throughout the research period as a litmus of changing attitudes. Television shows and films were particularly useful. Media presentations did not have to be police-oriented to elicit responses that were valuable to my research, but the police-oriented shows yielded myriad responses, as did news programs. I had found a way to direct areas of information gathering and diminish the reluctance of certain individuals to discuss issues about which they were formerly guarded.

Discussions that centered on these media presentations appeared to be totally nonthreatening (unlike the more formal interviews). They generated substantive discussion of more abstract issues and precipitated reminiscences of similar or counterexperiences. Even officers who had previously been guarded in their responses spontaneously and vigorously volunteered their opinions of tactics, acts, storyline, personnel and the reality quotient of the media presentation. Not surprisingly, police officers do not like most of the shows on police. When they do watch them, they tend to do so for the entertainment value and release gained from ridiculing them. It has been interesting to compare the comments made by the same officers to similar stimuli—the television news and entertainment programs—in different contexts: in the station house coffee room, in public places, and in their own homes.

Being able to use this nonthreatening technique encouraged revelation and provided me with insight that was a major contribution to the continuation of my research when I felt bogged down and defeated by my lack of success with more formal interviews. The formal interviews, when they actually occurred (recall the scheduling problems), were fine.

Note Taking

I focused on the ways in which police interact with each other. I thought that if I could not ask them directly about the issues that interested me, maybe I would be able to get sufficient data to understand and document their social world through careful and diligent observation and documentation. However, I soon found that, in many instances, I had to abandon even minimal public note taking. To bring out a note pad virtually had the same effect that switching on a tape recorder would have had. It simply ended all discussion and literally drove people away. In place of open note taking I often retreated to the restroom to jot down the essentials that were verbalized by officers.

Ultimately toward the end of this second stage of research, I was able to take notes openly with some informants, and I did tape many of my interviews. I wish that I had been able to tape some of the early conversations, which were really oral free-for-alls and potentially rich sources of data. When there were many officers present, all added their opinions and examples to the wide-ranging discussions. It may have proven interesting to be able to keep track of who instigated specific stories, who embellished, who turned the story into a joke, who listened and who ignored the whole thing.

In this stage of my research I was unaware of the distinctions that form the police worldview. I did not realize how much depended upon the particular informant and the phase of the career that he or she was experiencing. The alignment of my stages of research, skills and abilities with each officer's phase of the job, the priorities and issues important to him or her made for interesting dynamics in terms of the research project—for my part it was just this side of total confusion.

Directed Questions

When I started to ask questions, I quickly discovered that there were only certain kinds of questions, asked in certain forms, that would elicit thoughtful and honest answers. For example, questions for which the honest answers would be critical or reflect badly on another officer would not be answered at this stage of my interviewing. Thus, questions that were perceived as inappropriate or asked inappropriately would be ignored, answered with a joke, or responded to with a stock or ideal answer. Many helpful officers tried their hardest to tell me what they thought I wanted to hear.

A question could be deemed inappropriate due to timing, people present, context in the flow of conversation, or a multitude of other features outside my awareness. Eventually I became more knowledgeable, skillful and sensitive to the subtleties of roles and personalities as well as the guidelines that provided the hidden agenda of police conversation. It was only at this point, toward the end of the second stage of fieldwork, that I felt that my work could begin in earnest. I am aware of no short-cut for reaching this happy state.

Revelations and Realizations

When I started getting more data I had a horrible revelation. Everything I knew up to that point in time was wrong. After focusing on conformity and homogeneity I kept finding counterexamples—officers who simply did not fit the patterns I had so carefully extracted from the data. Often they seemed the opposite. I felt I knew nothing. I began to feel my entire anthropological effort was a house of cards. Actually, I was learning that officers in different phases of their career have different views, behave differently and emphasize very different issues than do officers in other phases of their career. At this point I almost gave up the project. Only basic stubbornness, the fact that I had already invested so much time and energy and was too embarrassed to have spent so long to no avail, coupled with the feeling that I really did understand much more than when I started, led me to persist.

The officers knew that I taught anthropology (although few knew what anthropology entailed, and of those who did, the consensus was that it had something to do with digging up bones and finding arrowheads). They knew that I was writing some sort of paper and that many of my questions, and much of my attention, were for this paper. The word dissertation did not mean anything to them; they regarded anyone writing about police, singularly or collectively, with great suspicion. My writing worried some officers. However, most seemed relieved once they knew that my study was for scholarly and not journalistic purposes. Police tend not to take scholars very seriously, but they are less trusting of journalists. Still their anxiety over what I was doing, coupled with their clannishness, continued to be a problem. I had access, but they still did not completely trust me—I was still an outsider. Being female slightly mitigated this problem but created some others.

Being a Female Researcher

A great deal has been written recently on the role of female researchers and the contributions they have made to the discipline of anthropology. Anthropology has the distinction of being the earliest of the social sciences to value the potential contribution of women, and to encourage them to enter the field.

The fact that I am a woman was in many ways a distinct advantage while conducting this research. Because I am not a man, I did not have to meet the police officers' criteria for being an acceptable male: I did not have to be athletic, a skilled fisherman, or have mastery over large and powerful motorcycles. It was fine for me to eschew risk taking, but witness their contests and tests. I was not expected to have command presence. I did not have to have an acceptable profession, such as police officer, firefighter or professional athlete. I did not need to embody any of the macho attributes so often highly valued among police officers. These are stereotypical criteria, yet the lack of these attributes, and many others, could be considered defects in a man. As a male, I would have fallen short of the mark. For a woman researcher, these criteria simply do not apply.

Police officers have a more expansive scale in their evaluation of women (unless of course, they are also police officers, in which case similar criteria apply). Even the men who were somewhat anxious about the process of talking on the record were pleased and flattered by the attention. In some instances, officers did not view the project as a serious one. I suspect they envisioned the research as leading to a term paper—perhaps uncompleted, possibly unread, and certainly of little consequence. These officers were in the minority, but could have been a real problem for me had they taken me more seriously.

An obvious disadvantage to being female was the fact that I had to establish, early on, that I was not a groupie, did not wish or expect to be courted and, in fact, did not date policemen. The fact that my attention to them and presence at so many of the social functions mimicked some aspects of classic police-groupie behavior was an unfortunate coincidence.

I had to convince them that I did not fit in the groupie category and was not interested in dating them. It was a point that had to be stated, confirmed, tested on their part and restated and reconfirmed. Many of the officers initially approached me for social reasons and were interested in me as female. They found it difficult to understand that I was always around and available for talking, coffee, parties and all sorts of events—but not dates. Establishing myself as a researcher/friend was a difficult task and one which needed constant reinforcement.

For the first five years of my research I adhered to the rule of fairly intensive social and personal involvement, but no dates, no flirtation, nothing that I felt would compromise my position as a researcher. I was explicit about the nature of my research and never attempted to conceal my data gathering activities.

As time passed I became a normal part of the extended police community. Five years of involvement lent the mantle of respectability within the group. I was not one of them, not a police officer, but I was an acceptable outsider, and certainly a member in good standing of the police community. Many officers became almost enthusiastic in their participation in my research; others answered my questions willingly. Many interviews could now be taped.

The Research Relationship

I believed that I had established rapport and could, therefore, proceed with the serious job of data collection. I did not, at the time, realize that establishing rapport is not like achieving a state of grace: it is a never-ending process that requires constant attention—just like friendship. Once you have established a relationship with a friend there is more latitude for demands as well as neglect—within certain fluctuating limits. In a friendship it may be necessary to reestablish or revitalize the relationship. The same durability and fragility holds for the field relationship. However there are several essential differences.

The research relationship is a conditional one in a way that friendships are not. The researcher has an agenda. There are data to be gathered. There are clarifications to be made. The researcher knows "there's method in his or her madness." Perhaps there is a follow-up study in the wings, but the field relationship carries the seeds of its own terminus. The researcher wants something from the informants and, other than some scholarly addition to the literature or increased understanding, there may be very little given back to the informants. As Richard Borshay Lee (1969) indicates in "A Naturalist at Large: Eating Christmas in the Kalahari," even the parting gift designed to give something back to the !Kung san resulted in more data for the researcher. The researcher, in my case, was getting good data as well as interesting companionship. I would ask questions and participate in many activities, but offered little other than my company in return. The interaction was on my terms, not theirs. It was sometimes tempered by vague anxiety over my "real" purpose in asking questions, and the fear that, ultimately, revealing too much to an outsider would prove unwise. I had to prove myself constantly, not only to those with whom a relationship already existed, but also to new participants in the study.

After reaching a state that is best described as having good rapport within the police community, I was able to go into the field while my informants were working, to observe them in action. However, as mentioned previously, this was not the focal point of the study. I discovered that when officers known to me were working, they performed just as I would have expected. They were professional, competent, courteous, and often curt. They clearly responded in predictable ways to various encounters with the public as well as the context of each encounter. At this time, it became clear that my study would focus more on the effects of occupational socialization: the off-duty manifestations of conformity and solidarity and the police officers' interpretations of their jobs, rather than their on-duty performance.

Observing officers on duty did allow me to engage in a bit of reality testing, or reality comparing. After making my own observations, I listened to officers describe the events of their watch to others. For the most part, I found these officers to be extremely reliable in terms of describing chronology, action, setting and participants, and outcome; that is to say, our perceptions of what happened were very similar. The only major differences between their perceptions and my own hinged on their perceptions of intent and causality, which seemed to be influenced by the number of years they had on the job. Their reporting of the incidents frequently impressed me as being more cynical and negative than my own. At the time this did not strike me as significant. After all, I would expect that officers would become somewhat hardened and less sympathetic in their responses to those persons they considered to be trouble makers, criminals or simply irresponsible. It appears to be part of the police worldview that people are responsible for what they do. There are very few acceptable "excuses."

I was astonished by their own dispassionate or even joking manner of reporting events that were clearly tragic moments in other people's lives. Police descriptions treated these events as almost mundane, everyday occurrences. It became clear that for police officers these awful events, while not everyday occurrences, are certainly not uncommon. In order to deal with the situation, they must remain somewhat detached. This extends even to the telling of the event. I also witnessed, on many occasions, a very different response. Police officers in small, intimate groups (with their close friends or family) frequently lost that detachment and facade of cynicism and became quite emotional in the retelling of an incident.

It is difficult not to become caught up in the drama of police work—the tragedy, the excitement, the uncertainty, the danger. It is intense and radically different from most of life's experiences or, at least, radically different from the life I had experienced up to that point. Here were the events of television and film—tomorrow's news items—and I was getting all the details of the "real" story. I became used to seeing my informants on the evening news and quoted in the morning paper. It was heady stuff.

I became more sympathetic toward the officers as the difficulty of the job became clearer to me. I learned that it was not just the physical danger that made the job difficult—in fact, the exciting moments were really few and far between. The majority of time the officers were working they were not engaged in exciting work. They frequently described their jobs as truly boring. One of the great difficulties they reported was dealing with the job in such a way that their response was appropriate. For example, an officer must be ready for a watch in which nothing of note may happen for the entire watch, or it may "get hot" in an instant and not let up. It is easy to become complacent, but officers must remain ready for anything.

Policing Literature

By this stage of my research I had discovered that there were several problems inherent in trying to use the existing literature as the foundation for understanding my informants. The literature did not deal with off-duty police. Literature concerned with attitudinal data appeared to imply, in the absence of any clear discussion, that the attitudes and behaviors exhibited by on-duty police represented their off-duty attitudes and behaviors as well. Most of the attitudes described in the literature are negative. The literature appears to tacitly assume that officers are impersonal, cynical, violent, racist and authoritarian while in uniform and, further, that these on-duty attitudes are a "given," totally internalized part of being a police officer. My data did not support either of these assumptions.

The officers who were known to me exhibited significant off-duty differences from the descriptions of officers that emerged from the literature. I feel that some of the differences may be due to regional, agency, or individual variation, but mostly I think the difference is due to a combination of misinterpreting both the working persona and the degree to which individuals who are performing the job of policing internalize the working persona. Police officers are not as totally inculcated with the police role as has been assumed. The degree of immersion in and internalization of the working persona are largely a function of the phase of the career of the individual officer, and police officers certainly differentiate between on- and off-duty behavior. What is appropriate on duty is not only inappropriate but can also be socially disruptive off duty.

Surprises and More Questions

As I came to know the officers in greater depth, I was amazed to realize how idealistic many of the officers were. I had not expected high degrees of sensitivity, idealism, or creativity. There were other similar surprises, frequently as a result of incongruence between the images of

police officers in the literature and the officers I knew. This produced a
new crisis in the study. How, I wondered, could these police be so different
than most of the other police as presented in the literature? Was this simply a matter of the difference between police studied on duty and off duty?
Was I missing something? Was it due to geographical or agency differences? Was I deluding myself about the people I had come to know, like
and respect? Were their attitudes and behaviors part of the uniform, to be
put on at the start of their watch and removed before leaving work? How
much of the job is internalized, and what affects the rate or the content of
internalization?

Three issues became highlighted toward the end of this second stage
of research. First, I discovered that I was interested in too many aspects
of the police officers' world. I gathered information in a greedy fashion,
convinced that surely the truth would emerge from the data. I was fearful
that there would not be enough data on certain topics and/or that I would
miss essential clues to greater truths if I omitted a scrap of information.
I quickly found myself inundated with unrelated bits and pieces; some of
them were gems, but not useful. I was overwhelmed and confused. This
confusion resulted in frequent shifts of focus and scope as my interests
and the sources of information changed. I searched for something that
would help in comprehending the data—the discovery that the policing
career had distinct phases was the key.

The second issue involved logistics. The discovery of phases in the
police career created a new problem. I needed to reinterview officers to
determine if the perceived phases were real. Rescheduling officers was a
nightmare, but well worth the effort. The reinterviews demonstrated the
phases to be valid, and remarkably useful. It brought order to the data,
and better yet, accounted for the variation that had been so perplexing.
Such verification would not have been possible if I had not been able to
reinterview the same officers.

The third issue, and area of concern, was my creeping awareness
that my attitudes and perceptions changed as a direct result of my exposure and involvement with police officers. I became more aware of my
surroundings with an eye toward not becoming a victim. I became much
more suspicious and even cynical. These were not welcome changes on
one level, because I liked the person I was before this transformation better than the transformed version—I was nicer, friendlier, less critical, less
suspicious. On another level, however, I believe the changes had a certain
amount of survival value. This too reflects more of a "police" worldview
than anything else. Not surprisingly, this is exactly the transformation
that takes place in the lives of police officers. Because of my own transformation I felt better able to understand similar changes among officers.

III: TAKING THE VOW

After five years of fieldwork, and having finally established my relationship with the police community as a friend and researcher, everything changed: I went for a motorcycle ride and lunch with a policeman. The man was an officer whom I had met early in my fieldwork and had become a good friend as well as a key informant. Along with other officers he had visited my home, met my family members, and shared meals. We had been platonic friends for five years and I did not anticipate any change in that status—however, I was wrong. Three months later we married. By this time, he had moved out of my sample division, and I thought the bulk of my fieldwork was finished. The fact that I was now married to a policeman had again changed my status vis-à-vis the police officers and opened many doors for me. This happy consequence was not at all planned but has had a profound effect on my research.

Being married to a police officer markedly minimized, although not totally eliminated, the insider/outsider problem, among others. One policeman who had been very difficult to interview and who had, in fact, not shown up on two occasions for scheduled interviews virtually demanded to be interviewed after my marriage.

Thus, as a direct result of my marriage, I became privy to other aspects of off-duty life for officers. While I am not considered an outsider, I am not a police officer either. My marriage has further validated my standing as someone who understands—I'm not, of course, "one of us," but very close. I have been able to confirm many of my findings for which my data was scant or incomplete. In many instances the easier entrée simply gave me access to gems of substantiation that I am reluctant to omit. Some of the facets of the job, which are of great interest to me now, were totally unknown to me prior to this level of interaction within the community. For these reasons, as well as my new perspective that enables me to give a more accurate version of the reality of police officers' lives, I am including data gathered after my marriage.

My husband is only one of many officers who permitted me to tape formal interviews of two hours or more or permitted me to take notes. I have not used him as an informant since well before our marriage. I have taken great care to insure that the data are not skewed by our relationship. In fact, one of the problems of being married to a police officer and writing about police officers is that people are prone to think that I am writing about my spouse. As with all of the other participants, there are ways in which he is typical and ways in which he is atypical, and I have tried to give him the same degree of privacy as my other informants.

Formal interviews supplement the extensive data gathered through participant observation. Currently I have formal interviews of one to two hours or more from 73 officers. Another 120 officers permitted me to make notes while we spoke—there is some overlap in these two groups. Many officers were interviewed several times over the years. In addition, my analysis benefits from less formal interaction with a much larger group of officers and their families and the information gleaned from those contacts. All of the quotations in the book have been taken from taped interviews.

My marriage, coupled with the fact that I was already established in the police community on my own, opened virtually all areas of police officers' lives and concerns to me. Following the marriage my participation in the police community predictably became an even greater part of my life. For six years I took dinner to my husband every night at the station. Usually I took extra food, and often we would share the meal with other officers in the lunch room to the station.

Sharing meals at the station placed me in the center of the action, so to speak. While I had not planned this as a data-gathering technique, I learned a great deal over the dinner table. Due to the nature of the job, often I would arrive, set up and wait until my husband could "clear for seven." During the waiting time I would talk to other officers and take in the atmosphere of the station. It is difficult in retrospect to attempt to determine how many hours were spent in this way, just as it is similarly difficult to compute how many hours were spent at sporting events, at family dinners, at weddings, picnics, on rides, at hospitals, attending funerals. Suffice it to say, I was fully immersed in the field.

IV: AS EASY AS IT GETS

After completion of my doctorate in 1991 I returned to active interviewing required for several projects (Barker, 1993; Womack and Barker, 1993). I was astounded at how easy it was to get interviews—even with officers with whom I had no previous contact. During this stage I interviewed more women than in the previous stages. Over the twenty-one-year period I was able to interview officers at several different phases of their careers and document individual progression through the phases. I have actually followed some officers for their entire careers—from the academy through retirement—which is a benefit from having access to a wide range of officers for such a long period of time. I could put data gained during the first stage of my research, which came from informants who were predominantly in early phases of their own careers, into perspective in this fourth stage of my research.

Over the past two decades I have seen many changes in the L.A.P.D.; one of the significant changes is the marked decrease in the sense of camaraderie. Much of this is due to the continued fragmentation of the department and the community. As the city becomes more a patchwork of economic, ethnic, racial and religious enclaves so too the department reflects similar divisions to a far greater extent than in the past—of course, this is also partly due to the fact that historically the force was much less diverse.

In the past, the status of being a police officer was the cross-cutting tie that bound all officers as a group. Today, police solidarity has been replaced by special-interest subgroups within the department. For example, police officers tend to socialize with age groups—age being determined not by chronological age, but by years on the job. This is not to say that other types of divisive factors, such as gender issues, did not exist in the past; of course they did. However, one of the key differences in the department between the past and the present is this loss of a sense of community among police officers.

THE GOAL

Michael Agar says, " . . . part of the ethnographer's role is to give some sense of different lifestyles to people who either do not know about them, or who are so bogged down in their own stereotypes that they do not understand them" (1980:27). In the case of police officers both conditions apply: people do not know about them, their jobs and their lives *and* are so bogged down in stereotypes, their own as well as those provided by the media, that understanding police is highly unlikely. The entity "police officer" is fully public and intended to be so, but the individual who fills the public role frequently seeks to remain as anonymous and as private as possible in terms of lifestyle. The goal of this book is to flesh out the public figure police officer through an examination of the police career as it is perceived and described by the people who live it. The phases of the police career are significant, not only for understanding the officers themselves, but for understanding the dynamics of change in the department, occupational socialization, issues of social control and the policing endeavor in general.

3

The World of Policing

Although the Los Angeles Police Department is one of the best-known law enforcement agencies in the country—for good or ill—the average street patrol officer is largely anonymous to the public. Individual personalities of officers are obscured by uniforms, the exigencies of their job, and by their own efforts to maintain a professional image. Police are meant to be seen presenting a uniform appearance and image. This uniformity encourages the public to assume that visual homogeneity is associated with behavioral homogeneity. Not only do police look alike, presumably they also act and think alike. To a great extent, this impression is encouraged by how police officers present themselves; effecting a certain image increases the ease and efficiency with which they perform their job.

Police officers understand the importance of the art of impression management, which plays a major role in their interactions. Police officers—to the degree that they are able—set the stage, don the appropriate costumes (they are very much aware of the impact their costumes have on their audience—they refer to ordinary street attire as "soft" clothes), learn their lines, and become masters of improvisation. However, they must be careful not to deviate too far from the stage directions or their fellow officers will not be able to play their roles in the performance. They are aware that they have a choice in how they present themselves. They consider the appropriate presentation of self (Goffman, 1959) to include command presence, which is defined as presenting such a formidable presence that no one will challenge their authority.

Patrol officers are the department's representatives on the street and the people whom the public—guilty, innocent and victimized—meet. Policing requires that patrol officers be highly visible and easily distinguishable from other people. The uniforms they wear and the cars they drive are effective ways of achieving this visibility. Officers are often reminded of the public relations aspects of their jobs and are urged to be a credit to the uniform. On another level, they are warned that simply wearing the uniform makes them a target.

Police must focus on the experiences they encounter on their job (for example, scenes of violence or brutality) in a different way than the public; police may appear callous as they gather data at the crime scene; they can be abrupt in their questioning; later they have to review their findings and write them up. Report writing emphasizes detachment and excludes emotion. Police are subject to extended contact with events that provoke strong emotion, but are generally deprived of an outlet for expressing it.

Police believe their ordering of reality is essential for social—and literal—survival in a job characterized by extraordinary risks and high levels of uncertainty. Officers consider an ability to learn to "see like a cop" a crucial element in the makeup of a potential police officer. In this agency P1 is a rank of designating an officer still on formal probation—still in training. One officer responsible for training says:

> What I look for first in P1s is simple: Is this a reasonable, observant person? Anyone can see things, but can they learn to see things like a cop? Can this person learn to see the street and read a situation, not in the normal sort of way, but the way you have to on this job— see the situation for what it is, see the options, *all* the options, and know what to do?

Another officer with seven years on the job, who frequently trains neophyte officers, remarks:

> The name of the game on the job is learning how to be an officer. Not just how to do this or that, but how to see and think like a copper. If you have a poor learning curve, then you're going to take your lumps. And some of them, not all, God knows, but some of them are avoidable if you see things for what they are. If you don't see clearly, the way an officer has to, you're going to be part of the problem because you won't see the best course of action in a situation. The way to handle a situation may not be dramatic—mostly it isn't. On the job, it's the dramatic stuff we're mostly trying to avoid, whenever possible. Drama gets between you and going home. Often the best solution involves listening and talking. More listening than talking. And caring. You've got to care about what you're doing or what's the point? You'll never understand it, and never do it well.

Seasoned officers, those who have done the job for at least five to seven years, are remarkably consistent in their view of the best way to approach the job, and they agree that policing calls for restraint. In the following extract, "Code 3" refers to a high-priority call requiring lights and sirens. It typically involves a crime against a person rather than property, and typically means the crime is in the process of being committed and the perpetrator is still at the scene.

> Officers fresh out of the academy expect drama, and they think it's like in the movies. Their eyes light up when they finally get to go Code 3. They get all excited. They have to learn to chill out. To see it and process it and not get caught up in it. It's a real balancing act.

While restraint is critical, another officer explains that the inability to view situations as an officer is dangerous to everyone concerned:

> A person who just can't see it, who can't learn to see things and put them together in the way that's absolutely essential on the job just isn't going to make it. He'll never be a cop. He can't be a crime buster. He can't serve the citizens; he can't even protect himself or his partner. He can't see the problem clearly, so how's he going to deal with it? He's going to get hurt and get someone else hurt, too.

DANGER

Of all aspects of the police worldview internalized by officers, none is as compelling—or as stressed at the beginning of the career—as the concept of danger. It is a given in the job, and patrol duty is one of the most dangerous of assignments. Patrol officers are the front-line officers—the most likely to be injured or killed, the first on any crime scene and, usually, the first representative of the department encountered by victims, suspects and witnesses.

Officers are acutely aware of the dangers of policing, which they experience both as physical danger and as a threat to their image. It is the function of police to enforce the law, and that involves making arrests. Though police have a degree of discretionary power in deciding whether to arrest an individual, once the decision to arrest has been made, they are committed to that course of action and the person will be arrested. If the person resists, the resistance will be met with force. If the resistance increases, so will the force. In the view of the police officer, the incident has become dangerous. Any time an arrest does not go smoothly, there is potential for it to go very badly indeed.

Any serious resistance on the part of a citizen signals to the police officer that potential problems could arise on several levels: physically, there is more likely to be an altercation; legally, there is a greater chance of complaints or even lawsuits; logistically, more paperwork will be required; emotionally, an arrest that involves use of force is unsettling, even for police, who deal with arrests on a regular basis. None of these considerations, however, will affect the outcome: an arrest will be made.

Patrol officers deal with people in a highly charged emotional atmosphere. In the heat of battle, they are part of the action, and they are also part of the clean-up that follows. An officer who misreads the situation or makes the wrong decisions endangers not only himself or herself but other officers as well. For this reason, the concept of danger is central to police attitudes toward decision making.

Because of the focus on danger in the worldview of police, formal and informal codes of conduct designed to protect officers and citizens are not

likely to be either flexible or negotiable. Formal codes refer to those portions of department policy, which are taught at the academy and
reinforced in roll call training and special training days, and involve codes
of behavior and tactics devised with an eye toward the safety of officers.
Often these formal codes and the training are fairly minimal and are
based on somewhat ideal models. After the academy, the informal training begins and a far more extensive set of codes of behavior is stressed
among officers. These come out of the shared experiences in the streets
and are more likely to develop from the kinds of compound situations in
which many things are happening at once. Often, over time, informal
codes become formal—but it can also go the other way.

Patrol officers value unpredictability in many aspects of their lives,
but not if they consider it dangerous. They attempt to minimize unpredictability when they feel they are in danger. The variable most easily
within their control is knowing what to expect from their fellow officers.
This goes beyond expecting the company line response to situations,
defined by department policy. Patrol officers also want to know how individual officers are likely to behave in a given circumstance. Officers'
responses are shaped by standardized training administered in the police
academy and are honed by their shared experiences in the streets.

To know one's fellow officers is essential. This necessity leads to
emphasis on a high degree of conformity in behavior, if not belief. This
also means that a high value is placed on knowing a working partner's
personal life, since events in an officer's personal life can affect decisions
and actions on the job and could possibly interfere with making a clear-
headed decision in the face of danger. Partly because of the perception of
all kinds of danger, officers' off-duty lives are often quite private. Sharing
one's personal life with a fellow officer is regarded as a sign of trust and
camaraderie, as well as a working necessity.

The concept of danger organizes the life of a police officer in all its
aspects; from economic behavior to choice of companions, recreation, and
residence. Because police perceptions of danger shape their interactions
with each other and with citizens, it is essential to understand, not only
what they consider dangerous, but also the way these definitions change
over time as the officers pass through different career phases. As officers
progress through their careers, anxiety over physical danger is replaced
by other issues and other definitions of danger.

PERFORMING THE JOB

Though management officers have a higher rank, earn higher salaries, occupy higher-status positions in the hierarchy, patrol officers enjoy
a seemingly wider range of options in the performance of their duties. To

a very real extent patrol officers determine acceptable levels of order and can also be somewhat selective in the enforcement of the law. The discretionary power of patrol officers has received a great deal of attention in academic writings on police work (Banton, 1964; La Fave, 1965; Black, 1980; Bittner, 1980, 1983, 1990; and many others).

From the moment an officer walks into the roll call room at the beginning of his or her watch until the end of watch, there are conflicts and contradictions between the directives of the department, the requirements of the job, the expectations of citizens, the realities of the streets, and the desires of the officers. The officers' job for the nine to twelve hours of watch is, among other things, to reconcile these conflicts while maintaining positive relationships with as many of those involved as possible. These varying relationships are not equally important. Of all the relationships, the one most critical to the patrol officer is the one between himself or herself and the other officers.

In his study of police officers, Jerome Skolnick (1966) notes that most police officers prefer patrol duty even though they rank it among the most difficult of assignments. One reason officers consider patrol to be difficult is because of the inherent danger. In addition to the danger, it is also exciting and viewed by the officers as important and real police work.

DUTY

Officers are deployed with an eye toward mobility, and can be shifted into configurations that meet the logistical and political needs of the department. Within the context of department-mandated and controlled allocations of personnel, the officers can also request assignments to different duties, watches and divisions. Officers can also change jobs through promotion.

Street officers patrol in cars, on motorcycles, or on foot. In some specialized units they may also patrol on horseback or on bicycles. The mode of travel significantly alters the nature of the job and the kinds of situations the officers are likely to encounter. For this reason, there is a selective factor at work, both in terms of the officers who seek such work and on the part of the department in making assignments. Officers who work these different duties tend to view that particular duty as the essence of police work.

Car Patrol

After a probationary period during which officers get their first assignments, they are placed in a two-officer car and sent on patrol. Many officers will spend the major part of their careers in these car patrols, although it is rare for an officer to complete a career having worked this duty exclusively. Car patrol, referred to simply as patrol, is the duty performed by the majority of the uniformed officers in this department.

When many of my informants first started patrol work they say they actually patrolled; that is, they drove around an assigned area looking for things that appeared suspicious and generally tried to prevent crime. Now those days are gone, except for some more specialized units that do not respond directly to radio calls. Usually, as soon as the car-patrol officers log on at the beginning of a shift, they receive a call for service, meaning that something requires their immediate attention; a crime has been committed and, as soon as the officers get into their cars, they are already deployed. In fact there is usually a backlog of requests for service that must be handled before dealing with more recent requests. Thus, these officers do not have the luxury of patrolling and they are unable to prevent crimes, because they are busy responding to crimes that have already been committed.

Patrol officers deal with the broadest range of duties and are also expected to serve as back-up for more specialized tasks and units. Patrol units handle everything from time-consuming lost-adult calls (which usually involves driving around trying to locate the homes of persons who, for one reason or another, are not capable of finding their own way to family dwellings, drug or mental health facilities or halfway houses), to preliminary investigations of murder. They are expected to adjudicate disputes; defuse gang violence; discourage vandals; remove public nuisances; and apprehend burglars, muggers, robbers, rapists and murderers. They may also issue parking citations if a complaint has been lodged, and they may cite violations of traffic laws.

Among other things, patrol officers have been required to instruct parents in child rearing, quiet loud parties, and answer burglar alarms. The list is endless. Sometimes officers answer calls for service initiated by people who are simply lonely and want to talk to someone—anyone. Department policy requires that every call for service must be answered; patrol officers are responsible for making the response.

Clearly, while patrol officers are expected to deal with a wide range of concerns, whether they are trained or skilled in one area or another appears to be relatively immaterial. They are expected to respond to each call and make the best of it. Every patrol officer has favorite stories about the job, and there is an illustrative story for almost every occasion. Almost anything can happen on patrol.

The watch can be characterized by unadulterated boredom, chaos, terror, or frustration, or a combination of all of these and more. Humorous events are not infrequent, although police humor is typically drawn from the darker side of human experience.

Motors

Motorcycle officers are essentially traffic officers, primarily concerned with violations of traffic laws and with apprehending speed violators, drunks, and dangerous and irresponsible drivers. It is part of their job to respond to reports of traffic accidents. They are usually the first units on the scene, attend to the injured until the ambulance arrives, and oversee the initial investigation. Motors, as they are called, will often work "deuce watches," devoted exclusively to looking for drivers under the influence of alcohol or drugs.

Because they focus on traffic violations, motors tend to find their own work. Although they must also respond to specific complaints, they are not tied to the radio and are not expected to respond to the kinds of calls handled by car patrol units. The fact that they work more independently is important to motor officers and is often mentioned as one of the main reasons for transferring to motors. Motorcycle officers often see

themselves as doing the job the way it should be done: They can "be on the prowl" and be on the crime scene as the crime is taking place.

Motor officers resent and resist attempts by supervisors to monitor their productivity through implementation of quotas. The officers claim that quotas are yet another example of the way in which the city and their own supervisors make unrealistic demands and insult their integrity. They say that, as soon as officers produce to full capacity and meet the standards of performance set by supervision, the city will demand higher and higher levels of performance. Motor officers also state that quotas encourage some officers to write tickets when they would otherwise issue a warning.

Car patrol officers philosophically support motor officers in their resistance to quotas. Quotas are regarded with skepticism by most patrol officers both for the reasons mentioned and also because they are sensitive to citizens' frequent sarcastic references to officers making their quotas by issuing an unwarranted or capricious ticket. However, patrol officers also feel the motor officers are not always working as hard as they could. Partly because of the highly discretionary nature of their job, there is also ample opportunity for motor officers to "find a hole," or relax, and not remain "on the prowl."

Foot Patrol

Officers who work foot patrols are highly visible, resulting in more routine exchanges with citizens. Unlike car patrol officers, who deal primarily with victims, and motor officers, who deal primarily with traffic violators and accidents, the majority of contacts made by foot patrol officers are with ordinary citizens who are just going about their business. The visibility of foot patrol officers and their consistent interaction with people living in neighborhoods give citizens a chance to feel that the community and the police work together to prevent crime. Foot beats are sometimes regarded by car patrol and motor officers as being primarily a public relations position, rather than real police duty. Officers who choose to work foot patrols acknowledge the public relations function of the job, but they also see it as a reversion to an earlier style of policing and therefore conforming more to the way it should be done.

Specialized Units

Specialized units investigate and suppress major crimes, gang violence, drug trafficking and various kinds of vice activities. Recently demand has created units that deal exclusively with responses to burglar alarms, called "alarm calls," and a one-officer car that spends an entire watch taking reports of home burglary. Specialized units usually draw their personnel from the ranks of the various patrol officers—car patrol (most frequently), foot patrol (occasionally), or motors (rarely)—either at the request of the officer or at the discretion of the department. This means that an officer must be prepared to deal with a different duty on fairly short notice. Thus, his or her skills and techniques must be able to conform to those of his or her peers, whether on car, foot or motor patrol.

RANK

Patrol officers can be engaged in one of several different duties, but they all have essentially the same rank: police officer. On the L.A.P.D., there are actually four categories of patrol officers, but these are relatively insignificant in the overall departmental organization.

More significantly, differences in the rank of patrol officer often identify those who are concerned with upward mobility. Officers who move rapidly through these small differences in rank are likely to apply for management positions or duties that might make them more attractive candidates for management positions. Police officers with this orientation are often viewed by other patrol officers as simply passing through.

Sergeants also interface with the public, and their status marks a significant difference in rank. Sergeants are officers who have advanced through the ranks of police officer and who have passed written and oral examinations. The exams cover law and enforcement tactics, as well as knowledge of managerial and public relations techniques.

The role of sergeant is somewhat marginal within the department. Sergeants are viewed as management by the patrol officers, but they are viewed as part of patrol by upper management. Sergeants are seen as much closer to the street officers than other supervisory personnel, in literal proximity and also in orientation. Detectives are not at all regarded as management, but possess specialized investigation skills and work closely with patrol. Many patrol officers view detective duty as important police work and hope, someday, to join their ranks.

Sergeants vary tremendously in their management styles, a phenomenon which may be due to the long-term goals of individual sergeants as well as their differences in personality. Those who see themselves as management behave differently than those who identify with patrol officers. Some rarely leave the station unless their presence is required. Others actively patrol the streets and participate in, monitor, and supervise the activities of patrol officers.

Differences in personality and management styles create dynamic and sometimes tense relations between police officers on the street and their direct supervisors, the sergeants. However, for the most part, patrol officers and sergeants socialize off duty with little regard for differences in rank.

Officers holding a rank higher than sergeant are usually viewed by the street officers as no longer directly involved in policing as they see it and, almost by definition, are out of touch with the streets. Higher ranking officers are viewed as management, having loyalties and commitments to the political structure and to their personal careers rather than to street officers and their concerns. There are, of course, exceptions, but higher ranked officers must consciously work on maintaining their ties with officers to avoid being viewed simply as "management," and no longer one of them.

Patrol officers consider decisions made by management to be guided by different priorities than their own. A recurring theme in the conversations and mythology of patrol officers is that management is more concerned with economic and political considerations than with the safety of officers. Since perception of danger plays such a prominent role in the worldview of policing, it is not surprising that it plays a metaphorical role in expressing patrol officers' frustration at management policies. The story below, often told in several versions at different times, suggests that an officer was shot as an indirect consequence of receiving "days." (Recall that the terms "days" and "days off" refer to days that officers are required to work without pay as punishment for an infraction of the rules.)

An injured officer was working the end of a ten-day stretch and was on patrol when he and his partner received a call that a small local restaurant felt it was being "cased by two Black males in a dark-colored car." The officers observed a light-colored car with two African-American males in the area close to the fast food restaurant. They called in the vehicle plate, but did not wait for the response—the first mistake. One officer approached the driver's side of the car and began talking to the driver. The driver explained that he was unfamiliar with the neighborhood, but was looking for a street (nearby and known to the officers) to which his sister had recently moved. In response to the driver's question, the officer made the second mistake. He looked away to point out the direction of the street and the driver shot him. The partner was so upset that, although he did put out an officer needs help call, he did not transmit useful information about the suspects—this was regarded as another error. When other officers arrived, he was still unable to give a good description—this compounded the problem. He was very upset and not very articulate. It later turned out that, had the officers waited for the response to their license plate call, they would have learned that the car was regarded as armed and dangerous: that is, the car, and presumably its occupants, had previously been involved in an incident involving weapons.

When a report on a car comes back classified armed and dangerous, it includes the admonition to "hold all occupants," or "hold for prints," the stop is titled a "Code 6 Charles" and handled very differently—as a felony stop. According to proper police procedure, both officers should have approached the car with weapons drawn, and ordered the occupants out of the car and onto the ground. Other units would be notified of a Code 6 Charles stop and ideally a backup unit would be on its way.

Although the injured officer failed to follow police procedure, he received little criticism from his fellow officers, who considered the error as resulting from bad management decisions that put the officer on the street for too long without a break. Though many said they would have handled the situation differently, they identified with the "officer down." Management, on the other hand, considered the incident a case of breach of policy and "failure to anticipate," placing the blame on the wounded officer.

Though the officers generally absolved the wounded officer of blame, the same was not true for his partner. The partner's actions, attitude, and personal attributes were subjected to heavy criticism from his fellow officers, though not so much by management. This is another way in which patrol officers and management view the case differently. Management assigned primary responsibility for the incident to the more experienced, wounded officer. Patrol officers considered that, after management made decisions requiring the one officer to work ten consecutive days, the partner was at fault not only for having failed to read the situation properly and protect the officer who was ultimately injured, but especially for losing control—he responded emotionally when he needed to respond professionally.

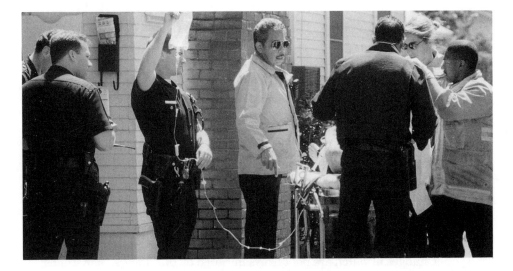

The evaluation of peers can be more important to the careers of the officers involved than that of management, as evidenced by the partner's subsequent career. He changed divisions, perhaps in an attempt to put the incident behind him, but that was impossible. Within one year of the incident, the partner quit the job. As one officer puts if: "When a jacket is hung on a guy, his reputation precedes him to the next division he goes to. Everybody knows what there is to know about the guy, at least enough to form opinions."

WATCH

Although varying slightly from division to division, there are several overlapping watches, or shifts, within which officers can be deployed to meet the demands of the division. During the bulk of time research was conducted, these watches were based on three eight-hour-and-forty-five-minute shifts covering the twenty-four-hour day. These were supplemented by "mids," watches that double up officers during some of the busiest hours of the day. Depending on the division, time of year, general deployment, and other factors, there may be two or three mids per division. All these watches are regular patrol shifts. Specialized units may be deployed on the same schedule or may be on a totally different schedule.

Different watches have distinctive characteristics, as do the officers who choose them. During the probationary period, officers are moved through most of the watches and, during this time, most officers choose favorites or discover which watches they intensely dislike. Throughout his or her career, an officer's watch preference may change as his or her personal situation changes. This is one way in which the police career offers some vital flexibility. Officers can arrange hours to accommodate a spouse's schedule or to be available for children.

Aside from having its own character, the watch often determines the composition of one's off-duty recreational group, as well as recreational possibilities. Police officers frequently engage in recreational activities with the officers who share their watch. Changes in friendships or in hobbies may be marked, instigated, or acknowledged by a change in watch. One officer stated that he decided to change his watch because he realized he was drinking too much after work. If he changed his watch, and therefore the time at which he finished work and the group of people who would be available after work, he felt he would find it easier to break what he saw as a destructive pattern. He was able to alter his off-duty behavior to omit marathon drinking.

Changes in watch are not always initiated by the officers. Sometimes an officer will be moved by management from one watch to another. These moves can be difficult for the officers, not only in resetting their biological clocks, but also in terms of the nature of the work, compatibility with other officers, and the constraints and conflicts created by outside commitments, such as family, school, social pursuits and other jobs. Changes not initiated by the officers themselves are often regarded as punitive.

Daywatch

Daywatch is the shift that most closely corresponds with normal working hours, from approximately 7:00 A.M. until about 3:30 P.M. Crimes encountered by daywatch patrol officers typically include business disputes, shoplifting, purse snatching, forgeries, citizen complaints (regarding vandalism or other disturbances), traffic accidents and bank robberies. Many burglaries, auto thefts, and stealing items from motor vehicles take place during this watch but often are not reported until the following watch, when people are likely to discover their losses. Assaults, rapes and homicides occur during every watch, although the circumstances tend to differ. During daywatch, these are more likely to be associated with businesses or other institutions that operate primarily during these hours.

Officers who choose this watch say they feel it is easier on their families. Daywatch is often the choice of people with school-age children, because watch more or less coincides with the school day. Officers on this watch often say they feel more normal and in synch with the non-police world.

> You can lead more of a normal life. I mean as normal as life gets
> when you're on the job. Parents' night, you're there. Take the kids
> trick or treating—no problem. You want to see a movie—name the

night. Baseball game Saturday morning, there you might have a problem. Maybe you get your days [off], maybe not. But you're still in much better shape than some poor joker who's trying to have a normal family life and begging for the days off.

There are advantages and disadvantages to every watch. Sometimes the same feature mentioned by one officer as an advantage is cited by another as a disadvantage. One example is going to court. Officers receive subpoenas to testify in court on a regular basis. An officer on patrol duty expects to testify at some court procedure on all of the cases in which he or she is involved as an arresting officer. This includes hearings to determine whether or not a case will go to trial, as well as the resulting trials. Going to court can be very time consuming.

Working daywatch means the normal time of watch includes the hours spent in court. Court time is just part of the normal working day. For officers not working days, court is also a normal part of their working day, but they receive overtime compensation for court appearances—either in time or in money. Time is time on the books, which they can draw on at a later date when they need a "special," an unscheduled day off, or a "deduct," permission to come to work late or leave early. Regardless of how long officers spend testifying or waiting to testify, they are compensated for four hours. For the officers not working days, then, court time can help build up cash or time surpluses.

However, court appearances can be extremely inconvenient, cutting into an officer's off-duty time. Officers who work days know that any court time will fit conveniently into their normal work schedule. However, they also do not have as many avenues for collecting overtime due to court appearances.

P.M.s

P.M.s is the watch from 3:30 P.M. until 12:30 A.M. Many officers choose this shift so they can do other things during the day. Several officers used this watch to attend school; some took occasional work—department-approved jobs—providing security for movie productions, private parties or individuals, and sporting events. Court appearances sometimes interfered with their studies or other activities, but they were spared the necessity of juggling days off with the demands of their schedules.

It is easier for sergeants to employ this strategy than for patrol officers due to the greater numbers of court appearances required of patrol officers. However, because there are fewer sergeants in the division, a sergeant can be moved from one watch to another with little warning.

Many officers work P.M.s because the hours make the commute to work more pleasant and time-effective. Los Angeles is so large and so

hemmed in by suburbs that the morning commute can be quite an ordeal. Most officers do not live in the city or even close to its boundaries, and they have to allow another hour or so of commute time if they drive to work during rush hour.

The P.M. watch is most likely to deal with crimes carried over from daywatch—crimes committed during the earlier shift, but not reported until the P.M. watch. Burglarized cars and homes and stolen and vandalized cars are key among the carry-overs. In addition, the P.M. watch has its own distinctive array of crimes. Among them are even more burglaries and thefts (although these are not the most numerous crimes on the watch), business robberies (especially restaurants and other businesses that are closing at the end of their day), gang activities, problems with juveniles, cruising, drug trafficking, drive-by shootings, problems involving prostitution, complaints about parties, and other noise complaints.

Late in the P.M. watch, or early in the morning watch, there is an increase in suicides and reports of drug overdoses. Homicides that occur during this watch tend to be the result of robberies, family disputes or, late in the watch, gang-related killings. Most, but certainly not all, of the rapes that occur during this watch are of the "date rape" sort. Usually the victim knows her assailant.

Morning Watch

Morning watch, which falls from roughly 11:30 P.M. to 7:30 A.M., is known as the "tightest" watch, which means the officers who work this watch tend to exhibit even more solidarity than those of other watches. Traditionally these officers socialize more with each other off duty and seem to have more intense friendships within the watch. This watch is also somewhat smaller than the others, partly because there are far fewer citizens out and about during the hours of this watch and, therefore, it is not necessary to have as many officers ready for deployment.

This watch also facilitates the commute to and from work and makes it easier to take on other activities. Many officers choose this watch so they can go to night school or take part-time jobs in the early evening. It is also known as the singles watch, partly because it is possible to have an active social life and still get to work on time, and partly because most married police officers find it unworkable. Many officers mentioned that before they were married this was the best watch for them, but after their marriages they switched to P.M.s or daywatch.

The officers who work this watch describe it as one in which it is easier to separate the "good guys from the bad." During much of the watch, most citizens are sleeping, or at least not out and about. This makes it easier to spot suspects. It is also much easier to get around the division and keep track of what is normal and what isn't. Most officers who work morning watch do so because they like the watch. It is small enough that it can usually be staffed by officers who appreciate its distinctive character, liabilities and advantages.

The crimes that characterize this watch are business burglary, grand theft auto, theft from motor vehicles, grand theft from construction sites and vandalism. As with P.M.s, there may be some gang activity, drug trafficking, and "people just floating around, up to no good."

Morning-watch officers are always on the alert for "hot prowl" burglaries. These crimes are of particular interest to police because they involve burglars who choose to enter and burglarize homes they know are occupied. Police believe that, unlike burglars who are surprised by the untimely homecoming of the tenant, hot prowl burglars enjoy the excitement of knowing the victim of the burglary is present while the crime is being committed. To police, this makes these suspects more dangerous.

Hot prowl burglars often have an m.o. of rape, assault, or even homicide. Short for *modus operandi*, an m.o. entails the distinguishing characteristics of the way in which the crime is committed or elements of the crime itself. These often provide keys to investigatory leads and apprehension of a suspect. Most successful or career criminals develop characteristic m.o.s that work for them. This can work against these criminals once the police discover patterns in the m.o. Sometimes the burglary escalates into rape, assault or murder, not because the burglary was interrupted, but simply because the opportunity presented itself. Rape, in particular, is often a crime of opportunity with hot prowl burglars. Hot prowl crimes generally take place just before daybreak. Other crimes—including homicides, family disputes and intruder calls—also occur throughout the watch.

Partly because the watch is so small and closely knit, the officers tend to keep in closer touch with each other through their radios and the computers that have been installed in their patrol cars. This is not feasible on other watches, where the radio is much busier and there are many more police officers on the streets. On morning watch, or "mornings," the officers are more likely to let each other know what they are doing and to roll out (join in) as back-up whenever there is any kind of activity. Part of this is motivated by the desire to back-up fellow officers; part of it may come from boredom if the watch has been slow; part of it is because it is so much easier for the patrol cars to get around during the morning hours. The fact that the officers directly share more experiences in the course of the watch also binds them more closely together than officers on the other watches.

YEARS ON THE JOB

Of all the features of the social organization of policing that have significance to police officers, years on the job is paramount. It is the single most defining characteristic of the officer independent of his or her individual temperament. Officers consciously use the number of years on the job, known as "years on," to evaluate another officer and to set the tone for interaction with that officer.

Officers count their years on the job from the first day they enter the academy. This date, called the anniversary date, will be the most significant marker of their police career, serving as a quick device for other officers to evaluate their skills and expertise. For minority officers, this date is especially important because if they were hired before court mandated minority hiring, they do not have to work as hard as new police to establish themselves as members of the working watch, and their commitment to the job is taken more seriously. They are assumed to be more competent than the majority of new officers, minority or otherwise, hired since qualification and training standards have been relaxed.

Another reason for the significance of years on the job has to do with the predictable rhythm of the police career, which becomes evident when we examine the years on the job in terms of separate career phases. Over the span of a career in policing, an officer passes through five successive phases of idealism, competence, disillusion, resolution of conflicting attitudes toward policing and, ultimately, retirement. The following five chapters identify these five phases in the careers of street cops and explore how they impact the lives of officers. "Phase One: Hitting the Streets," begins with training in the police academy and continues through the probationary period, when the new officers are earning part of their "jackets," the reputation that will follow each of them through the rest of their career. "Phase Two: Hitting Their Stride," begins about two or three years after the officers begin street duty, when the officers develop confidence in their ability to patrol the streets and gain the acceptance of their companion officers. In "Phase Three: Hitting the Wall," officers become disillusioned by the department and the job, but find they have few other options, since they have devoted themselves to the life of a police officer. During "Phase Four: Regrouping," officers come to terms with the difficulties of their job and begin to look forward to retirement. Finally, in "Phase Five: Deciding to Retire," a senior police officer who has earned the respect of this colleagues faces the decision of whether to stay on the job or to "pull the pin," collect a pension and leave the police organization. All the phases are fraught with various forms of danger; they are distinct primarily in terms of how the officers define that danger and the strategies they employ to deal with it.

The phases emerge clearly from the clustering of key events that mark the officers' lives, as well as the feelings and attitudes the officers express in talking about their lives and careers. Virtually all officers pass through these phases, although the individual experience may vary significantly in terms of the length of time spent in any one and the time of onset of the phase. Delineation of the content of the phases—the kinds of experiences, issues, perceptions and changes the officers undergo—arose from the data gathered during my fieldwork and was subsequently confirmed by the officers themselves. It is not possible to similarly delineate an exact time schedule, but the approximate onset and duration of the phases similarly emerged from the data. While these phases are not strictly of uniform length, they correspond closely with the number of years on the job—part of the reason that officers focus on this information.

Phase One
Hitting the Streets
The First Three Years

Phase one is most easily understood when subdivided into three stages. During the first and second stages, the officers are on probation. The first stage, making the grade—involves the formal preparation for the job and relies on police academy training to train, test and evaluate candidates. The second stage—making the cut—involves an initial period of informal, as well as formal, training and their first experience on the streets as police officers. The rookies are scrutinized and evaluated by other officers. In the third stage, officers are on the road to proving themselves—as officers—to their comrades as well as themselves.

Stage 1: Making the Grade

Many recruits to the L.A.P.D. are drawn by a romanticized, exciting, and even heroic vision of police work. These recruits are often shocked by the training they receive in their first formal introduction to the job.

Other recruits, who have family members or friends on the force, already know what to expect. There are numerous examples of police families within the L.A.P.D. or officers with family members working for other law enforcement agencies. For these recruits, academy training is much less dramatic than for those who have not been exposed to the harsh realities of the job.

Academy training is designed both to turn neophytes into functional police officers and to weed out inappropriate candidates. This process is fraught with pressures from many directions. L.A.P.D. management and city administrators press for passing as many of the recruits as possible to save money; training officers view maintaining standards and producing well trained officers as the goal. Sometimes these desires are at odds. Training is expensive for the city and every recruit who fails to pass muster represents a net loss.

At the same time, training faculty at the academy are experienced officers who know the importance of having well-trained, disciplined, competent, and dependable personnel in the field. Their internalized understanding of danger—in the physical sense for the officers and in terms of morale and reputation for the department—guides them in training and evaluating new recruits. They have a vested interest in eliminating inappropriate candidates.

However, it is unclear what constitutes an appropriate candidate. Demonstrated ability and willingness to undergo rigorous physical and academic training are obvious criteria. The most valued attributes of a police officer include the ability to respect authority and to get along with one's colleagues, since patrol officers rely on each other in all aspects of police work especially in times of danger. Collegiality is very difficult to assess.

In the academy, officers are drilled in police procedures, the law, physical training and officer safety. They are taught how to take a report, how to take fingerprints, and are trained in other aspects of crime scene investigation. They learn how to drive—police style—which includes the safe and fast way to turn, how to broadcast a location, and the rules

and techniques of pursuit. They learn about their weapons—how they work, how to maintain them, their limitations, when and how to use them and when not to. They learn control holds and combat wrestling. They also learn, if they do not already know, how to take orders.

THE MILITARY MODEL

Most urban police departments in the United States are organized according to the military model. Recruits are taught to rely on and relate to each other along the lines of this model, which includes respect for authority and rank, and for the flow of the chain of command. They are expected to accept the military model as appropriate for police academy training and the structure of the department.

Recruits are taught that the unit is only as strong as its weakest link and are urged not to be the weak point. Weakness and failure to follow the model can place the entire endeavor in jeopardy. They are taught that they owe their allegiance to the badge, the agency, and their fellow officers— not on the basis of personality, but because that is the only way the system can work. The chain of command cannot be broken. Officers respond to "rank," not to the individual. Recruits are taught that they must fit into this system. In the past, officers who were unwilling or unable to accept this structure did not graduate and did not become sworn officers.

The academy experience is similar to that of a military boot camp in many respects. Recruits spend a great deal of time in close order drill (coordinated marching). They are subject to inspections of their drills, their dress, and their weapons, as well as their personal grooming and deportment. The resemblance to military structure is intentional. In the 1960s and 1970s, all recruits had military experience and were well acquainted with this format. An important difference between traditional and new police is the military background of the former officers and the absence of military training among new officers.

Traditional officers view this as possibly the most significant difference between the two groups. They believe the absence of military training is reflected in a lack of respect for rank, lack of comprehension of the chain of command, the inability to follow orders, lack of discipline, and an indication of lack of commitment to the department and their fellow officers. Traditional officers believe this laxity could potentially result in endangering the safety and well-being of other officers.

In initial training two kinds of danger are emphasized: the physical danger inherent in the job and the potential danger of inappropriate social liaisons. These two dangers will remain constant concerns throughout the police career, and both are likely to take their toll on the officers.

PHYSICAL TRAINING

The primary emphasis in academy training is on conveying a sense of the physical danger of the job, and on teaching the proper way to manage or minimize risk. Recruits are urged to build up their physical endurance with the admonition that their physical conditioning will make the difference between life and death.

Recruits are sent on forced runs of several miles, often through adverse conditions. Informants report being required to run ten miles through extreme heat in the hilly environs of the academy wearing heavy gun belts from which batons hang, flapping and rubbing the officers raw. Officers talk of doing sit-ups on the field until their tailbones are likewise raw. This strenuous training took place in the "good old days" of standards. While traditional police officers complain about the physical training they received, they are simultaneously proud of having completed the rigorous course. They criticize new police because they were not similarly tested and trained.

Still, recruits engage in hand-to-hand combat drills and practice with various pieces of police equipment: gun belts, guns, batons, and monadnocks (a martial arts weapon). They are gassed with tear gas, so they will know what to expect, since any time tear gas is used, the officer also gets a dose. Trainees practice in pairs, both armed and unarmed.

Traditionally, recruits would take turns "choking out" each other. "Choking" refers to a control hold designed to make violent suspects compliant. The control hold is done from behind the suspect. The officer puts his or her arm across the suspect's neck, pulling tight with that arm assisted by the hand of the other arm which is used to give greater power to the hold. By cutting off the blood flow to the brain, choking renders the suspect unconscious long enough to make an arrest. Until the late 1970s, every police officer in the agency had been rendered unconscious by this hold during training.

Officers are trained in the various stages to follow in maintaining control of a situation and gaining compliance. The sequence they are supposed to follow is: verbal, touch, pain compliance, control hold, baton, deadly force. In this agency, ideally officers are to use only the force necessary to safely attain compliance or make an arrest. In describing the sequence, one officer includes an often-voiced negative comment on the new police:

> If someone complies with a verbal request, fine. If not, then the officer attempts to convince the person. If he complies with a verbal argument, fine. If that doesn't work you try "touch." Sometimes all you have to do is move in closer to them, but sometimes you need to keep your distance; it kinda depends on the situation. Next is "pain compliance." Finger holds. Next, "control hold," commonly referred to as

"choke out." In place of this control hold, new recruits are now taught
. . . to use their batons or monadnocks to gain compliance. If the "verbal" doesn't work for them, they're trained now not to get in close. The
new training with all the A.A. police emphasizes baton, because so
many of the new police are female—smaller muscle mass and generally short, or shorter—and small males, guys that would never have
made it on the job before. It's not safe. They're too easily overpowered.

The use of "deadly force" is the last resort, and the rules governing
this most serious of police sanctions are numerous. Partly due to changing
conditions in the communities policed and in the nature of the police
force, several significant changes have occurred in the kinds of weapons
allowed as service weapons and back-ups, in the kind of ammunition
allowed, and in shooting policy. For example, traditional police were
trained to aim for and shoot the largest part of the body: the trunk. They
were trained to fire multiple shots, because in real-life shootings shots
often go astray.

Today, police officers are also trained to make head shots. This is a
more difficult shot because the head provides a smaller target, but the
shot has greater stopping power. This shift has been deemed necessary
because of an increase in suspects wearing bulletproof vests, and because
drug intoxicated suspects (especially those on PCP) can take several
shots and continue to resist for prolonged periods of time, according to
police lore. While most officers never fire their weapons at a suspect,
when they do, despite their training, I suspect they still aim for the easi-
est target—the torso.

Academy training dramatically underscores the dangers of underes-
timating the strength or stamina of one's opponent. One officer describes
his reaction to a training film depicting a stabbing:

> It was unbelievable. Unnerving. It was worse than the worst horror
> movie. This suspect was on the back of a police officer, stabbing him
> with an ice pick. The officer had to reach around, put his arm across
> his body and try to shoot the suspect while the suspect was still stab-
> bing him. And he shot him and the suspect said, "Yeah, you got me
> good that time." And he stabs the officer again and the officer shoots
> him again and he says, "Yeah, got me again," and keeps on, stabbing
> and talking. Like he's not going to quit, and he's not going to die. He's
> talking to the officer while the officer's shooting him, and he's stab-
> bing the officer and it goes on and on, stabbing and shooting, and each
> time the guy gets shot he's telling the officer about the shot.
> Unbelievable . . . the officer lived. He lived, he was on the tape and
> you could see in his description how heavy it was. Hard to believe, but
> there was the guy talking about it. Imagine some guy just talking ca-
> sually as you shoot him, and he's still stabbing and not stopping. Un-
> believable. Now that's scary.

Other officers tell of similar experiences, either firsthand or, more often, accounts they have heard in roll call training periods or on the police grapevine. Most of these scenarios involve suspects under the influence of drugs who are capable of superhuman strength. One example is the story of a suspect who, when taken into custody, grabbed a shotgun from its holder and bent the barrel.

Sometimes superhuman strength is not a matter of drug use. Officers are particularly worried about the physical size of large suspects. One officer reported:

> The big guys, really big guys, you've got to watch. Some are real cooperative, like they know they're big and they don't want us to feel threatened or like we have to come on heavy, and that's fine. That's good. But if a big guy goes off on you, you have got a real problem there. It jumps you into hyperspace. You have to think *so* far ahead, because this guy can win. Well, no, he won't win, but it's going to take a hell of a lot to stop him. You better pray for back-up and even then, those big guys . . . [shakes head, shrugs shoulders]

Sometimes, legends of the physical prowess of suspects who have to be apprehended travel from one police department to another:

> In Hawaii they changed their ammunition because some of the suspects they come in contact with are immense. The Samoans. Huge. There was one guy they had to shoot nine times and it didn't stop him, he still killed the police officer, and he'd already killed his whole family.

In their academy training, traditional police learned that the degree of force necessary to gain compliance depends, to a large degree, upon the "command presence" of the officer.

COMMAND PRESENCE

In addition to classroom work and physical training, recruits are also taught the importance of command presence. This training is part psychological and part physical, and some officers maintain that some of it cannot be taught at all. Command presence is a quality that conveys supreme authority, confidence, competence, and the physical ability to back it up. It is essentially an exercise in the presentation of self.

On many levels, command presence is intimidation, but it may not always be coercive. Command presence also includes the capacity to be persuasive, diplomatic and convincing. It is the ability to make others respond quickly and without incident to your directives. One officer stated: "All you needed on the street was the brains God gave you, your gun, and command presence. If it came right down to it, you could do without the brains and the gun, but God help you if you didn't have command presence." Police officers dress, walk and talk in ways they feel create and enhance command presence. Officers who embody this quality are assumed to have fewer problems on the streets than officers lacking command presence.

Traditional police express doubts about the ability of new police to present a physical image that motivates suspects to comply without resorting to more forceful means of persuasion. Traditional police lament the absence of command presence among many new police, especially the women, and see this as a serious deficiency in them as police officers.

In the view of traditional officers, command presence coupled with police skills allows them to control almost every situation. It is this control which is supposed to permit police to do the job efficiently and safely. When control breaks down, they believe, police must apply the sequence of escalating force (described previously by one officer)—verbal, touch, pain compliance, control holds, baton, deadly force—designed to gain compliance and, with it, control. In the view of many new police command presence is initially seen as a macho trapping of an earlier era, but by the time they have been on the streets for at least two years, most of these officers come to value it as a vital police tool.

Command presence is synonymous with control, and that is why it is so important for police officers. They cope with the unpredictability of the job by maintaining control whenever possible. To lose control is dangerous, as indicated in the following statement, representative of many:

> When you lose control of the situation, that's when people get injured. We're supposed to win. We try to talk to them; it's easier on all of us. We always try that first, but then some people just don't want to comply. I don't know why they don't, but they don't. People see a couple of officers, got some citizen down. And we've got the guns and the sticks and the gas and all. And that citizen, he doesn't have diddly. Hell, he [the apprehended suspect] could have all kinds of shit and they wouldn't see, and they get all in our face because it's two on one, and it isn't fair. Isn't fair? Isn't fair! [At this point, the officer became agitated.] We're *supposed* to win! They *pay us* to win!

INJURIES

Recruits not only learn about physical danger in the abstract, but also firsthand: there is a good chance they will be injured in the course of their training. Thus, their lives have already become more dangerous.

Recruits learn in the academy that it is not a good idea to complain about injuries, or to question the way things are done. Complaints about discomfort or injury are likely to result in the entire group being required to do more of the same activity. The theory is that, if the activity is properly done, it should not result in injury. Therefore, obviously the person complaining, and perhaps the entire group, would benefit from more practice.

The hapless complainer may also be subjected to public ridicule. Being branded as a "wuss" in the academy is an inauspicious beginning to a police career and, in the past, could result in the candidate being found "unfit." A wuss is defined as a person who is a quitter, a complainer, one who is inept, unreliable, and untrustworthy (recall from chapter 1 the female officer who did not want to be deemed a wuss). Officers refer to people who wuss out with contempt. According to one officer, police owe it to their comrades to be physically fit because of the dangers of the job:

> I don't think about the danger every day when I go out because I think that if you get that paranoid about it, you can't be free enough to work. But you know it's there, so I wear my [bulletproof] vest every day. I will be far more alert in some areas than others, but I don't wake up and wonder if I'm going to get shot today . . . One thing I do, I work out because I want to be in really top condition. I'd work out for myself, for my own personal health, but I also do it because you might need to run a little faster one day, or have the strength to pull somebody out or do something to help you or your partner. I hate seeing fat, lazy cops. I figure, how are they going to help anybody? How are they going to help me?

Machismo is deeply imbedded in the value system of police academy training. It is not socially acceptable to be injured since injuries are regarded as proof that the officer has done something incorrectly to cause or permit the injury. Officers who make errors of any sort are dangerous to themselves, their partner and others.

For all these reasons, it is considered inappropriate to complain. This aspect of policing will continue relatively unchanged throughout the first three phases of the career. In later phases, officers acknowledge their injuries and discomforts with close friends and working partners but will not dwell on them.

SOCIAL DANGERS

The indoctrination process for recruits also emphasizes the social danger of their new status. At this time it is first suggested to them that their best, and perhaps only, defense in a treacherous and dangerous world is someone else who understands it: another police officer.

In addition to being encouraged to rely primarily upon fellow officers, the recruits are taught to regard non-police contacts as potentially dangerous. At this stage, outsiders are dangerous because they can compromise the officer professionally. One officer describes his experience:

We were good buddies in high school but, hey, he went one way and I went another, and now I don't fraternize with him. If he's smoking, or owns a hot stereo, or even if he only hangs with the bad guys, you just can't be there. You're at a party and someone lights up, you're out of there. If you stay, you condone the use. If they're busted and you say you didn't know about it, what kind of cop are you? You couldn't smell it? You didn't see it. Come on. It's your job. You can't risk it.

Another officer, still on probation, describes an incident that he felt might cost him his police career:

. . . when we took him [the suspect] in, we were still doing the paper-work, there was a commotion at the desk, so we were out in a flash, and I could have shit on the spot. My ex-girlfriend—well, a girl that I knew before—was there with these low-lifes to bail this guy out. Well, I thought, "That's great. Here goes my career." I knew she was going to blow it—I knew she was crazy from before—and she got this big smile, kind of a sly smile, on her face, and called across—my training officer was one step behind me—and she calls me "Honey Bear," and says she's so glad to see me, because now I can help, and all this stuff—and I'm not believing this is happening to me. She was drunk or stoned. And I wanted to be somewhere else . . . I wanted to tell [his training officer], to explain to him, that I hadn't seen this girl for years, and I knew I was going to be out of here, because they told us in the academy that that can happen if you don't clean your house. And there she was. . . .

Recruits are told that they, as police officers, cannot afford to make the errors in judgment that other citizens are allowed. They are told that, as police officers, they can be compromised by the mere appearance of wrongdoing. They are urged to consider the implications of guilt by asso-ciation when choosing their friends or planning their activities. It is sug-gested that they reevaluate friends and acquaintances vis-à-vis their new status, and recruits are instructed to avoid any semblance of activities that are "unbecoming an officer."

LEGAL DANGER

The potential for legal problems is not emphasized in recruits' acad-emy training. Recruits are provided with the basics of law, the parameters under which they will work, and the somewhat idealized assumption that, if they conduct themselves as officers ought to and enforce the laws as directed, the entire judicial system will support them and protect them. In this view, police are officers of the law, on the side of law and order, and work hand-in-hand with other officers of the law in the judicial system.

Academy training does not address adversarial relationships between police and other branches of the judicial system (lawyers in particular), which is so pronounced in other phases of the job. One officer offered this description. The term "duce" comes from the old penal code section for drunk driving, 502, hence a "duce" is a drunk driver:

> The academy did not prepare me at all for court. I had no idea what to expect from court. No one acted like [a well-known attorney], one of the best duce lawyers in L.A., in a courtroom. He totally burned me out. Turned me off to working duces.

Officers who have been trained to view themselves as upholders of the law may come to see themselves cast in a very different role after a particularly difficult courtroom encounter.

ECONOMIC DANGER

In the past, academy classes were warned of the economic pitfalls that can accompany the job. Currently economic incentives are a leading recruiting tool, and economic perils are seldom mentioned.

Many traditional police were drawn from the lower economic strata and viewed the job of policing as lucrative. Not only was the pay high, but credit for police officers was easily obtainable. Police officers could obtain 100 percent loans on vehicles and other goods simply on their signature. Many traditional police, unaccustomed to buying on credit, over-extended themselves. Many new police are also drawn from the same economic group, and the starting pay of close to $40,000 with only a high school education required is quite seductive. While it is no longer as easy to get such generous loans, it is still easy to get into economic trouble. New police grew up in an era of buying on credit and frequently find themselves in economic peril even with, as one officer commented, " . . . more money than both of my parents brought home put together."

Usually, problems developed from the purchase of expensive luxury items: boats, fast cars, motorcycles, and recreation vehicles. Officers would often buy top-of-the-line toys—guns, fishing equipment, and archery or other sporting equipment. Police officers tend to spend freely on equipment seen as aiding their relaxation, recreation, or personal protection. All of these are viewed as being interrelated and essential to the successful performance of the job.

PSYCHOLOGICAL DANGER

As in the case of potential economic problems, the issue of psychological peril is somewhat soft-pedaled during formal training, but it is at least mentioned. In the academy there are frequently conflicting goals:

instilling skill and confidence, but warning officers that they are vulnerable at all times. Cooperation and the need for operating as a team are stressed while, at the same time, individual initiative is emphasized. Though cooperation and individual initiative are not necessarily in direct conflict, recruits report confusion over what was the most appropriate or most desirable behavior in a given situation.

It is difficult to instill the balance necessary to graduate a class of enthusiastic, skillful officers, who are ready or even eager to hit the streets but also are cautious and mindful of the risks entailed in the job. Recruits are warned repeatedly about being over-zealous. In spite of the warnings, over-zealousness is one of the most frequent problems with new officers, one that is a potential source of trouble for themselves and their training officers.

Over-zealousness is referred to as the John/Jane Wayne syndrome. Officers who are too aggressive are regarded as a potential danger to citizens and other officers. This is also seen as placing the officer in psychological jeopardy. Recruits are warned against being "badge heavy" or overly impressed with their status as a police officer. Recruits who are badge heavy may fail to complete their training:

> This guy was so full of himself, he kept flashing that badge like it was the keys to the city. I guess he thought that was what this job was going to be. We heard he even badged his way into the movies. ["Badging" is a process by which an officer shows his badge to gain admittance to an area.] Honestly, the movies! He'd flash that badge for anyone who would look. He lasted about six months, six, maybe seven most. That's what it took for him to see, for everyone to see, buddy, he was in the wrong line of work. That crap just doesn't go around here. You can't do that. He didn't belong doing police work. He tried the fire department next, and they kicked his ass out, pronto, too.

Officers are also subject to the "Dirty Harry Problem," which centers on the question, "When and to what extent does the morally good end warrant or justify an ethically, politically or legally dangerous means for its achievement?" (Klockars, 1980). At this budding stage in the recruits' career, they rarely consider that this could ever be a real problem for them.

UNDERSTANDING THE PHYSICAL DANGER

The physical danger of the job is underscored on the last day of academy training. Before leaving the academy, neophyte recruits, now almost considered to be rookie officers, are subjected to the capping moment of their instruction—a dramatic presentation of what can go wrong in policing.

The last day consists almost entirely of slide and film presentations, along with some firsthand accounts, of officers who have been ambushed, maimed, or involved in incidents fatal to other officers. There are photographs, films and videotapes of dead and dying officers, as well as scenes of severed limbs and crushed bodies. The exhibitions are designed to be graphic. Audiotapes gleaned over the years from actual police calls are chilling. Officers are heard pleading for help, but unable to give their location so that any help could be deployed. Wounded officers call for back-up which does not arrive on time. An emotionally wrenching scenario for neophyte and seasoned officers alike, these tapes are also occasionally played during roll call.

These stories are used as educational tools, but often cause some trainees to reconsider their choice of profession. Police say that every academy class loses some potential officers after this presentation. Many informants mentioned that they were frightened by it, but also said they thought it was appropriate and necessary. They seemed to feel this portion of the training put the rest of what they had experienced into perspective. One officer describes a disturbing incident that took the life of a classmate only three months after graduating from the academy.

> I had a classmate that was killed in the line of duty. This is his memorial bracelet; I always wear it while I'm on duty. [Says the dead officer's name and shows the bracelet, reminiscent of the MIA bracelets from the Vietnam War era.] I talked to some officers who graduated two or three years after I did, and they told me in the class where they show officers who have been killed, and as part of this presentation, they had a picture of my classmate laying on a table in the morgue. He was killed about three months out of the academy, during probation. It was in North Hollywood; he and his partner responded to a burglary call. On arrival he and his partner split up. His partner was going to watch the front; he was going to go to the rear. The suspect tried to escape from the back and some kind of confrontation occurred in the back. He ended up getting shot with his own weapon, so I can only assume the suspect came out and he pulled his weapon and told him to stop, but the person must have been too close—he ran up on him—because the first round, he was shot in the groin or upper leg area, and he went down partially, and then the next shot was in his forehead. I know a lot of officers in my class who have been shot or died. I just had another classmate die a month ago in a traffic collision.

The following is from a normally relaxed, articulate, and talkative police officer. He had difficulty speaking while trying to describe the occasion when he was shot. Clearly, although twenty years have passed, the event remains fresh in his mind:

> ... my first assignment was Southwest Division. I had ten months on the job when I got shot. It, uh, it's difficult to talk about even now and

it was twenty years ago . . . they killed a young officer. The call involved was a "nude man with a rifle" call. They roll up. The senior officer tells the probationary, "You go around the back." The probationary takes the shotgun, starts around the back, and the suspect ambushed him. A back-up unit rolled up just as the shotgun blast rang out. They saw the officer fall. So I'm the third police unit to roll up there. I have ten months on the job. My partner is a two-week probationer. We're so short of training officers. I was a senior officer with three months in the academy and seven months on the streets. Anyway, with ten months on the job, I go and look for the suspect and got shot in the arm and the shoulder. I still carry the buckshot in there. I was in the hospital for a week.

The officer describes the reaction of other officers, including a graduating class of recruits, to his experience:

The academy asked if we'd stop by the academy when we were being discharged. . . . They asked if we'd stop by and talk to the next recruit class. Give 'em a few words of wisdom. I didn't have any wisdom, I was just shot. . . . I went up there and my right arm was probably twice as big as it is—looked like one of those muscle-builder's arms. It had little holes in it where blood had dripped out . . . it looked really bad, bruise marks were around the hematoma so it was showing where. . . . My hand was all puffed up so I took my jacket and covered it as best I could. I couldn't put on the jacket . . . my jacket arm got all messy and so forth. I walked into the classroom. . . . I'd been there seven months earlier, myself. I said, "I know nothing about weapons. My training in the military was an M-14 rifle." I said, "The only thing I know about a handgun is what they taught me here at the academy. . . ." I said, "Here's what a 410 shotgun will do. . . ." And I shoved my jacket off. I tried to be dramatic—I did intend for it to be that way. It was so quiet in there. I never heard that classroom so quiet before. Guys weren't breathing. I said, "I don't know what to say to you. I don't live for the streets, I've only got ten months on the job." I found out that after we left, one guy got up and quit that night, and another guy quit the next day.

In every class there are some candidates who decide before graduation that police work is not for them. For many, the decision to leave follows the last day of the academy when the idea of physical danger is firmly implanted in the minds of the rookies.

GRADUATION

At graduation, the novices, now transformed into rookie police officers, are officially recognized in their new status and welcomed into the family—the "brotherhood" of law enforcement agents—a large family, consisting of men and women, with a strong sense of community. They are greeted by the upper ranks of the agency hierarchy amid great pomp and circumstance. Their families are present. They are told that they are now in fact police officers. They have joined the police family, not only of the specific agency, but of the larger brotherhood of law enforcement officers worldwide.

This will be a recurring motif throughout their careers. Police officers will hear repeated references to the brotherhood of law enforcement officers at training sessions, important civic events, funerals, and virtually any event focused on police officers or the job of policing. The new police officers are made to feel they are superior to those who were unable or unwilling to finish the police training.

The new officers are instilled with a sense of pride in the department bordering on elitism vis-à-vis other policing agencies. Again there is a double message: the ideal of the brotherhood of all enforcement officers and the sense that they are the elder brothers, superior officers working for a superior agency.

For traditional officers, graduation was the culmination of a process that began on their first day at the academy, when they were issued a badge and a gun and tested to see how they would handle these two very potent symbols of power. Misuse of either the badge (being badge heavy) or the gun usually resulted in expulsion from the academy. The recruits' reaction to their new status was considered part of the training, and the weeding-out process included sanctions on abuse of power.

New police are not issued badges until graduation. Traditional police say this change of policy was brought about by the high number of abuses of the badge by new police—a way of sidestepping the issue of weeding out. If the new police are not issued the badge, they cannot abuse it.

The new practice may actually be more a matter of economics. Traditional officers were sworn in as police officers on the first day of the academy and began receiving full benefits, including medical coverage, throughout their training period. Although the new police are hired by the city from the moment they enter the academy, they are not sworn in as police officers and given badges until their graduation and, therefore, are not eligible for full benefits until they are sworn in as Los Angeles police officers.

Stage 2: Making the Cut: The First Assignment

By the time recruits have entered the second stage of phase one—making the cut—they have already passed through a culling process. Many would-be-officers have dropped out or have been washed out. Those who have made it through the academy training now must prove themselves on the streets.

While in the academy, future officers submit a list of preferences stating where they would like to be placed during their introduction to the streets. However, this may have very little bearing on their ultimate destination. They can be assigned to any of the eighteen divisions in the city for this initial breaking-in period which usually lasts about six months.

Unlike the scenarios presented in the police academy training, situations on the streets are rarely clear cut. Worse yet, police officers are encouraged to perform their duties so that all concerned will be satisfied with the outcome. This is not often realized. Officers must make quick decisions and, often, must respond to a situation before they have enough data to fully understand what is going on.

In an effort to work quickly, efficiently and safely, police officers attempt to reduce the ambiguity inherent in every situation. In so doing, they often gloss or generalize, and may rely upon stereotypes and statistical probability. This is not appreciated by the community at large, and certainly not appreciated by groups regarded by police officers as presenting the greatest threat. This is not to suggest that individual officers are not aware they are generalizing, but they feel there is little else they can safely do. Police officers operate on the meanings configurations of people and situations have for them.

If police are making a traffic stop, they respond differently depending on the configuration of who is in the car. Sex, ethnicity and race are interpreted as providing different potential for danger. There are marked differences in the assumed danger quotient of each configuration, although all traffic stops have some potential to go badly. In the police view, to ignore these potential differences is to behave in a way that is dangerous not only for themselves but also for their fellow officers. Peer pressure brings recalcitrant officers into line on this issue.

Patrol officers are responsible for enforcing laws, dealing with emergency situations of every sort, resolving conflicts, creating order, and conducting social work, as well as sometimes serving as quasi-psychiatrists. Many different skills are required, and few are taught at the police academy. In spite of the best efforts of academy trainers to present examples of compound and enigmatic situations an officer must expect to encounter, real-life street patrol is far more perplexing, confusing and therefore potentially more dangerous than most rookies have anticipated. Thus, the "making the cut" stage is another, more dangerous and sometimes deadly stage in the training of police officers.

PROVING THEMSELVES

This second stage of the first phase of the police career is the real introduction to the working group. For the first six months on the streets, officers are on probation. During this time they are assigned to a division, a watch, and a duty, and will be closely supervised as they begin to apply what they have learned. Almost immediately, they learn that life outside the academy is much more difficult than in the sheltered learning environment. Also during this time, it is supposedly possible to weed out unsuitable officers. Few are actually fired during this period, but some are. Traditionally, officers have failed probation for behavior deemed dangerous to their fellow officers, such as incompetence or over-zealousness. Currently, officers are most likely to fail probation because of involvement in illegal activities, abuse of illegal substances, or for failure to show up for work or court.

Rookies are rarely welcomed into the working watch uncritically. They are subjected to close scrutiny and carefully evaluated by other officers. Some rookies are preceded by a reputation or "jacket" earned while still in the academy. The officer's performance and personal attributes—for good or ill—are often discussed at length. Rookies from police families have an advantage, since they may draw upon the reputation of their forebears. It is also presumed that officers who have been socialized into the police life by their families are better able to understand the conditions of the job.

Because traditional police came from more homogeneous backgrounds—having military experience and primarily coming from white, lower-middle-class families—acceptance came easier for them. Because the current crop of recruits does not necessarily share similar backgrounds, they are subjected to more critical evaluations and are often referred to by veteran officers as "A.A. police" or "Tupperware police" (female recruits). Both labels may be used in a way that is either pejorative or merely descriptive.

Traditional and new rookie police officers must prove themselves in countless ways. They receive criticism, both constructive and otherwise, and their response to criticism, praise and instruction is noted by others on their working watch. Whether they take initiative, how well they listen to and follow orders, their personal habits, grooming, and, in fact, all their actions during the breaking-in period are discussed by their peers.

The rookie officer is assigned to a training officer who will be responsible for close supervision of his or her introduction to the streets. Almost immediately the officers are rated formally by their training officers and informally by the other officers on the watch. Police commonly seek information about other officers, and the comment "You worked with Johnson last night?" is understood to mean, "Tell me about Johnson."

No specialized training is required of the training officers. The classification "training officer" is likely to reflect experience doing the job and a step up on the pay scale rather than any desire to train neophyte police. In fact, all police with senior status are training officers in the experience of the new recruits, because anyone who has been on the streets longer than the newcomer has important information to impart. As in the case of the officer who was shot in his tenth month on the job (discussed earlier in this chapter), it is possible to be the senior officer in a car with very little police experience. Rookie officers believe there is something to be learned from every contact, whether police or civilian, and they value colleagues who are experienced, articulate and good teachers.

Many police commented on the importance of both a good training officer and the input of other veteran officers. The guidance of veterans is needed to integrate the somewhat idealized training of the academy into the considerably more complicated and bizarre situations encountered in the streets.

Recruits expect seasoned officers to offer suggestions and critique their performances—and they do. Experienced police know it is dangerous to work with a new officer, and this is one of the reasons many do not opt for the training officer position, even though it means more money and facilitates future promotion. Many officers feel the disadvantage of working with new recruits is not worth the extra money or status. Being a training officer involves more paperwork, working constantly with inexperienced officers, increased danger and aggravation.

All officers are closely supervised during their training period, so it is relatively rare that they become seriously injured. However, there have been major injuries and deaths involving officers during the period of first

exposure to the streets. Many of these injuries, deemed "avoidable" by veteran police officers, are the result of brashness and over-confidence, mixed with large doses of wanting to impress fellow officers. One veteran officer commented on the feelings of invulnerability many inexperienced police officers feel on first hitting the streets:

> They call it "tombstone courage." You feel invincible. You're wearing a vest, you've got a gun. Like in a barricade situation—pull back—it's like a castle, they're trapped. Just wait. You'll win. Pull back. Don't storm it. It's an unnecessary risk. No police officer should get hurt in that situation. To go in, that's not courage, that's stupid. It makes the six o'clock news, but it's stupid. We're supposed to win and we don't have to get hurt. Most of the time there's just no need to get hurt.

INTRODUCTION TO THE WORKING WATCH

Training officers work one-on-one with the new officers and, if they are good at their job, also help in the socialization process in terms of the watch. The training officer can facilitate the entrée of a new officer, or leave the officer on his or her own. Either way, new officers are usually so overwhelmed with the magnitude of tasks to be learned that they tend to feel pretty much on their own, even if the training officer is leading them by the hand. Most officers seemed to feel their training officers were very directive, yet did not give them as much information and support as they had expected.

Part of this seeming contradiction is inherent in the training goals. Training is for independence, but within certain guidelines. Officers must be able to make decisions quickly and sometimes literally under fire. However, their actions must be clearly understandable and predictable, so that other officers can coordinate their activities. Decisions should not come as a surprise to one's colleagues. An officer must learn very early to make the proper decision, which is in many ways synonymous with the expected decision.

Inculcation of the police worldview, an ongoing and lengthy process, is one of the important determinants in reaching proper, predictable police decisions. How do rookies learn this? By paying attention. By listening to the way other officers handle the situation. By imitating the actions of veteran police officers. In the view of other officers, there should not be much variation in the basics of doing the job. There is tremendous agreement about the best way to handle many routine duties.

Rookies also learn how to handle less routine, and even extraordinary, events through listening to the experiences of seasoned officers. They learn to value war stories, jokes, even gossip. All shared information is valuable. Through it they learn the more elusive values underlying the actions and attitudes of their more experienced colleagues. Only a limited number of personal experiences are possible, but officers' shared experiences are limited only by the number of tales they have time to hear.

One of the most valuable things a new officer can learn is to pay attention to the elders in the department. Just as the new officers get "jackets," so too are the older officers well known to each other, and very quickly to the new officers as well. Those who are considered "flakes" are so noted. Those who are "hard chargers," "quitters," or "goldbrickers" are known, and one's personal attributes and the way in which they are viewed by the police community are considered essential knowledge for new officers.

Supervisors try to ensure that new officers are partnered with outstanding officers when they are not with their training officer. In fact, most rookie officers will log more time in their first year with "non-training" but excellent officers than they will with their training officer. However, there are some officers who are never assigned a rookie as a regular partner.

Some traditional police claim that when they came on the job, officers would be fired if they did not distinguish themselves during the probationary period. However, the data I have gathered do not support this perception. My data do support the contention made by one officer, "All you do is produce the recap, please your training officer, listen to the veterans, and keep your package clean." It would appear that a number of lackluster officers successfully passed through the probationary period during both time periods, but officers who are considerably deficient in performing the job are now advancing to normal status, which was not the case for the traditional police.

Stage 3: Off Probation: Establishing a Jacket

The six months spent in the academy coupled with the six-month period of the initial assignment satisfies the formal requirements of the department, which has a one-year probationary period. (However, in the eyes of veteran officers, this period lasts much longer.) After passing probation, officers move on to another formative stage of their police career—the first assignment. Moving rookies to a division where they are not perceived as being fresh out of the academy gives them a second chance if they did not distinguish themselves during their early training period. If lapses in collegiality are minimal, new officers can learn from their mistakes, rectify their behavior, and have a more successful experience at the next division. This last stage of the first phase of the police career lasts approximately two years and is an extremely critical period for the officers. At this point, they are viewed by their colleagues as understanding more than the basics of police work, but also as being unproven.

The possibilities of what a watch will bring are literally limitless: it can be characterized by total boredom or the exact opposite—an assortment of natural disasters, terrorist attacks, or spectacular and bizarre murders. It can be punctuated with gang shoot-outs, or sprinkled with doses of social work, psychiatric work, and finding lost adults. It can include responding to burglaries, robberies, batterings, rapes, and assorted mayhem. Police officers have been called to "use your master key and open up my apartment." The officers who received this particular request joked that their "master key" consisted of a battering ram and three guys from Metro Division.

In an entire career, no police officer could encounter all possible situations. Even officers with many years of street experience meet new situations and circumstances that test their skills. Still, an officer with five years of experience is far better equipped to handle difficult situations than an officer who is still learning the streets.

Because no one can be trained to deal with every conceivable situation, much of the training rookies receive in this period is focused on determining how quickly and how well they can figure out appropriate solutions to whatever they may encounter. Officers working with a rookie in this stage will frequently take the time to explain why they took one course of action and not another. After the watch is over, any notable event is shared, analyzed, commented on and generally processed by the entire watch. If it is noteworthy enough, it will be discussed during the next day's roll call, which is scheduled during the first forty-five minutes of every watch, and the merits or shortcomings of the officer's actions will be debated at that time. New officers need to display good listening and learning skills to be regarded as serious about the job and as having the potential to be a good officer.

During these two years of being permitted more latitude in their decision making, and given more opportunities to work with less stringent formal supervision, police officers find their own rhythm on the streets and with their partners. It is also during these two years that most of the injuries that might be avoided occur.

DEALING WITH INJURIES

Many injuries sustained by officers are unavoidable. Physical altercations are common, especially early in the career. Bodily damage caused by vehicle collisions and long hours spent carrying heavy police gear also appears to be somewhat unavoidable. Many officers become so damaged during this period they operate defensively, trying to protect their injured backs, elbows, and knees (the most common complaints).

Officers learn during this early period how to minimize the damage in the future. After their early physical experiences, they become more careful and less physical in their policing. This ushers in a mode of enforcement characterized by greater reliance on negotiation rather than physical prowess.

Thus, during this stage of phase 1 of the career, they become slightly more conservative in their approach. They are learning to improve their command presence, which assists in making arrests without the need for aggressive physical or verbal action. When it is necessary to become physical, as it often is, they are clearer and more decisive in their actions. They are learning how to gain control of a situation without damaging themselves. They are more accomplished in their physical control of suspects, and they are better at interpreting and reading situations. Officers often say the whole key to policing is control, and every day they spend on the streets, they learn how to have more control—over themselves and others.

At this stage, police are exposed to unnecessary danger and injury both on and off the job for a variety of reasons: Key among them is the necessity to demonstrate that you are a "stand-up" guy, not a quitter or a wuss. This concept is similar to Keiser's description of "heart" ideology in Vice Lord culture.

> It is apparent that generally "heart" means bravery, but it means more than just this. It also means bravery in terms of being "game," that is, being willing to follow any suggestion regardless of personal risk. Having heart contrasts with punking out. A person who acts in a cowardly way—that is, who is not "game" for any suggestion—is a punk. Vice Lords believe that having heart is good, while being a punk, or punking out is bad. Heart, in other words, is one of the values of Vice Lord culture. (1969:49–50)

Partly because they are young and resilient, the officers mend fairly quickly and are not likely to seek medical treatment after becoming injured. Part of this is the John/Jane Wayne syndrome, but it also due to the fact that officers at this stage do not want to use sick days, or to be "out I.O.D.," off work and classified as "injured on duty." It looks bad on their ratings and may have social consequences as well.

These officers are subjected to almost daily scrutiny and analysis and receive written ratings that become a permanent part of their file. Every rating report includes the number of sick days the officer used during that rating period. Officers, who are allowed twelve sick days per year, are discouraged from using them. From their first rating, they find out that an officer who uses sick days is not viewed favorably. The officers are told that using sick days will damage their chances of promotion and assignment to special details.

Officers who use sick days are a liability to the working unit, because they are considered to be officers available to work in the division and yet are unavailable for duty. This puts a strain on the rest of the working watch. It means their partner must work alone or with an outsider. It is construed by the other officers as sandbagging, or avoiding their duty and not honoring their commitment to their colleagues. Officers must be willing to cover for each other, in the sense that they must be willing to be extra vigilant and warn others if there is a real problem in a colleague's performance.

In their first years on the job, officers are usually anxious to please, flattered that they are included in the recreational events, and generally trying their hardest to do their best. This too, in the police context, is having heart, being a stand-up guy, trying hard. In recreational activities or on the job, doing your best counts, even when you fail. When lives are at stake, it only counts if you are also successful.

SOCIAL RELATIONSHIPS

Policing takes a heavy toll on the social relationships of the rookie officer. While the officer is preoccupied with learning appropriate police responses and attitudes, this shift in focus is rarely welcomed on the home front. Officers often feel they have little to talk about with their non-police friends, and marriages frequently break up in this period. This further reinforces the idea that no one but another officer really understands the police officer—or, in fact, the "real" world, the world of the streets.

Marriages that existed prior to the officer's joining the police force are especially at risk. Very few survive. The normal process of growth and change is exacerbated by the experience of being a police officer. The occupational socialization that officers undergo is radical and all-encompassing. They are told how to dress and how to groom themselves, and they are punished if they do not comply. They learn a walk and a tone of voice. Specialized vocabulary becomes integrated into normal speech, as do the meanings, interpretations and realities conveyed by the language. The further into the process of police socialization an officer goes, the less comfortable the fit with non-police.

Officers experience a progressive shift away from more generally held perceptions and views, toward greater self-isolation and reliance on police definitions and perceptions. Some officers learn to find balance, but many do not. Among the obvious problems attached to this lack of balance is becoming progressively out of touch with the majority of the citizens with whom they interact.

5

Phase Two
Hitting Their Stride

By the time officers have been working the streets for three years they have experienced enough police work to be able to do it well, if they have the aptitude and have been paying attention. Their colleagues regard them as officers—period. Whether their performance is viewed as good or lacking, they are police officers, in a way they were not prior to this period. In police worldview, experience is extremely highly valued—essential. In their performance of the job, encountering the realities of the streets, and proving themselves to colleagues, officers have passed the probationary period mandated by their colleagues. Usually this part of the career is genuinely enjoyed by most officers:

> I love doing police work. I love getting up in the morning and I have no idea how the day will go, but it's not going to be dull. I know what it's about, and even though there are things I haven't done before, it'll be fine . . . I'll be fine. I'll know what to do when I have to do it. Working with [an experienced officer] has been good. We do it together, a pretty good team, and . . . I'm just going to follow his lead and back him.

GAINING CONFIDENCE

Officers at this phase believe they know what is expected of them, and they believe that they can meet and exceed these expectations. They feel the camaraderie and support of the police community. Officers tend to spend much of their off-duty time with other police officers and the extended police community (although there are significant differences between traditional and new police regarding this feature—new police spend significantly less time in the company of other police officers). The police community is made up of retired officers, police family members, and others who are embedded in the police community, such as the doctors and nurses who staff local emergency rooms, firefighters, and other people who interact with officers on a daily basis. Officers feel that they understand how the real world works, and with this understanding they can now get down to the business of being excellent police officers.

Some officers become confident to the point of arrogance. It is in this period that an officer runs the risk of getting "salty," or assuming that he or she knows all there is to know about police work and that other officers who are not as "gung-ho" about the job are merely "drones" or "burnout cases." Officers who become known for their salty attitude soon find that other officers, particularly officers with more time on the job, are less likely to want to work with them.

This self-confident attitude toward job performance is balanced by greater caution toward the dangers of the street. It is rare to encounter an officer at this stage of the career who has not already received injuries that result in further discomfort and medical attention. By this time, the injuries they have incurred are likely to make them more cautious.

> . . . the first injury was to my eye, and that was pretty traumatic. I lost sight in my eye for a week, I was in the hospital in intensive care for nine days, I had my head between sandbags. It was a scary thing . . . that I could lose my eyesight. So I'm real careful . . . if a guy gets away, the guy's going to get away. No big deal. He will get caught eventually. There's no sense sticking your neck out. I've been like that ever since I got my eye punched out. Right after I got off probation. I've been a very cautious person ever since . . .

They are much less likely to act impulsively: plunge headlong into brawls or leap over walls without knowing what is on the other side. In addition to their own experiences they are well aware of many other tales of woe. One such tale involved an officer with eighteen months on the job, who followed a suspect down an alley and over a short stucco wall. The wall was only four feet high on the side the officer could see, but there was a twenty-foot drop on the other side. The officer was not familiar enough with the neighborhood to know that such an apparent discrepancy was possible. Increased experience on the job and increased knowledge of that specific neighborhood may well have tempered the officer's decision to jump the wall.

Other instances where officers learn to use caution involve family disturbance, or domestic violence, calls. Domestic calls are particularly dangerous for many reasons; key among them is the degree of uncertainty and the lack of control. Almost by definition, the officers are working in the suspect's home, they do not know who or how many people are involved, if they are armed and/or under the influence of alcohol or drugs, who might walk in on the situation, and how any of the participants might react. Frequently, even though officers have been called for service, once the police actually arrive they are no longer wanted or welcome. Nevertheless they must handle the call—a situation where passions run high and people do not always think clearly. Often weapons are involved, and

often these are turned on the officers. Frequently, once the police start to effect an arrest, the complaining party will have a change of heart, and quite often attack the officers. Quite often other bystanders may join in. Domestic disputes are also more likely to generate "beefs"—complaints about the officers' conduct. The oft-quoted statement is, "I wanted them to do something but they didn't have to arrest him!" A domestic violence call can spin out of control very quickly and become extremely dangerous for all involved. Despite training to the contrary, rookie officers underestimate how dangerous these calls can be. With experience, officers become more prudent in their handling of all calls, and learn never to underestimate the potential for danger in any of them. This makes it easier and safer to work with these officers, an obvious plus for their partners.

Criticism of their performance by their colleagues is reduced because officers in phase two of their careers have learned how to do the job to the satisfaction of their peers, not just their supervisors. They have, at this point, learned the working vocabulary as well as the appropriate attitudes and behaviors on the job. The learning and eventual mastery of these concepts, attitudes and behaviors make it easier for officers to do their job safely. Using these concepts and attitudes as guides for their own behavior also means that officers understand and can anticipate each other's actions and perceptions. This is useful in any workplace but assumes even greater importance in a situation in which teamwork is required for the successful performance of the job and discussion of the course to take is often impossible at the moment action is required.

As officers learn and internalize the attitudes and behaviors that facilitate the performance of their job, they find themselves drawn more closely into the police community. This in turn reinforces these attitudes and behaviors, and the process of internalization of this worldview can be accelerated for officers with reduced ties to the non-police community.

Officers in this phase are viewed as being capable and likely to make the right decisions in a given situation—that is, to act in concert with the internalized values and belief system with which they have been inculcated. Officers learn to act in the way any seasoned officer would act based on a shared interpretation of the meaning of an act, situation, or occurrence. Variations from the norm in the way police work is conducted are quickly noted and discussed. If the deviant behavior is deemed dangerous there will be great pressure to eliminate it or modify it to conform to the norm, or at least to a less dangerous form of non-normative behavior.

Officers do not like to work with someone whose behavior is inconsistent or unpredictable. In a job where it is impossible to anticipate all that could happen, or even predict when something is likely to happen, officers strive for the only source of control over the situation they have: control of themselves and their partners. Straying from normative patterns is at least unsettling and often dangerous. Of course there is some variation due to personal style, but personal style is something other officers can accommodate with little stress. Uncertainty on the other hand is not so easily dealt with. By definition, uncertainty is dangerous if an officer is doing something the other officers do not understand.

DISCRETION AND STYLES OF POLICING

Police discretion and the threat of unfair/uneven treatment is one of the greatest sources of anxiety among citizens. Police officers also worry about their discretionary powers. Although policies and guidelines direct police responses in different situations, officers are given some latitude to vary their response.

> The police make policy about what law to enforce, how much to enforce it, against whom, and on what occasions. Some law is always or almost always enforced, some is never or almost never enforced, and some is sometimes enforced and sometimes not. Police policy about selective enforcement is elaborate and complex. (Davis 1975:1)

Clearly this is a truly awesome responsibility. Because of the ripe ground for abuse, officers must exercise their discretionary power wisely. While in almost any police encounter there is a preferred, "by the numbers," way of handling the situation, analysis after the fact is of course a much easier task than the kind of on-the-spot, instantaneous decisions officers make daily. The policing style of an officer is one factor that determines the way in which he or she handles calls and uses discretionary powers.

Geoffrey P. Alpert and Roger G. Dunham note the factors which converge to produce patterns of police discretion:

> While we know that discretion exists, and often know the results of discretionary decisions, we are unable to pinpoint the exact reasons police exercise it the way they do. However, we know in general terms that police discretion is partially determined by a combination of several factors, including the interests and styles of individual officers, the nature of the law and the legal system, and the institutional work environment. (1997:164)

There are many different styles of enforcement and they change to some extent from division to division, and even among officers depending on their mood, the phase of their career, and the kind of situation with which they are dealing. The major split in policing style in this particular department is often referred to by the officers as the "hard charging" and "social work" split.

Some officers favor a hard-charging, less interpretive style, a style in which there is little room for judgment calls or listening to explanations or excuses. Officers speak of this style in many different ways, and indeed there are degrees of hard charging. Some officers who subscribe to hard charging see it as proactive police work. It has been variously described by officers as: "hardliner," "hook 'em and book 'em and don't look back," "kick ass and take names," or "arrest 'em all, let the courts sort it out." This approach is regarded by those who practice it as the best way to do police work. One officer, who was an officer in New York for four years before joining the L.A.P.D., stated:

> They don't pay me to figure it out. That's some other person's job. They pay me to enforce the law and catch the guys who break the law. I get called out, I catch the guy carrying the goods. . . . It's not *my* job to figure out if he bought the stuff from some guy on the street. He fits the description of the perp, *he's* the guy that's holding the stereo equipment, and *he's* the guy *I'm* taking to jail. Let those other guys sort out the whining, and the reasons for it all. That's not my job, my job is to put him in jail . . .

Other officers refer to this style with disdain, as the "easy" way to do police work. This hard-charging style is commonly found among officers off probation but in the first phase of their career, and especially among those officers considered to be salty. They are anxious to prove their mettle, and work toward having a large recap (many arrests) by the end of the month. However, this style of policing can be found among

officers in every phase of the career. In addition, styles of enforcement are not mutually exclusive, and are often a response to the circumstances surrounding or even peripheral to the encounter. That is, an officer who normally takes more time and makes it a point to carefully and methodically weigh and evaluate all the possibilities may well adopt a hard-charging style of enforcement if he or she is under time constraints or has been specifically directed to do so. Officers who describe themselves as burned out are often characterized by this approach.

The interpretive style is, in the short run, less efficient and certainly more time-consuming. Response time, the length of time it takes, on the average, for a patrol car to respond to a call, is often used as a measure of the level of police service. A shorter response time is assumed to be indicative of better police service. When minimizing response time becomes a major concern, officers are sometimes urged to streamline their calls. Employing the first style accomplishes this goal; the so-called "textbook" style does not. This is the style that officers were taught in the academy as the way to do police work. For this reason it is often found among rookie police officers still on probation, as well as many of the more experienced officers who find this to be an appropriate style. This is a more analytical and considered style. The emphasis is on gathering all the facts available, weighing them, and assessing the situation before settling on a course of action.

> It takes time to do any investigation properly. I'm not talking about your basic smash and run or something like that. Most of the calls we get, you've got to know the "knowns." If you don't take the time to find out what the true situation is you can make a big mistake. You've got the crime scene itself and you've got the people involved, and they are going to be upset. All of them. They'll be operating on adrenaline and fear or grief, or panic, and whatnot, but your job is to find out the "knowns" so you can get the person who caused the problem. It takes time. Sometimes it takes a lot of time but that's just how it is . . .

Both styles of enforcement can work well, and both can get an officer into trouble. The first is a real time saver but can result in an increase in the number of "kickbacks," which are criminal cases that are not filed upon and therefore never result in court cases or the arrestee being "held to answer," doing time or being incarcerated. It is also a style which tends to alienate citizens and is viewed by the department as terrible public relations. For obvious reasons many police officers find this style antithetical to their purpose. The second style is more careful. However, it may be more dangerous for the officers, because whenever they make a judgment and openly interpret, they are more likely to make people angry with them, are more likely to get sued, and are also on the scene longer. This style takes much more time, but is more likely to result in proper filings and successful cases (convictions).

Circumstances, the kind of situation one is dealing with, the kind of crime that has occurred, and the partner with whom one is working, all influence the policing style the officer might employ. When two officers are working together, the style of the dominant officer is most likely to be adopted by the pair; due to the value officers place on time on the job, this is usually the senior officer. However, which style to adopt may be subject to the situation, as suggested by the issues and dynamics of the classic "bad cop/good cop" mode of interaction. Policing styles are perceived by the public as: bad or good, effective or ineffective. Suspects also respond to these different styles in profoundly different ways. Sometimes one style works well, sometimes the other. Sometimes what works is a dynamic that occurs when a combination of styles is used. Most officers are capable of and have used both styles. However, individuals are usually drawn more to one approach than the other as a general pattern.

FINDING THE RIGHT NICHE

During the course of this second phase, the officer has learned the basics of the job and is now free to find his or her niche. This is where different watches and duties may come into play. Officers find that they prefer certain tasks to others and are better suited to certain kinds of detail than others. At this time officers are generally given the opportunity to find out which watches and duties they prefer.

It is in everyone's best interest to allow the officers to self-select their watch and duty whenever possible. Most officers are allowed this choice; some are not. The officers who find themselves transferred to units, watches, duties, and even divisions against their will are generally those with whom no one wants to work, or officers who challenge management. Thus, officers may transfer as a result of many different circumstances. These circumstances are quickly known, discussed, and become common knowledge within their new division, watch, duty or detail (a small temporary group of officers deployed to deal with a specific problem). Whether an officer is considered charismatic, a troublemaker, unpopular with management, or unpopular with other officers will generally precede the officer. If an officer is considered to be dangerous by others, this information and the reasons for it will not stay private for long.

Some officers are tapped for special duties based on special individual attributes, including physical appearance. Officers who have a particularly youthful appearance are likely to be approached to do undercover narcotics work, which is highly dangerous. During this study officers were selected to work vice, narcotics, or to infiltrate various organizations that were known to engage in criminal activity, because these officers' demeanors would fit in with the group to be infiltrated. There are other considerations as well, however, and sometimes it is a combination of features that leads to the selection of an officer for a particular task. One Anglo officer was assigned to work the gang detail because of his fluency in Spanish. Spanish-speaking gang members did not expect this, and, upon being arrested by the officer, spoke freely to each other, mistakenly secure in the assumption they could not be understood. Usually gang members are quickly separated so they cannot communicate with each other with great ease, but to facilitate data gathering, officers might simply be slow in separating the suspects, so that their conversations can take place with a minimum of difficulty, within earshot of a particular officer. While this was not a department sanctioned strategy, it was effective.

On the traditional force, officers who were members of groups that were under-represented in the police population—women, African Americans, Latinos, Asians and Jews (and officers who appeared underage)—were effective undercover officers because they did not fit the police stereotype. Many of these officers were selected on the basis of their sex, race, ethnicity or religion either to play against or fit in with the suspect group. Officers used to joke about the "hate" car, a patrol car that housed two officers, also good friends outside of work, who had just completed their undercover assignments. One had infiltrated a militant Jewish organization and the other had infiltrated a neo-Nazi group. Today, the diverse physical appearances of the new police officers facilitates data gathering and infiltration techniques.

COMING TO GRIPS WITH WEAR AND TEAR

While phase two is generally a time of high productivity and personal satisfaction, with young officers feeling very much a part of the police tradition and community, it is also a time when they must come to grips with the danger of the job. This is not in the sense of the excitement which can be a component part of danger, but with the lasting physical effects of having been injured—aches and pains which do not go away. Officers become physically more conservative as the impact of their own mortality and their physical limitations become more obvious to them. They learn that they are vulnerable.

> It was like I finally got it. Like turning on a switch. I realized that my body was getting *very* hard use. "Rode hard and put away wet"— that's what they say. I'm really getting hurt here. My body was not designed to do the things I'm making it do. I like what I do, but I sure don't like the way I feel.

Officers in this phase tend to take on a more conservative style of policing. They are less trusting, and have experienced enough on the streets so that cynicism and suspicion may become part of their working persona. They are aware that they have some, though not complete, control over some of the potential hurts they may receive. On the more dramatic end of the spectrum of their experience, they have had firsthand experience with death and dying, and find it bears little resemblance to sanitized, depersonalized media representations.

Attitudes and attributes which have a definite survival value on the job rarely enhance off-duty relationships. Wives and other family members, as well as friends, are often stunned by the changes in the officers. Officers sometimes express surprise over the changes in themselves.

PHYSICAL DANGER

In this phase of their career officers have an excellent understanding of the physical danger involved in the job, and they take measures to protect themselves. Officers who do not wear a bulletproof vest at the beginning of their careers decide that it may be a good idea after all. Officers who previously felt that a back-up weapon was not worth the discomfort involved decide to get used to it.

One of the mixed blessings of having conducted this study over such a long period of time is to see some of the changes that have occurred. When I started this project in 1976, most of the officers did not wear bulletproof vests. They had many reasons for this: vests are extremely uncomfortable, heavy (at that time they were very thick and weighed about ten pounds), hot, bulky, did not "look good" under the uniform. By the end of the seventies virtually all street officers wore vests. Some officers even bought larger uniform shirts to accommodate the vests. Uniform shirts at the time cost about forty to fifty dollars, so this was not an inexpensive purchase.

The vests remained essential equipment throughout the early and mid-eighties, when they were greatly improved. Bulletproof vests became less bulky, lighter and more effective. At present, the vests are regarded as essential equipment. As is true of all things dealing with police, there is some variation in this perception. Increasingly there are cases in which suspects use armor-piercing bullets or automatic weapons. In these instances the normal reasons for wearing a vest offer more psychological reassurance than real protection.

Police officers also often comment that in the past perpetrators made body shots—it is, after all, an easier target—but now due to increasing awareness of the use of vests, suspects are more likely to take head shots. So while the vests may be more effective than ever, the use of vests is shunned by some officers who feel that they are not likely to help unless a shot goes wild, that is, into the torso.

This focus on the physical danger is both typical of this second phase of the career and symptomatic of a general perception of a marked increase in the physical danger of the job since the mid-eighties. With the easy availability of more powerful weapons, officers assume more people are likely to be "packing" or "carrying"—both refer to the possession of weapons, usually concealed, and usually firearms. This makes police officers feel they are in even greater jeopardy than in the past.

There were some officers—all with a minimum of twelve years on the job—who felt that the danger level has remained somewhat constant. Their perceptions also appear to be tempered by a degree of fatalism. An exchange between two of these veteran officers focused on the increased number of bullets that automatic weapons are capable of firing in the same time span that it takes to get off a few shots from a revolver. One veteran officer argued, somewhat fatalistically, "If it's your time, it's your time and nothing's going to change that. If a bullet has your name on it. . . ." Another officer with sixteen years on the job replied, "The bullets don't know the difference. No bullet has your name on it, but you gotta watch out for those general deliveries." The conversation shifted to police officers as targets, and another officer commented:

> . . . there is very little difference between being a political target in the seventies, or a drug or gangbanger target in the eighties. It doesn't matter how many bullets are flying. Dead is dead. The threat hasn't changed, they're just better at pulling it off then they used to be. There are more of them than there are of us. Outnumbered and outgunned, that's how it is.

Police officers receive numerous threats and rarely take them very seriously. Disgruntled motorists, drunks and people involved in all manners of confrontations will express their displeasure in threats, but these are regarded as blowing off steam, and barely register.

On the other hand, some threats, especially threats to "the uniform" are viewed very differently. Sometimes through direct messages, various forms of intelligence gathering, or citizen tips, the department, or other agencies, will be made aware of a threat which they believe will be acted upon. Sometimes the information will simply be that a certain gang has set the death of a police officer, any officer, as part of an initiation ritual. Other times there will be threats that any car with any identifying police insignia—in particular private, off-duty cars, with visible police affiliations such as stickers and license plate holders—will be targeted for vandalism or attack. These threats are taken very seriously, discussed at roll call, and remain a concern for the officers and the entire police community.

During this phase of police work, the officers experience a stronger sense of community and commonality with other police officers, while at the same time they feel increasing alienation from other branches of the criminal justice system. Their idealized vision of the criminal justice system is put to the test from the beginning of their experiences on the streets and in the courtrooms, but in this phase of their careers they often come to see the relationship between police and most of the rest of the criminal justice system as primarily adversarial. This is particularly true of the court (especially lawyers) and prison systems.

COURT

Court time is regarded quite differently by officers: some regard it merely as a necessary task, some enjoy it, others hate it. No matter how they feel about courtroom appearances all officers have experienced court time interfering with vacations, special events, illnesses or simply their rest time between working shifts. More importantly, all officers have and share stories of courtroom experiences which they view as undermining their job. They know that if they have made any errors in the way they collected, described, or handled evidence, this may result in the case being dismissed or never coming to trial. Challenges to police procedure and legality, even to the competence or intent of individual officers, are common. This can be particularly unsettling for young idealistic officers. What is or is not admissible is subject to change. Likewise, changes in the search and seizure laws, police policy and public sentiment make the courtroom experience a constantly changing one. In the rather long citation which follows, an officer describes a case being challenged by a lawyer attempting to have the case dismissed, first on procedural grounds and later by questioning the honesty of the officer's testimony. The officer describes the following scene and the courtroom experience. Interestingly, he slips into courtroom jargon in the telling of the event:

> Here's an example. It's four in the morning. I'm driving down a side street with my window rolled down, and I hear a pickup truck running. I look and the lights aren't on and I don't see a driver. On my passenger side of the street is a building under construction. We decided to investigate because we know that there are a lot of things that get stolen from construction sites, tools and such. So we went past the truck and came along around behind it, for a position of advantage, behind the vehicle. Put ourselves code 6 [unavailable for another call—investigating at scene] over the radio. Walk up to the vehicle with flashlights and light the truck bed. In the back is a pillowcase, all lumpy. Simultaneously we notice that the back plate [license plate] is doubled. Two of them are bolted together. Walk up to the cab, and light the cab to look in and observe the sole occupant laid over in the seat. Passed out with a hypodermic needle in his arm. We arrest him. There was a TV set and household items in the pillowcase. The arrestee was booked, filed on for receiving stolen property and possession of narcotics and now we're coming around to the court thing.
>
> When my partner and I went to court they had him on the stand first. We had about the same amount of time on the job. We both knew what we were doing. Courtroom policy is that witnesses are excluded from testimony so they only hear one testify at a time. They don't want you to be influenced. This was in the preliminary, so they were trying to determine it if the evidence was obtained lawfully. That's what they're supposed to be doing—making sure everything is legal and what is the evidence, and is it enough to file on. So they asked him the basic scenario: what is your employ, what were you doing, were you passenger or driver. Basically tell what happened. And then at some point the defense attorney asked what time of night it was. "Four o'clock." "Isn't it true that at this time of year its very cold outside?" Partner said, "yes." "And wouldn't it be unusual for your partner to have his window down at four o'clock in the morning?" He said "no." And the attorney just kept after it. Well, it was January and it was cold. If you drive with the windows up you're already at a disadvantage. Everybody can hear you coming a mile away and if your win-

dow is up you can't hear anything. Lots of guys drive with the windows down and the heater on, or just with the windows down freezing their ass. If the heater's on, sometimes there's a lot of noise too. Sometimes even when it's cold, if it's raining, guys will drive with the air conditioning on so their windows don't fog up, 'cause that puts you at a disadvantage too. It depends on what you need to do.

Well this guy, he's worming his way around trying to get it thrown out. Because that night it said in the report that the reason this truck came to our attention, was that first I heard the sound of the truck, then I noticed that the lights were out, construction site, the whole deal. This is this guy's [the lawyer's] tangent. He figures that if he can get my partner to say my window was up, then he can get his guy off. He thought he'd get us caught up in a falsehood. He kept hammering away at my partner, who said that, yes it was very cold, and his window was rolled up, but my window was rolled down. And the guy kept it up, and wanted to know how my partner could be so sure, and if it was so cold why was my window down, and my partner said that I was chewing tobacco and spitting out the window.

Then it was my turn, and finally he got around to his point. What time was it, the window, how cold, why was it rolled down. And I told him about being able to hear better, and, of course that doesn't mean anything to him. He wheedled and asked me it wasn't unusual to have the window down when it was so cold and I said, "no." He leads up to it, and he thinks he's going to lay you out and, bingo, "I had my window down because I was chewing tobacco and I was spitting out the window." The court fell out, everybody broke up. They could see where he was going, and they knew what my partner said, and it was an unusual answer. The guy was held to answer, but that attorney, we were kind of dumbstruck, because it didn't really matter, but he was trying to show that we weren't telling the truth.

Early in their careers officers have had enough experience with court to know they may be badgered, belittled, contradicted and otherwise challenged in the courtroom setting. Their honesty, intelligence, competence and ethics are called into question continually. This is never a pleasant process, but it tends not to bother officers to a great extent when they are in this second phase of their career. During this "Hitting their Stride" phase they tend to think of it as simply part of the process of going to court. While police officers must deal with going to court on an ongoing basis, those lacking in verbal eloquence may be overwhelmed or intimidated by being questioned on the witness stand. Many officers are tense and edgy before court or immediately afterward, but with no lasting effects. During phase 3, "Hitting the Wall," this tension and disquiet will be transformed into anger and distress.

There is no way for police officers to avoid court, but sometimes it is possible to participate more on their own terms. One of the most common challenges to an officer's competence during his or her testimony can be circumvented by becoming an expert witness, by being taken under *vox dire*. In this process an officer becomes expert in a field such as gang activity, assessing drunken behavior, spotting various altered states (narcotics, alcohol), by mastering D.O.T. (Department of Transportation) regulations, judgment of speed or D.U.I. An officer can become a court-recognized expert in many fields and often expertise in one field lends itself to expertise in a closely related area: expertise in narcotics and gangs go hand in hand; expertise in D.U.I. and traffic are also related. Working a detail often provides the officer with an excellent practical background for applying library research and training acquired in the courses he or she attends to become certified. According to one officer,

> If you worked that detail then you can become the expert. You have to be able to expound in exacting detail, exactly what the symptoms are, if it's, say, D.U.I. or narco [narcotics], the court interviews the officer. Asks any questions they might have, really grills him. If the officer shows it, really knows his stuff, then, "I'd like to take this officer under *vox dire*," from then on he is regarded as an expert [certified]. The court then says, this officer knows the difference between a youngster on the street and a gang member, he knows dressing down, bindles, he knows enough to know what he's talking about and we acknowledge his knowledge. You can say, "I am recognized as an expert in this field," and they may not want to open that can of worms. It can cut out a lot of hassle, sometimes not. There are some areas where you can't be taken under *vox dire*, like driving, shooting, fingerprinting. Those are mechanical aptitudes.

Some cases are lost or never go to trial because of procedural errors or lack of sufficient evidence. Officers often speculate on just what it takes to finally get someone in jail:

> First off you have to catch the player, the guy committing the crime. That's first, and that can take a long time. If someone is just starting out it's not like they don't have someone to pave the way, to prepare them. . . . So they may hear for a long time how to pull it off, and then they give it a try. Take your burglar. Residential burglar. Lots of people make a living as burglars, and they don't pay any taxes either. Well, lets say this guy tries it, he gets away with it, 'cause most of them do. Why not again? It beats working for a living. This city is like a smorgasbord for burglars, they can pick and choose. . . . By the time we get lucky and catch this guy it's not his first caper, and it's for sure not his last. We might get him after a year of living off burglary, or after five years. You go figure it . . . he does okay. . . . First time caught, no priors [arrests or convictions for burglary], he's loose. He won't see a day of jail time. No jail time until the court can say, "Well, Johnny, I see you've been here before," or until he bashes in some lady who comes home too early. Then, even when we've got him, [the dis-

trict attorney's office] file on them for "receiving" [receiving stolen property, rather than stealing the property] because that's all they can prove. We've got a city full of people who "receive" but they can't remember who sold it to them, nobody stole it, they all just "received" it. It is such bullshit. It is so frustrating. . . . They know and we know, and the court even knows, so why aren't these guys doing time? What is my job really? Why am I chasing these guys down and going through . . . all the hassle, if no one really wants to deal with the problem. I'm the front line . . . I have to deal with these guys, but after the arrest it's just one big show. They play at being innocent, the court plays at being . . . this "firm but compassionate" father, or uncle or something, and then everyone finishes their paperwork, collects their pay and goes back to what they were doing before. I go back to trying to catch this guy, he goes back to capering, and when I catch him again, the court goes back to letting him go.

Many officers believe that the first time suspects are caught they are unlikely to be incarcerated if the crime is not a felony. If the crime is a felony the prevailing belief is that the suspect may or may not spend time in jail depending upon the specifics of the crime. This is particularly frustrating for police officers because they assume that most people who commit crimes get away with them for quite a while, until they are caught, die, or move out of the area. For the most part, police officers feel that the court undermines their job, which is as they see it, to put "bad guys" in jail.

Police officers view the practice of plea bargaining—pleading guilty to a lesser crime to avoid prosecution for a more serious one—as unfair. Officers feel that they take the risks—the injuries, the waiting, the paperwork and often the emotional and sometimes literal cleanup of victims—yet suspects rarely go to trial for the crimes they have committed. The victim's grief or loss is not reduced. The police officer's risk and work are not reduced. One officer observed:

There are no real winners in the [criminal justice] system, but the only ones who make out at all are the bad guys and the lawyers. . . . it's hard to say, of those two, who does better, and it's hard to say which one of them is worse. Sometimes there's not a hell of a lot of difference between them.

During this second career phase officers see many standard court actions as undermining the work that police have done and as hindering or even subverting justice.

LAWSUITS

Along with physical danger, it is in this phase that officers generally experience for the first time the dangers of the legal system for themselves. Although officers are frustrated by plea bargaining, they tend to blame the lawyers and the judicial system, not the suspects. I suspect that, in some ways, they feel the criminals are more honest than the lawyers. The new danger encountered by police officers at this phase of their career is the lawsuit—being sued.

During this phase it is not unlikely for officers "to be beefed," or to have a complaint lodged against them. It is somewhat rare for an officer never to be faced with a complaint. Complaints can be generated by arrestees, associates and family of arrestees, other officers, citizens, victims, special interest groups—they can come from anywhere. Some complaints are "buried by the desk"; that is, whoever is responsible for taking the complaint either manages to convince the complaining party not to file a complaint or indicates to the watch commander that the complaint is without merit. All complaints are supposed to go to the watch commander but in reality some do not. Current policies have been designed to prevent this from occurring and insure that all complaints will be investigated and acted upon. The success of these policies remains to be seen—there were, after all, similar directives in place in the past. Complaints received by the watch commander and entered in the records can prevent a promotion or result in disciplinary action, days off, or even in firing if the allegation is a serious one. They can also result in investigations by Internal Affairs, the self-policing unit of the agency. As troubling and problematic as these complaints may be, they pale in comparison to one of the street officers' most dreaded nightmares, the lawsuit. Beefs have the potential to turn into lawsuits.

The nature of the job is such that officers who work the streets are likely to be sued sometime in the course of their career. For many of the officers, their first suit is incurred during this second phase of their career. Sometimes officers are sued years later for an event that occurred during this phase. Most street officers who have been on the job for ten years have been sued.

Usually officers are sued in their capacity as police officers, representing the city. In these instances, if the case goes to arraignment and it is determined there is enough evidence to go to trial, it is city policy to settle out of court to avoid the cost (in dollars, time, and public relations) of a trial. City officials are concerned that juries are more likely to find police officers and the city culpable and award large sums of money to plaintiffs. Historically, the city would rather pay than fight a lawsuit. This is totally demoralizing for the officers involved. They feel the city is not backing them, that they are being punished for doing their jobs and, most hurtful of all, that their reputations have been damaged.

To avoid going to trial, the city enters a plea of *nolo contendere*, which technically is not an admission of guilt. However, it might as well be in the view of the officers. It means that the charges against the officer will not be contested, that there will in essence be no trial. The officers do not have the opportunity to present their evidence or call any witnesses. In not contesting the award the city sustains a small financial loss, regarded as smaller than the potential cost in time and money of fighting the charges. To the officers involved, however, it is a much more serious and lasting loss. For them it is the same as saying that the department thinks they were guilty or doesn't place a very high value on either the job they do, the reputation of the department, or the individual reputations of the officers involved. For police officers, reputation is extremely important. Unlike circumstances involving most other professions, court proceedings or even allegations of impropriety against a police officer are likely to draw media coverage as well as become a part of the officer's personnel file.

The officers are told they can sue the person who sued them, but they will have to do it on their own time and with their own funds. If they do decide to file a countersuit, the city's out-of-court settlement pretty much dooms their case unless they have absolutely conclusive evidence of their innocence. This may be difficult to obtain many years after the fact. After settling with the city out of court, the plaintiff may sue the police officer as an individual (independently from the police department), seeking even more compensation.

RESIDENTIAL PATTERNS

Usually by this stage in their careers, officers have relocated to "safe" communities. They have left the city where they are employed and moved their families (if they are still intact) to areas deemed safer. These neighborhoods are usually in the suburbs and are often quite distant. During this research many officers moved their families twenty or thirty miles away. Today it is not unusual for officers to live forty to sixty miles from the division in which they work.

One consideration in residential patterns is economic. Housing is less expensive in outlying areas. However, this is not the only motivation. Police officers move to more remote areas because they feel that they are inherently safer than the urban center. Police consider it foolhardy to live in the city and almost totally out of the question to raise children there. They feel safer in an area populated by a concentration of police officers. Many buy their houses from other officers and learn about available property through other officers. A number of police wives make a good living in real estate selling to police and firefighters. Law enforcement officers consider a neighborhood with a concentration of these occupations as a bonus. To some extent, this attitude may be generalized to the public. Real estate salespeople mention to prospective buyers that police officers live in the neighborhood and even point out their houses. Police officers are not pleased with this practice unless the potential buyers are also officers or firefighters. After all, officers go to some lengths to guard their private lives. They often have unlisted telephone numbers, although they may list them in their nicknames; they register their vehicles to the police department.

Police officers welcome living in a community of shared concerns and feel safer in this social surrounding. Not only do they avoid the kinds of crime associated with urban blight by living outside the city limits, but they also remove themselves from the likelihood of encountering someone they have arrested while they are off duty and with their families. Although outlying areas are certainly not crime free, the crimes and criminals are, to a much greater extent than in their own division, unknown to them.

During roll call at work, a recap is made available to the officers, which sums up incidents of crime. These are attenuated crime reports listing just the basic facts: the crime, where it occurred, when, briefly what happened, name of victim, name of suspect (if known), m.o., any special comments, or persons to contact. Thus, before they go out on their shift, they have already had the opportunity to make themselves aware of many of the crimes which have taken place in their absence. Anything of particular note, in the division or in the city, will be commented upon by whoever is conducting the roll call.

On their shift they are constantly aware of the police radio or the m.d.t. (mobile digital terminal—a computer) which informs them of calls for service as they come in. This is in addition to the unofficial reports of their fellow officers, commenting on the various crimes committed throughout the city. Police officers are keenly aware of crime in their working area and in the city in general. This amounts to a staggering amount of crime and, of course, the most heinous crimes are talked about at length. As a result, officers perceive the city as a very dangerous place. The same officers are less likely to be as well informed about crime in the area in which they live. Some officers have said that they do not want to know. Others make it their business to find out.

In addition to choosing areas which they consider to have low crime rates and a concentration of police community people, officers pay special attention to the fortification of their homes. Police officers tend to choose homes that are already structurally secure and then refine them to make them even more so. The preferred police officer's home includes, but is not limited to, solid core doors; metal reinforced door frames, hinged so that doors cannot be removed from the outside; outdoor mail boxes; dead bolt locks with removable keys; no louvered windows; windows that can be secured and cannot be removed from the outside. Officers remove the handles on their garage doors. They install outdoor lights, some equipped with motion detectors. Most of the places in which officers purchase homes do not have alleys. Where they do exist, officers generally avoid buying houses on alleys. Fully fenced properties are popular. High fences are popular, as are dogs—substantial dogs. Officers say they do not want to be surprised. Breaking into one of these houses is possible, but the house next door would be a better bet, unless, of course, it too belongs to an officer.

In addition to living in these fortified structures, officers add to the security of their homes by actively watching out for each other's homes. Firefighters work shifts that require them to be away from their homes for long periods of time, as do most law enforcement officers, so they are quite used to watching out for each other's families and homes. This enhances the image and essence of the police community as an extended family.

SOCIAL CONTACTS

In addition to providing a safe haven or residential community, these areas also provide a recreational and social hub for police families, especially those with small children. The image of the police community as some sort of idealized small community from past Americana is an incorrect one. The police community consists of many dispersed pockets, united only by the ties the officers share. This functions as a community of sentiment with several different physical loci. Sometimes social events even take place at the division or at the academy, but the favored location of most off-duty recreation is in one of these police community areas.

Social events, like picnics, swimming parties or barbecues, are attended by several police wives and their children, as well as other police families and community members. Women who get tired of explaining to their friends why their husbands are absent yet again from some planned activity do not have to go through any lengthy explanation in the police community. Everyone understands the nature of the job and the absence of officers. At one such occasion a police wife whose husband had been on the job for about five years said that she hated accepting any invitations from anyone who was not familiar with the job because she was tired of trying to explain why her husband was absent from the event, and to reassure people that her marriage was still intact. She indicated that people who are unaware of the police lifestyle often took offense at her husband's absence. Rather than go through the difficulties caused by his absence from events, she simply declined invitations "until they stopped coming." This is a common response among police families, and it contributes to the pulling away from non-police and strengthens the bonds with the police community.

Friendships from pre-police years tend to become more distant, while those among other officers on the same working watch become stronger. This formation of alliances appears to start sometime during the second phase and extend through to the end of the career. Not only do officers become familiar with other officers' families, they also indicate a greater degree of closeness linguistically (symbolically) through the use of nicknames or diminutive forms of the officer's name.

This naming behavior usually occurs between partners or officers who work together on the same watch for a prolonged time. It is a sign of friendship, which goes beyond the on-the-job camaraderie. It is an indication that the officers have a relationship independent of their working watch. They usually enjoy the same off-duty recreations and spend time together off the job. Officers who are William or Bill to family and other close friends are Billy to a small number of close coworkers. David becomes Davie; Frank becomes Frankie. This is an indication of intimacy and genuine caring for each other and only happens with really good friends. Nicknames—Squeeky, Daffy, Mad Dog, Flameout—can be used by anyone once they become known, but these diminutive forms are only used by close friends. Also along the same lines, among themselves female officers often refer to the males as "boys," and conversely, among themselves, male officers often refer to the females as "girls." They do not do this in mixed groups, or in the presence of outsiders.

It is difficult for non-police persons to understand the kind of investment officers have made in their job. Police may complain about it, or even make plans to leave it, but on varying levels they have made a strong commitment to doing the job as best they can. Part of the job is learning to rely upon your fellow officers. Just the fact that someone is involved in law enforcement commands a degree of kinship.

The inability of citizens (non-police) to see officers as individuals drives wedges between police officers and non-police, and also demonstrates to police that life is safer and easier when they interact primarily with police and police community persons. Police are also offended by the tendency of non-police to gloss over all of the many distinctions relevant to police officers (especially the agency involved, but also the time on of the officer involved, the watch, and other significant specifics) in asking questions or requesting explanations or justifications of police actions. The citizens in these cases are doing precisely what police officers do every day when they gloss over categories of people and do not acknowledge the individuality of the citizens they encounter. Neither group likes being on the receiving end of this process.

One officer commenting on this feature of police life became progressively more agitated as he explained:

> God! The words I hate to hear are, "well [his name], you're a cop, I was just wondering . . ." explain this . . . justify that . . . it's all attack and parry. It's not my idea of a good time. I avoid situations where that's going to happen, and believe me, that's anywhere I go where someone lets on that I'm an officer, a cop. . . .

Hubbard Buckner (1967:471) comments on his experience of feeling set apart in social situations during the participant observation portion of his fieldwork when he attended social gatherings as a reserve police officer: "I got a hostile reaction at social gatherings from people who had not known me 'before,' and incredulous reactions from people who had."

Conversations with non-police persons are exasperating for the officers because their views are so incongruent as to make communication difficult. The message the police hear is criticism. In their view it is criticism from people who do not know what they are talking about because the average person is, to the average officer, hopelessly naive and untutored in reality. Officers are weary of the reality they deal with daily. They have no desire to convince their friends and neighbors how dangerous the world is. It is bountifully clear to them that, even with media coverage, people are constantly surprised when violence and crime strikes close enough to affect them.

It is difficult for non-police friends to understand the job and its effect on the officers who perform it. Officers can become quite defensive about the job, their performance, and the department. Officers complain that friends from off the job always want them to justify or explain the actions of some other officer—sometimes even an officer in another agency or state.

One officer describes the problems of interacting with citizens:

> . . . the next thing I know [someone] is on me about every controversial thing any cop in any jurisdiction has done over the last ten years. But, this is the thing, he doesn't want to hear what I have to say, he wants to show how hip and liberal and knowledgeable he is, and what an illiterate, inarticulate, cold-blooded bastard I am. I won't be part of the show anymore, I don't go where that's going to happen to me. I don't need that kind of harassment. When they talk about "police harassment" that's always what I think of.

Another officer also commented on the difficulties he had encountered in interaction with non-police persons: "How can you answer them? However you answer, it's not what they want to hear, and you just get too tired of having to defend every action, of anybody who ever put on the uniform."

Officers take criticism levied against other officers or against virtually any facet of police work as a personal criticism if it is offered by someone who is not in the police community. Officers do not spend much time among people who are critical of police, and often this results in estrangement from their own families and former friends. Many changes in the attitudes and demeanor of officers during this phase of their career result from criticism from former friends.

Attempts by officers to relax and get away from these pressures sometimes backfire. Visits to family and friends designed to rekindle feelings of solidarity often serve merely to emphasize the transformations the officer has undergone. This is especially true for those visits in which there has been a prolonged absence of contact. Such visits may prove much less of a tension reliever than anticipated.

As officers find it more difficult to conduct a social life with their friends from the time before they became officers, they turn more to police friends and police community friends, such as firefighters and nurses. This process of self-segregation is often accompanied by an increase in the number of identifying items collected and displayed in officer's homes. These include articles of clothing, functional objects and accessories that identify the person as a member of the police department, sometimes as performing a specific duty, sometimes acknowledging rank. They also look more closely at older officers as models. Just as they have used them as guides to learning the essentials of the streets and the job, they begin to turn to them as guides for learning how to integrate being an officer into the rest of their lives, or how to separate the two.

Separating their working lives from their personal lives is rarely successful because they are almost always introduced in social settings as police officers. They are not permitted to interact with others in social situations without their occupation being noted. Once an officer's occupation is known, there is usually some job-oriented conversation, often similar to the ones reported above. More often, officers limit non-police contacts and turn more toward their fellow officers for socializing. This is a conscious turning toward the police community and away from non-police contacts.

At this point in their careers, an intensification of focus on other police officers, especially veteran officers, strongly reinforces the police worldview and reduces alternative explanations of events. The shift involves three ongoing processes: (1) There is less input from people whose views are likely to be at odds with the police version. The farther at odds an opinion is, the less likely it is to be listened to with serious consideration. (2) There is an increased belief that the police community is the only context in which an officer will be truly understood. (3) Officers feel that, if their colleagues were right about x then maybe they should listen more to what their colleagues have to say about y. The result is that officers become less critical of what they hear from other officers and more critical of outsiders who might espouse different ideas. When reality is formed by consensus, then the consensus will be the party line of the police community.

Looking more closely at the off-duty lives of other officers, officers in this stage of their careers find new models for their personal and professional lives. They begin to pay close attention to the "veterans"—officers in the fourth phase of their careers. Sometimes they will attach themselves to one of these veteran officers, and this will usually be one of the officers who has found new commitment to the job, and welcomes both the attention and the opportunity to share what he or she has learned over the years.

MARRIAGE, DIVORCE, AND THE JOB

This is a time when the job is often more satisfying and comfortable and makes more sense than officers' off-duty lives. Most of the officers who were married when they joined the force will be divorced either soon after probation ends, in their second year on the job, or within the first five years—during the last stage of phase one, or during this second phase of the career. One officer describes the break-up of his marriage:

> About the time my probation was up, they moved me over to a mid-P.M. watch [six P.M. until three A.M.], which was really a killer, because I had no time, no time for anybody. I worked, and I went to court, and I worked, and I went to court, and when I was home, I was sleeping. There were a couple of times, I didn't get home 'til eight or nine o'clock in the morning, when I was supposed to get off at three at night. Didn't work out too well. She'd [his wife] get upset at me, getting home so late, and there was nothing I could do about it. . . . Can't always be contacted when you're at the station. She would call, and couldn't get me. She talked to all her girlfriends and they kept telling her I was screwing around on her. I didn't know about this until later. They kept telling her I was screwing around on her, and then one night we got some drunk woman that smelled like she took a bath in some strange perfume, it was the cheapest stuff I've ever smelled, and we had to kind-of fight with her to get her in the car, and I was just [exasperated pause] . . . smelled great, I didn't bother to even think about what might happen when I got home. All hell went loose when she smelled perfume. It didn't make any difference what I had to say, she believed her girlfriends at this point.

> I got in an altercation one night shortly after that and got put in the hospital. I was in the hospital for nine days. The sergeant on the scene wanted to know if I wanted her to come to the hospital, and I said that I didn't know whether he should go get her or not, maybe he should just tell her that I would be home as soon as I could get home. He decided to go get her, and the first thing she said when she came into the hospital room was, "I told you this would happen." There was a kind of real cold and no-caring feeling coming from her and she just

kind of left me alone. That was the end of that marriage. It took a little while to complete it. I was off work for about two-and-a-half
months and then I went back to work, working light duty, working
community relations, went to work one day, came home in the afternoon, and the apartment was empty. I sat down on the steps when I
got home and said, "Son of a gun." It was a great big surprise to me.
The place was *absolutely* empty. That finished that one.

It is not uncommon for officers in their mid-thirties to be on their
third marriage, especially if they work patrol. Many aspects of police officers' lives place extraordinary stress on a marriage. The fact that now
many officers are married to officers certainly has not changed this.

ECONOMIC DANGER

This phase of the career is one in which many officers encounter economic problems, most often related to legal problems such as lawsuits
and divorce. There are also less dramatic economic problems directly tied
to overspending. These are often the result of, as one officer put it, "keeping up with the boys." Usually this involves purchasing the proper
recreational equipment, household appliances, vehicles, furniture, or toys
for the children. Sometimes officers will even overextend themselves in
the purchase of their homes, especially to have a home in a known police
area. Purchasing homes a great distance from the station means they
need reliable vehicles for the commute—new cars. Ideally cars should be
new and always well maintained, regardless of age. Similarly their
houses, clothes, indeed, all of their material possessions, should demonstrate their care and attention.

Wives who may formerly have had jobs they enjoyed may have left
these positions to move to a safer police community. Many officers do not
want their wives to commute for long distances, so these women often
take a lower-paying job close to their residence or stop working entirely.
While this may please the officers, it may not sit well with the wives. If
the marriage fails, these women are more likely to require financial assis-
tance (alimony or child support) than women who did not alter their
career plans. Officers who are paying one or more ex-wife alimony and/or
child support find there is very little left of the paycheck.

Officers may take second jobs, but it is more likely that they try to
work a great deal of overtime at the end of this phase, especially if their
wives are unemployed or underemployed. This is more likely to be the
case if they have children. Many officers are anxious about day care and
baby sitters. They do not want their children to be latchkey children, as
they know of too many examples of abuse, neglect and other unhappy sce-

narios. Those officers who do take second jobs are often tired and, in the case of divorced officers, depressed.

Many officers try to save more money or make investments as they learn from other police officers. They start making concrete plans for their retirement. Indeed, the concept of retirement starts being a more real concern for them. Along with this concern with retirement many officers receive counseling from veteran officers regarding one of the major pitfalls of divorce, losing one's pension: "Two bad ways to lose your pension. Die and not leave someone to collect it, and divorce and have someone you don't like walk away with it."

Throughout the job the officers joke about their pensions and their wives: "I've told my wife, 'if I die, find yourself a good man, and shack up with him, make babies, do whatever you want, just don't marry him. Make the city pay. The rule is just don't remarry, and there's nothing they can do. They have to pay.'" This remark is from an officer whose second wife is considerably younger than he, and was made prior to a city amendment which now makes it possible for widows to remarry and continue to collect on their husband's pension. He fully expects his wife to outlive him, and he speaks with apparent relish of the city having to pay out on his pension for many years to come, even after his death. This is not an uncommon sentiment.

In every division officers know exactly who "lost" their pension in a divorce settlement. Recounting these disasters ranks right along with the other police horror stories, featuring death and dismemberment. It is regarded as one of the worst things that can happen to an officer. If an officer has been married for over one year and divorces, legally the ex-spouse can petition the court to award him or her a portion of up to 50 percent of the officer's pension. The pension, if the officer leaves at twenty years, is 40 percent of his or her salary. Forty percent of their salary is usually not a great deal, but during their twenty-year careers, these officers have had plenty of time to think and rethink just how they will support themselves when they retire. Since most of them want to move to a more rural area and since they have planned carefully, most officers can get by on their pension with perhaps another job to put them in a healthy financial position. However, this is generally impossible if a divorce settlement leaves them with only 20 percent of their former earnings.

When officers first started losing 50 percent of their pensions to their ex-spouses in divorce settlements, they were incredulous. Sometimes an ex-spouse would opt for the pension rather than alimony, or sometimes it was taken because the officer did not have the economic resources to provide any other kind of settlement. Some spouses try to get the pension, in one officer's perception, "because she knew she could make my life miserable by doing it." Another officer, who had made elaborate retirement plans, all based on the full pension, said, "[She] knew exactly what she was doing. She knew that was the only part of the plan I couldn't fix, that she could totally destroy, and she did it. After seven years of marriage she knew the one thing to do to get her pound of flesh . . . 50 percent of my pension." Many times officers give up all of their financial interests in homes and other real estate in order to try to retain their pensions untouched.

In some particularly disastrous and legendary cases, officers have lost their homes and their pensions, and must still work second jobs to meet divorce settlements. In the division in which most of my research took place, one officer had at the time twenty-seven years on the job. Other officers jokingly said that the only reason he was still on the job was to keep his ex-wife from being able to draw his pension. The officer, when asked about retirement plans, said: "I won't retire. As long as I'm working my [ex-] wife gets nothing. It keeps me going just knowing that as long as I work she's outta luck." Now he has retired after more than thirty years on the job, and his ex-wife has received her portion of his pension.

Officers in the second phase of their careers encounter many other officers who serve as examples of the economic dangers of divorce and lawsuits. At this period most officers do not think that either scenario applies to them. In this assumption, most of them are mistaken.

6

Phase Three
Hitting the Wall

As we have seen, in phase one, as they hit the streets, officers learn the ropes and tend to be idealistic in their view of the job and their role in the criminal justice system. In phase two, as they hit their stride, they have mastered the things learned in the academy and on the streets. They are usually quite successful in this and gain confidence as they draw closer to the police subculture. As their work lives and social relations with colleagues improve, their home lives tend to deteriorate. During this second phase of the career officers begin to perceive shortcomings in the criminal justice system and in their own department, but are not overly concerned. They are beginning to feel the increasing physical toll of the job, but are unaware of the psychological toll. They enjoy being police officers and have mastered the skills required to do the job well.

In the third phase officers become disillusioned with the department and the role of police officer, but have few other sources of validation. Since it has been immersion in this definition of self as police officer that has sustained them, the blow is a critical one.

Phase three, in which they hit the wall, lasts approximately four years and is an extremely difficult period for the officers and their families. It is characterized by the angst which accompanies the disillusion officers feel with the department and with themselves. They say they have "hit the wall" and they "don't care" anymore. This is one of the most negative expressions in the police subculture. To say that someone doesn't care (or that the department does not care) is viewed as a negation of all that they do. Some officers become self-destructive and behave in ways that compound their distress over the job. This difficult transitional period ultimately results in change discussed later in the chapter.

SYMPTOMS OF DISILLUSION

Until they develop a coping strategy officers are likely to experience turmoil, distress and great confusion as a result of disillusion with their lives and occupations. They are used to making quick decisions and doing something about disorder; now, when they are invested in the out-

come on a personal and professional level, they don't know what to do. Without assessment and redirection this is the time when an officer is most likely to resign or develop severe problems with alcohol, drugs and personal relationships.

Often officers do not express these sentiments to each other at the time they are feeling them, or they tone them down when sharing them with friends. At this point, my data collection was greatly facilitated by talking to police wives. Wives compare notes, and, from these conversations, patterns of work-related complaints emerge. This is highly personal information, not polite conversation; still it is common enough that police wives see it as part of the job, albeit an unpleasant one. Many police officers in this phase of the career must on many occasions force themselves to go to work. Chronic complaints on work days include vomiting, diarrhea, severe headaches, gastric upsets, queasiness and double vision. Usually the onset of symptoms begins one to three hours before the officer is scheduled to leave for work. The symptoms may or may not subside as the officer's working watch progresses.

The following officer's comment illustrates the sense of desperation and urgency expressed by many at this phase of their career:

> I can't imagine doing this for one more day. It's like there is only to-day. Do the watch. Keep it all together. Keep everything in line. Nothing out of the ordinary. Just keep it from pulling apart. Now I just do that today, today is all I'm thinking and it will be all right.

According to another officer:

> It would start basically when I got up, but it would seriously be a problem as it got closer to the time I had to go in, and with an hour's commute, it gave me plenty of time to think about what was going on. Still for a long time I didn't put it together. I'd chosen this, I was doing what I wanted to do and I couldn't get it that it was making me sick.

The officer who made the following comment lived part of the time with two other police officers. He did not discuss his illness with them. Further, he said that when he realized this only happened when he was working patrol, he felt there must be something wrong with him because he couldn't take the job anymore. He continues to work patrol, and describes the pre-work routine at this time in his career:

> Throwing up. Like a baby. Time to go to work, "excuse, I gotta go to the john." It was embarrassing. And it was frightening. I thought maybe I had cancer like [another officer]. Scared the shit out of me. Didn't want to tell anyone. I knew it would go away or I would die. And it did—go away. It lasted on and off about four months, and then again a few times about a year later.

Another officer who has since become very active in the peer counseling program, formed by police officers as a support group, commented:

> I've been in casts—for [nonverbal indications of a very long time], but the area I have to deal with is the area of the psychological stuff. It used to be much, much more extreme. From 1977 to 1980 I was a sick boy. Heavy stress. Colitis. Insomnia. Memory loss. Migraines. Bleeding gums. A real rough period. I had no idea what was going on. It became normal to feel that way. I thought it was normal—I was always intense anyway. Eating always was an annoyance to me. I'd eat to refuel. I'd sleep when I had to. No limits to what I could do.

> After being under strain and personal abuse, at twenty-seven I just couldn't do what I could do at seventeen. I was really physically spent, used up. I was in big trouble. I used to leave the house, and I'd get to the station and find out I wasn't [scheduled to be] working, and I'd call my wife and say, "I'm not working today; where was I going when I left the house?" She'd tell me I was going to court. I'd say "thanks" and go off to court. That's the way it was—for too long. I'd leave the house

and I'd forget my keys, gun, wallet. It was like a crippling disease. I was doing such brainless stuff then—and that scared me.

The thing that drove me to the doctor had nothing to do with my walking around like a zombie. As I said, I had stress-related colitis. The pain would build up. I was so uncomfortable. The pain was terrible. . . . The insomnia and the migraines and the colitis, it was all there . . . I was really feeling sick, and I went to this old doctor. This guy was eighty years old. He told me, at twenty-seven I was the worst stress case he'd ever seen.

At the time this officer finally visited the doctor he was following a grueling schedule. He attended college full time, was working morning watch, among other commitments. He allocated six hours a day to sleep. He went to work around 11:00 P.M.; arrived home around 8:00 A.M.; ate; left for school; and attended class. He went home and drank alcohol to relax before going to bed. In the morning, he drank two or three cups of coffee, sometimes more, just to wake up and get going. He says:

I was doing everything wrong. I was surprised when the doctor told me how bad it was. I was surprised. I didn't have a clue. I got so used to feeling that way I thought it was normal. "This is what happens to people who work hard and have goals," that's what I thought. It took me a couple of years to turn it around. I had to leave patrol, take a desk job. I had to stabilize my hours. I had to stabilize my diet, and improve my diet.

This officer credits peer counseling with his recovery and more importantly as a means of educating other officers with the same problems. Young, active officers who regularly perform relatively athletic tasks do not easily think of themselves as either vulnerable to, or sick from, something as innocuous and meaningless to them as "stress." He continues,

The peer counseling was very important. I was really angry about it. If someone had told me what was going on I wouldn't have had to suffer. And it was sheer hell for her [his wife]. Now I know the signals my body was screaming at me. I didn't know what was going on. The reason I go through the peer counseling is there's no reason why I or anyone else has to suffer through this sort of thing. When I was talking with [another officer] the things he was telling me about how unhappy he was and how much he hated to go to work every day, and how his body felt, and the problems he's had swallowing. I just had to say, "All right, Buddy, Hands up! This is it. Just from what you've told me today, this is stress. *Stress* is why you're feeling this way and I know you can turn this around. You don't have to go through this. It doesn't have to happen." I heard him telling me the same thing that I'd felt, the same stuff. I could see it was lockdown for him.

However, not all officers are able to cope. Some officers commit suicide during this period. Approximately two active-duty L.A.P.D. officers commit suicide each year. They refer to officers' suicides as "eating the gun." Compared to the general population of Los Angeles, Los Angeles Police Department officers are nearly three times more likely to kill themselves.

This is a period when officers make dramatic changes in their lives on and off duty. Depending on the strategy they have adopted, they change divisions, watches, duties. They promote. They attempt to promote. They change their lives in major ways. There is another wave of divorces, changes in their social relationships. They withdraw from old relationships, perhaps start new ones. They get new significant others or new spouses. They have new children. They pick new hobbies, make new investments. They change their drinking patterns, their exercise patterns. They start new back-up jobs, return to school. They develop new skills. They plan new lives.

This is a period characterized either by decisive action or withdrawal from the struggle. It is a period of personal and professional rekindling—or burnout. Change is the key word. This seems to be the career version of a mid-life crisis—apparently precipitated by strong feelings of having been let down by the department.

One officer, noted for his positive outlook and highly respected by his peers, said of this period in his career:

> I was so unhappy and so sick . . . I was just going to do it a day at a time. I wasn't going to leave the house until head to toe, my grooming was perfect. There was nothing negative . . . I was prepared for every contact to go well, to be successful . . . when I did a crime report, it was as thorough and as neat and as proper and as right as I can do it . . . They get my report and say, "Good job." [If someone said] "I have a sodomized juvenile; I have to book the father," I'd buy the call. I'd take the juvenile to get m.t.ed [medical treatment]. I sought out and did the garbage work. T.A.s [traffic accidents], impounds, jail transfers, narco transfers, m.t.s. Nobody wants 'em. . . . Finally the watch commander just has to cram it down somebody's throat. I'd buy these. I did the work that no one else wanted . . . and when I was done, it was better, because it needed doing and I did it right. I wanted to attack and control my work environment, and I was busy all day long. The only goal that mattered—the kid didn't have to sit around five hours; we did it in two. Things were better. What needed to be done was done. That was the goal. Did the watch run smoother?
>
> I wanted to control the negative stuff—take it off the other guy's back. If you want success, then you have to work without any expectation of reward. You have to do it just because it needs doing. You do it the best way you can, with no negativity. It took a year or two to change

my life around. I did it out of desperation. It's a totally different mental attitude.

This third phase is a period of tremendous disillusion and frustration with the department. The source of this distress is not necessarily the work per se—not the daily job on the streets—but rather the structure and policies of the department and the officers' perceptions of them. By this phase, officers have been on the job for at least seven years, and have personally handled a very large number and wide range of situations. As police officers they feel confident of their abilities and perceptions. They think they understand what is going on, professionally, with crime in the city, but begin to question their role in the department and the department's support of them both as officers and as individuals.

Informants in this phase expressed feelings of having been "used" by the department. Many officers described themselves as "cannon fodder" or "put on the line to be the first down":

> I used to think the department cared about me, and about every officer. I felt that no matter what, the department would look after me, and if something happened to me, my wife and the kids would be all right, too. I believed that, really believed. . . . They have a never-ending source, especially today where it doesn't take anything to be a cop. They'll take anyone. That is the problem . . . they can just keep drawing, and drawing from the pot to get more police officers. If they cared about the officers, if they cared about me, the officers, the city, they wouldn't take what they're taking and calling them "police officers." You see, that's the problem. They don't care. They have a budget, and they have a need for bodies, and if they can get enough of them, just bodies, it doesn't matter, because no matter, they won't run out. Full deployment. They'll use me 'til I'm done, then use whatever else. It doesn't matter to them, and I didn't know any better. None of us did . . . we didn't know. . . . So now I don't feel like I owe this city anything. This city, the department owes me, but I'm not going to hold my breath. Some citizen might thank me sometime, but not the city. They got what they wanted. I did the job, I still do the job I was hired on to do, but I'm not so naive anymore. Now I'm in on how it works.

PHYSICAL INJURIES

Injuries incurred during the first and second phase of their careers, aggravated by the constraints and misalignments caused by the wearing of the police equipment, begin to become daily problems. In terms of punishing police equipment, the Sam Browne is undoubtedly the worst offender. The Sam Browne, or gunbelt, holds not only the department

issue weapon (currently a nine millimeter pistol weighing in at about three pounds), but also numerous leather cases which contain handcuffs, gas, restraints, magazines containing extra ammunition and sometimes other items such as flashlights and batons. The entire Sam Browne, fully loaded, weighs a minimum of fifteen pounds and is often considerably heavier. It is heavy, bulky and can easily cause permanent back injury and nerve damage. It makes sitting and running difficult and often painful. Officers get used to it and must learn to move quickly despite its cumbersome interference. Every officer interviewed, with at least seven years of working the streets, reported back pain attributed directly to wearing a Sam Browne or to other injuries failing to heal properly because wearing the belt prevents full recovery. Obviously the Sam Browne must be kept on at all times; hence it takes a toll on the body, when driving or riding in a patrol car.

As a direct result of these collective injuries their recreational patterns may be curtailed because they cannot physically do some of the things they used to do. These are men and women of about thirty years of age who are physically oriented and have considered themselves to be athletic. Most of them have back, elbow, wrist, and knee problems, or problems with their feet. Many suffer from ulcers, migraine headaches and colitis. Officers have pensioned off with severe back problems (generally only after repeated surgeries), with arthritis, heart conditions and cancers (possibly caused by contact with such items as radar guns, fingerprint powder, or gunpowder). Some officers who ignored ("powered through") various symptoms of injury or illness now find that they have permanently damaged their bodies by not attending to them.

A few officers apply for pensions on the basis of incapacitating injuries (usually acquired earlier in their career) or for psychological reasons—stress diseases or other psychologically rooted difficulties. One officer who joined the department at twenty-one and retired at thirty with a medical pension (broken back) mentioned that during his physical examination doctors found that his back had been broken once before. The first time he did not get treatment and, in fact, did not realize his injury was so severe. Lack of treatment for the first injury adversely affected the prognosis for full recovery in the second instance. The officer stated these were not the only injuries he received during his career:

> Primarily my injuries started out as nose and face injuries. That stopped. I started getting a few rib injuries. That stopped. Started getting broken fingers and broken wrist injuries and carried those pretty much throughout. In conjunction with things like kicked shins, stomped toes—basically because I let the other guy get in the first swing until I learned better . . . I learned to be a little more cautious about my back—and about who was behind me, and what they were doing. And then it worked out to be pretty much finger and wrist injuries. I broke my wrist a number of times. The shin injuries always happen, and the toes, because I still always let a woman take the first shot—and they're hell for kicking you in the shins, they really are. Of course you try not to get hurt and to stop anything before anybody gets hurt, but that can be real tough to do.

The injury in which his back was broken the second time and that ultimately resulted in his medical pension was sustained when he and his partner responded to a domestic disturbance call. When the officers arrived they were told that an armed man was holding two children. The officer saw the opportunity to overpower the gunman without further endangering the children and took it. As he lunged for the man and the gun the officer realized two important facts: first, that the gun might not be real, and secondly that they would most likely crash into a glass covered table. He tried to secure the weapon and twist their collective bodies to alter the trajectory of their fall in mid-air. He was partially successful; he gained control of the toy gun, but caught the edge of the table on the way down. Of the incident the officer said:

I pensioned off with a broken back, I.O.D. The end of that incident
turned out to be a Mormon deacon with a toy gun. I requested the attorney not file any charges on him and they didn't. He had never been
in any trouble before, just a classic case of a very normal citizen at a
crisis point in his life—he had a problem with his wife at that time—
he just went a little crazy for awhile. My broken back . . . that was one
of the hazards of the profession. It wasn't a malicious act on his part.

These officers are "working hurt" and often fearful because they
know they are physically not as fast, strong, or steady as they once were.
They also try to protect themselves from further injury and pain, while
attempting to insulate themselves from legal entanglements. For these
officers the goal becomes simple: to get off the streets. There are problems
with this goal. First, they find it difficult to express their desire to do this.
I suspect they are fearful that others will think they are wussing out, or
they think that everyone must want to get off the streets and feel it would
be presumptuous for them to try to do so. The second and more critical
problem is that there simply are not enough indoor jobs to meet the needs
of all the officers who want and need them.

Getting off the streets is a frequent topic at social gatherings. It is
so common that it is rarely taken as a serious sentiment. Officers will
recount a story and finish it by saying, "I have to get off the street." Others
will agree and the discussion will continue. The actual question of how to
get off the street is rarely investigated in any systematic way. The deployment patterns and requirements of the city do not make it easy for officers
to get off the streets. In fact, there is a strong political push to get more
officers "on the streets"—on patrol. In a classic example of the street cop/
management cop cleft (Reuss-Ianni, 1983), one officer states:

> You know, the administrators on the police department have worked
> and engineered themselves toward advancement, not toward police
> work. They're successful in the sphere of police management because
> a hell of a number of them weren't worth a damn as policemen—so
> there's a number of them that don't have any God-damn idea of what
> it takes to be a real policeman. By real policeman I mean somebody
> that goes out and really does a service toward the people who are pay-
> ing their salaries. Consequently, these people don't really understand
> the toll. Burnout is just a catch phrase. It's a new buzz word, but it
> fits a large category of people that want to get off the street. There re-
> ally is a burnout problem and they don't do anything about it. . . .
> There's a hell of a lot of street cops—I'm not talking about your ad-
> ministrators or audio-visual technicians who happen to have a
> badge—the guys out there on the street, that street-cop breed. We've
> got a lot of them. Big percentage of retired [officers] blow their brains
> out after six months, or they're squeezed to the last drop and then giv-
> en a pension, but they're totally useless to themselves or anyone
> else—used up—burned out hulks.

GETTING OFF THE STREETS

The perceived need to get off the streets presents another issue in which there has been a major change in the police career, directly due to the number of females on the force. Female officers who have been injured or are pregnant generally fill the small number of available inside positions. Pregnant female officers are automatically assigned to indoor spots. One new female officer expressed frustration with a practice she identified as reflecting badly on female officers. She was particularly irked because the officer she described was an academy mate and felt the officer lacked commitment to the job. She observed:

> . . . some of them have figured out that if they get pregnant they don't have to finish probation, and then they've got an indoor slot for as long as they want it. . . . [Name of officer] is pregnant again. On the job five years, this is her third kid.

While this is clearly not widespread behavior, this is a particularly notorious case in the assessment of both the traditional and new police; this officer has worked less than one full year of patrol duty in her more than five years as a police officer. The officer has said she is going to resign after the birth of her next child, but not until she has used up her pregnancy leave.

Officers are encouraged to return to work as soon as possible after an injury. Officers who really need to get indoor slots frequently cannot; this is particularly true of male officers. They use their sick days, overtime and vacations to stall returning to the streets, but when these are exhausted they must go back on the streets. They are usually willing to do so, but it may have negative consequences to both their bodies and their attitudes toward the department. One officer damaged his back in a car crash on the job, four years prior to being interviewed. His back had recently gone out as a result of that former injury. This has been painful, has cost him many sick days (he has used all of his 100-percent-paid sick leave days, as well as all of the 75-percent and 50-percent days the department allows) and has also caused him to reevaluate the department's policy regarding such injuries.

> I've been off and on for the last year and a half . . . and it's opened my eyes a little bit as far as the department is concerned. The people that do get injured on the job, and how well they do take care of you, and what they think about you. The department on the whole doesn't really care very much about you. They just want you back to work as soon as possible. They don't care what you need to do to get back. They . . . badger you and make you come back as soon as they think it's warranted . . .

In order to protect their bodies, many officers tend to pull back and are even more conservative in their style of policing. They become more passive and reactive rather than proactive. They become less physical, more verbal. They are less likely to pursue questionable situations with the same zeal that may have characterized the first two phases of the job. Officers are more likely to back down in situations that appear to be dangerous—especially if there is danger of being sued. They are especially leery of what they perceive to be "political stuff," that is, dealings with the numerous special interest groups that proliferate in the fertile diversity of Los Angeles.

Not only is the city a tribute to multicultural abundance, but Los Angeles is also an excellent venue for airing one's agenda with maximum media coverage. In addition to the sorts of opportunities for exposure that all major cities provide, Los Angeles is a mecca for media. The city's reputation invites media attention even on a non-news day. Many events that provide excellent settings for demonstrations and disruptions take place in Los Angeles and are reported nationally, even internationally. Presidential visits, parades, award ceremonies, film industry events, sporting activities, business centers, numerous museums and two major universities provide extra opportunities for groups to gather and promote various causes and issues. What makes these situations particularly tense and political for the L.A.P.D. is that due to the size, density and heterogeneity of the Los Angeles metropolitan area, virtually any issue is bound to draw opposition as well as support. Sometimes the conflicting interests are merely misunderstandings. In addition there are also real disagreements—not a problem of interpretation, but a genuine conflict.

The L.A.P.D. is often called upon to deal with confrontations between opposing camps. Often these encounters are volatile and unpredictable. Passions can run high. There are often mixtures of family groups and the added spice of alcohol and/or drugs. Often people who disagree and are passionate in their commitment are willing to break the law by failing to disperse, by trespassing or by engaging in any number of violations. Often getting arrested is considered part of making the statement and demonstrating commitment. Whether innocent misunderstandings or real conflicts, police view these interactions with special apprehension and aversion. This may stem not only from a desire to protect themselves physically, but also legally—which can also mean economically.

LEGAL CONSIDERATIONS

Legal concerns, which may have surfaced in the second phase of their careers, become more pressing in the third phase. Officers who may have assumed that they could never be sued because they have not done anything wrong now know that is not true. One officer commented, quite typically:

> It kind of really gets you. You think you're doing a good job and somebody comes along and sues you for something. Well you know you're right in what you did, and everything is fine, but yet they still are able to take this thing to court, and make it look like you're a bad guy, when actually you're doing the job that they paid you to do.

Police officers in both phase two and three of their careers see the possibility of legal action against them as one of the dangers of the job. However, officers in the second phase still believe that the department will support them; in contrast, officers in the third phase do not share this sentiment. Note the differences in the perceptions of the following officer with almost five years on the job, and then the next informant, quite representative of the third phase, with eight years on. First:

> I've been a soldier or police officer since high school and I don't ever worry about the danger anymore. I guess I may not be very typical. . . . The only danger I worry about is the psychological stuff. I don't have any concern for the legal side. Lawsuits fly like cannon fodder . . . people sue me all the time—for false arrest, false imprisonment and all that bullshit. The city will insulate me. That's the barometer of my actions: as long as I'm acting the way I know to act, and not maliciously or in bad faith . . . I'm not afraid of it.

And the other officer:

> We're living in a sad state. People will sue for anything. They will complain about you and try to sue you because you smiled at them at a traffic stop—I've been sued several times. . . . They think they can get away with something and they decide to embellish on everything that happened . . . and if they win, that even makes things worse. The city just decides they won't fight it and pays. The city has their quota system as to what they'll pay and what they won't. They have a ceiling on how much they'll pay and, rather than fight it, they'll pay a certain amount. I think it's bullshit, [laughs] because they're not backing up their officers, they're making them look bad . . . even when the officer's right—the city doesn't care. They don't care how the officer feels, they don't care what anybody else thinks about the situation. The city says its easier to pay them than to fight.

This officer went on to say that a key representative of the city's legal office described the policy and concluded that, "It's a crap shoot any time you go into the streets." According to the officer:

> . . . told me the city will only back you if they know a jury would find [rule in favor] for the city. The way juries feel these days there is no point in taking anything small to court. The city will lose. Even with

the large settlements, the juries are in a real generous mood. Any time it's the big guy vs. the little guy, they're going to give it to the little guy. Cops are the classic "big guy" and so is the city . . .

The officer went on to describe an account of another exemplary officer who no longer works the streets as a direct result of the city paying a suit that alleged misconduct on the part of the officer. He said,

That irks the heck out of me. That's what got [his partner] off the streets. He just hung it up. What reason does a police officer have to go out there and do your job when, on top of everything else, they're laying for you with the lawyers and the city will just pay?

Police officers in this third phase believe they may be sued without merit, so being sued is viewed as being somewhat independent of their own behavior. The officers most likely to get involved in legal problems are those who interface with the public—patrol officers. The officer who recounted the following episode became progressively more agitated as he told the story. He says it was the worst event in his twelve-year career:

We were on loan to Hollywood because they were having the Christmas parade. So we were working the crowd, people were just arriving and everyone was in a good mood. Lots of people. Families and such. And everything was fine when this citizen came over and told us that there was a man down and bleeding. We went to see this guy, and he was down, and out. All bloody. He was passed out, and when I leaned over to talk to him, he woke and said he'd been in a bar and got in a fight and got himself beat up; and then he saw who we were, that we were police, and became all combative. Calling us "pigs" and that sort of thing. He was drunk and not hearing at all what we had to say. He was swearing and spitting at the peds [pedestrians]. And now there were lots of people, mothers and their children, all coming to this parade.

Here's this beat-up drunk swearing and carrying on. This guy was saying real foul things, bad language and spitting at the people, the women and children as they passed—and we told him to "shut up," but we said it nicer at the time. The first time we did, then later it was just "shut up." But we handcuffed him, and he was spitting and kicking out at people, so we thought, "we can't have this." So we got out the restraints and tied him so he couldn't kick anymore. Had to pick him up and carry him to where we could get a car for transport. And the sergeant said we should take him to county and get him [treated] and absentee to book him, and we did. Eight hours, eight hours of paperwork because of this guy.

And that was it. We thought that was it, and then we get summonses. [His partner] and I got the summonses and we didn't even know what they were talking about. It had been five years since the incident. We didn't even recognize the name. It wasn't even familiar to me; I had to go through my officer's notebook to find out what had happened, and then I remembered the guy and what happened. Now, this is what he alleges. He alleges that my partner and I went into this gay bar, and pulled him out and beat him up, because he was gay, and then arrested him. He didn't even know what had happened to him, but that was his story. I actually think he really believed that we did it. I think he really didn't remember what really happened and thought we did it. He alleged this, brought this to a lawyer five years later. Five years! Half a decade. Where are we going to get the witnesses [even] three years later? Just [his partner] and me and the sergeant.

It was the worst time of my life, to be accused of something and not be able to prove myself innocent. To not even have the opportunity to prove myself because the city was busy covering its ass. [very agitated] I didn't do anything, and everybody knew it. I had a partner and a sergeant, and they took the deposition of [his partner], but didn't even call the sergeant in. They didn't even need us because they'd already decided. They just paid the fucker thirty-five hundred dollars, and it goes in my package that there was an action against me and the city paid. How does that look?

The partner when interviewed said it was this event that precipitated his decision to do whatever was necessary to get off patrol. However, he was not able to accomplish this immediately. Between the time he made the decision to get off patrol and the time he was able to do so, the officer followed the strategy of "withdrawal":

After that time I did as little as I could. Had as little contact with citizens as possible. I used to work the "L" car [a one-officer unit that handles reports most of the time], so I was only there if they asked me to be there. And there was a record of that. I didn't do anything else if I could help it. It didn't make any sense to do anything—any real police work. Not patrol. I didn't want to go through that again.

Many officers are sued, but many of the suits are unsuccessful or never make it through the court process. Regardless, police officers, especially at this phase of their careers, become very fearful of being sued. Being sued is emotionally draining, and can damage an officer's reputation. Just the fact that a suit has been brought against an officer becomes a permanent part of that officer's package. Officers are fearful that this could interfere with promotion, as indeed it may. They also have economic fears. One officer believed he would lose his house due to high punitive damages in a court action, until the person who was suing him admitted in court that the suit was without merit and called it off:

[An officer] was on the stand. [The lawyer] had him on the stand and he was accused of using unnecessary force with this kid. Here's [the officer], six-foot-three, motor cop, all in his uniform, and here's this seventeen- to eighteen-year-old kid, and the kid is alleging brutality. And the father's there. All the officers knew this kid. He was bad news. This kid was always in trouble. He was a burglar. A vandal. A doper. Boosted half the car radios in [an affluent area of the city]. He'd go over to the high school and get in trouble weekly. It was in [a well-known and very affluent area of the division], so mommy and daddy had plenty, but he would caper for his drug and drinking money. We thought the mother knew, but we didn't know if the father knew.

Anyway, [the officer] is sweating bullets because he thinks he's going to lose his house. The lawyer told him that—that they were going to clean him out. [The lawyer] was going for [the officer], trying to make him look bad, and [the officer] was so pissed off at the whole situation, but he couldn't do anything. He knew this little punk was lying, and the lawyer must have known it, too. Then the kid's father stopped it. The lawyer was so disgusting even the father couldn't take it. It was like nothing I've ever heard of. The kid's father talked to the lawyer and called him off. Said he knew [the officer] didn't beat the kid. No unnecessary force on the part of the officer. Kid had come home in fine shape. The father apologized, *apologized* to [the officer] . . . the dad couldn't stand it. It must of been the kid's idea. Hanging with some real princes. The kid knows all the angles, but the father couldn't take it. It was good that the father stopped it, but he shouldn't have let it start in the first place. It takes so much out of you being sued. Even when you know you did nothing wrong, it takes it out of you. [The officer] still gets hot when he sees that lawyer, or even just hears about him.

An officer who called being sued "one of the hardest times I had to work on the job" could barely get through his description of his experience. His voice cracked and he had to pause often. During parts of the interview he was barely able to contain his tears. He said:

. . . then I went to the jury trial—the two-day jury trial. So I'm not guilty. It was really—very traumatic. I mean—when—when the jury walks—walks in—and they say "will the defendant please stand"— you're the only guy standing—[becomes overcome with emotion, tears welling in eyes, choked up]—Oh, it was rough. But anyway—I was not guilty. Anyway—I got taken out for a drink afterward. I'll tell you, I sure needed a drink. I usually don't drink—so I got that out of the way, and then I got transferred. I figured, "Well, the handwriting's on the wall. I've been at the division too long. I've got shot down there. I've been to about four or five funerals of guys down there. My training officer got killed, and so forth—this is the worst. I'm gettin' out." Of all of that, the worst was getting sued and being filed on. Worse than getting shot. You get shot—there's no time to think about it. It happens and you deal with it. But the legal stuff eats at you and eats at you, and people look at you funny, like they don't believe you didn't do it—I got out of there and now I need to get off the street.

At this point in their careers officers feel fairly confident that they can handle most of what the street can hand out or, alternatively, that things can happen for which there is no defense. Officers are sometimes somewhat fatalistic in their views. They do what they can to prepare for, recognize and avoid physical harm. However, they also know there are some things that cannot be foreseen, planned for or circumvented. They feel they understand the physical dangers, but the legal dangers are inscrutable and almost impossible to avoid.

Feelings of being used or manipulated by court strategies surprised, confused or irritated officers earlier in their career, because they viewed the criminal justice system in a very ideal fashion. By the end of the second phase, they are less naive, and by the third phase, they are much more cynical. Some of the issues that emerge as major irritations as officers become better versed in the criminal justice system are: political pressures, shifts in department policy, the sort of adversarial relations that often exist between the different parts of the system, changing rules of search and seizure. They still resent attacks on their credibility and professionalism which are sometimes wielded in courtrooms. They often see what they do as rather futile—"We catch them, they let them go." Some officers never get used to what they view as demeaning, taunting and baiting personal attacks on and questioning of their integrity.

There is, of course, diversity in the way officers view court, as there is in all matters. The following rare example is from an officer who says he enjoys court. The other officers who enjoy court appear to be similarly motivated:

> I enjoy court. I like to testify. I know some guys don't like it, but with me it's a game. You're on the stand and they're trying to get you, and you answer but the whole time you're trying to out-think them and they're trying to out-think you, and you can see where they're going. They have to ask the questions and you have to answer them, but eventually they ask the big question. The one you can see they've been leading up to—and they think they've got you. They ask the big question and you get to give them the answer you wanted to give all along. You get to tell them what you want them to know, and it really frosts them. 'Cause then it's out. Their boy is dirty and you've said it, and they set it up. I love it. It's like chess. I'm never afraid of court.

According to another view:

> When I first started I tried my hardest to be as complete as possible and to be perfectly honest. *Big mistake*. They nailed me to the wall. I felt like I was the one on trial. I was trying to give full explanations and cover all the bases, and they were trying to show that I was a dumb policeman who didn't follow procedure and—I hated court. It's okay now, but then—then I learned. They ask a question and it's "yes," "no," "I don't recollect," and "to the best of my recollection." They

don't get anything from me, unless I want to say it, and then, *no* elaboration, *no* detail. If they want detail, they have to ask directly.

RESIGNATION

It is common for officers in this phase to state categorically that they would leave in a minute, but they cannot afford to do so. This is something of an exaggeration. While it is certainly true that police officers—especially divorced police officers—can find themselves in economic difficulty, this is not unique to the profession, nor is it a permanent condition. Most officers are still young at this phase of their careers—generally in their late twenties to early thirties—hardly a time when most people consider their most productive years to have passed. In addition, this is not a time when age would preclude a successful change of occupation. Something else is going on, something that has little to do with their financial profile and everything to do with the police worldview. Officers believe they are not supposed to quit, to wuss out, to desert their comrades. Officers who resign are regarded as quitters. They are no longer police and they no longer belong to the brotherhood of officers. This is not the case with officers who have pensioned off either at twenty years or due to injuries prior to the twenty-year mark. To use a military analogy, this is similar to the difference between an honorable and dishonorable discharge. However, either one is a far more public event in the closely knit police community.

In addition to the perceived stigma of resignation, the economic structuring of the job makes it difficult for officers to resign. They simply lose too much. If they resign they are allowed to take the money *they* have contributed to their retirement, but the funds set aside by the city are lost. Prior to 1982, if officers resigned for any reason, they were not entitled to their own contributions to their pension plan. Very few officers were willing to walk away from these funds, which represent a large portion of their paychecks. This provided an excellent economic incentive to stay in the department, even through extreme adversity and job dissatisfaction. Although that has changed, there are still few officers who resign.

At one time or another, most officers talk about quitting and say they would enjoy simply walking into the watch commander's office to do so—or, as an alternate fantasy, simply not show up for roll call. But it is only fantasy. Even though it is a common and alluring image, they would not applaud or respect an officer who did resign unless there were extremely extenuating circumstances. Quitting is seen as a defection. It is regarded as turning your back on your colleagues and not being there when they need you. Whatever your reason for wanting to quit, others have the same reasons. If you quit and they stay, you have let them down and set yourself apart from the rest of them. This violates a cherished value: you must always be there for your fellow officers.

Officers in this and later phases frequently complain among themselves about the job, coworkers, perceived disintegration of the department, policies, the courts, all of the elements which impinge on their professional and personal lives. They agree that the sooner they can get off the job the better off they will be. However, most have elaborate reasons why they cannot possibly quit. They express the sentiment that they would be leaving their colleagues, quitting, deserting. They do not want to remain on the job, but they do not want people thinking they can't take it or that they have abandoned their colleagues.

Generally by this point of the career, most of their social contacts are either police or people who have accepted the police lifestyle. If this were not the case, resignation would not be so poor a choice. At least, it would not have so many negative consequences for the officer. The officer may believe he or she would find little support in a decision to leave the department.

For the most part, by phase three officers are too socialized in the police worldview to leave. Between 1975 and 1990 only seven or eight officers, out of the approximately three hundred officers in the division that provided the bulk of the data for this study, quit with less than twenty years on. Almost all of these left after four to six years on the job. In that fifteen-year period, about twenty people per year moved to another division. Thus, from a field of three hundred officers, around 2 percent actually quit before twenty years. One officer asked to be reinstated after only a few months. This low percentage is remarkable considering the nature of the job, the stresses on the officers and the numbers of officers involved over a fifteen-year period. Other officers have left the division, died, been fired, resigned in lieu of being fired (viewed by other officers as being fired), or been pensioned off I.O.D., but only a few officers have quit.

Two of those who did resign were brothers from a "police family." The officers had worked in another metropolitan police force and had signed on to the department during the study. The officers "never fit into" the working watch, and both subsequently left the job after about three years. They moved to another city and neither is working in law enforcement. Another officer was a supervisor, a sergeant with nineteen years of service, who left to pursue another career as an insurance salesman. He returned to the job, but resigned a second time. He did not return again.

While even unpopular officers who retire are acknowledged, the officers who quit received no fanfare, no goodbye parties. They simply left. No special acknowledgement was made of resigning officers' departure, but neither were there signs of condemnation or vilification. As an infrequent occurrence, the resignations were discussed, but there was none of the condemnation the other officers assume would be forthcoming if they themselves were to leave the job. There may even have been more than a few traces of envy on the part of those still on the job.

In addition to real and perceived sanctions against resigning there are perks that come with retirement, and all officers want these perks badly enough that waiting to retire outweighs the reasons for resignation. How then do they get through this period and get to the twenty-year mark when they can retire?

STRATEGIES FOR STAYING

As the officers become aware that they cannot leave the job they also begin to realize they must make some changes. They pursue one of the four options: (1) recommitment—trying to work within the structure of the department and renewing their career plans, which often includes attempts to promote; (2) powering through—directing one's energy toward simply getting through, based on a perception that nothing can be done and whatever is must be endured; (3) withdrawal—investing less energy in the job and trying to minimize commitment to the department while maintaining commitment to other officers, rarely involving a literal resignation; (4) taking the "parallel track"—directing attention away from the job and the department and finding something to do off duty, outside of and independent of the job, to serve as a focal point. Sometimes their efforts to change their lives reinforce their feelings of alienation and despair, and officers may go from one strategy to another in an attempt to alleviate their discomfort.

Only recommitment combined with the desire to be promoted to a higher rank requires the officers to come to grips with their dissatisfaction with the department, then turn around and embrace it—work within its structure to gain their own ends while furthering the department's mandate. Officers who power through, or withdraw on the job, or focus outside the job do not have to work around the politics of the department or the constraints of the job.

Officers opting for strategies that distance them from the department tend not to put forth the same kind of effort in policing as they have in the past. It is still important to care about one's colleagues so safety practices are strictly adhered to. However, they often give up being proactive, being "a company man" or "a twenty-four-hour cop" and trying to "satisfy recap." At the end of each deployment period, and at other significant intervals, the department issues the recap. It is an accounting of all of the activity in the division over the time covered. This includes a breakdown of crimes that have been committed, as well as the arrests that have been made. The portion of the recap that concerns patrol officers deals with the number and kinds of arrests made. Officers are particularly pleased with high numbers of felony arrests.

The following comments are from the same officer at two different stages of his career. During the second phase, his assessment of his job reflected satisfaction:

> . . . this is the only job where guys do things together, really try to do good things together. I really like that; it means something. People talk about this male bonding, but there is something to it. It makes me feel differently when I go to work that I know who I'm working with and we're out there to be the good guys.

Five years later, during the third phase, the same officer expressed disillusion:

> I used to have goals, and I achieved them and they were meaningless. It wasn't what I thought it would be. Now I go fast, come back fast. . . . Now I just keep my nose clean, do as little as I can, don't get involved, clear, and wait for end of watch. I need to get retired.

On the other hand, by adopting the strategy of recommitting, street cops are in essence trying to get on the management cop track. This is not an easy task. Through their jobs as patrol officers they have distanced themselves from management. Theoretically, patrol duty is supposed to train them for management positions, but in reality it makes them "unfit" in the assessment of management.

Promotion

Not all officers who rededicate themselves to the job try to "promote," but many do. Those who do try to be promoted to a higher rank may find it difficult. For patrol officers promotion usually means trying for the rank of sergeant. This can be a lengthy process and, as Van Maanen observes, ". . . the competition for sergeant in most police agencies is keen, the results uncertain, and the material rewards to be gained slight" (1984:160).

In this agency any time an officer attempts to make a change, the first questions any supervisor will ask is why the officer wants to make the change and why he or she wants to make it at this time. This is especially true if the change includes promotion. On the last night of his last day on the job, at an informal retirement celebration, one officer described his attempt to promote after completing a master's degree in sociology:

> I didn't even try to promote for so long because I was doing that "roll call" thing [research for his master's degree focused on "roll call"] and . . . I had to be at roll call to do it. So anyway, I finished that, and then on my orals [for sergeant] they asked me the question, the "why now" question. And here I am. I've got the master's, which they *say*

they want, and they want to know why I waited so long to promote . . .
and I just had to tell them. I really told them, and well—[laughs]—
still on patrol. Still patrol—No more!

In the perception of the officers, management favors those who have
a consistent record of promotion or who have laid the groundwork for promotion, that is, requested many different changes of duty and work on
specialized units. Work on specialized units brings officers to the attention of management and permits them more opportunities for interaction,
as well as giving them the opportunity for learning new skills and information. This is regarded by patrol officers and management as some of
the necessary groundwork for promotion.

In the past patrol officers believed supervisors looked for a package
that represented the officer as a "hard charger" who also possessed a
sense of proportion and keen mediation skills. They also felt that chances
for advancement were enhanced by having varied experience in terms of
duty or division, being proactive. Traditional officers now believe these
are less important than other features:

> Well, you can beat all around the bush, but anyone who is honest has
> got to say that now, the way the department is now, there's no way a
> white male is going to promote. Well, they will, but damned few, and
> only after all the factions or the minority interests have been satis-
> fied.

According to another officer:

> I graduated first in my class [at the academy] in physical and academ-
> ic. First. I get bilingual. Bonus shoot [bonus pay for expert marks-
> manship]. My ratings are great, but they've classified us [Asian
> officers] as white, so I know I'm not going anywhere. Promotion-wise.
> I plan to go north—find some small p.d. [police department] and be
> the best thing that ever happened to them. There's no future for me
> here, on this department—I mean as far as promotion goes. The ex-
> perience, the experience is what I'm here for right now, but I want to
> promote and it isn't going to happen on this department, not now. I
> was told I'd have it made, but now that I'm classified as a white
> male—forget it.

If this officer had been a bit more patient it probably would have paid
off for him. Currently Asian officers are no longer classified as "white";
they are actively recruited as an underrepresented group.

In this department officers must pass written and oral examinations to qualify for the rank of sergeant. After passing these examinations
they are placed on a "Sergeants List" in order from the highest passing
score to the lowest. A candidate whose name appears on the list must wait
until there is an opening. Only a limited number of new positions are created, so vacancies are usually due to promotion, retirement or death. If

an officer is tenth on the list and only nine openings appear during the specified time, the officer must restart the application process from the beginning, which means he or she has to retake the sergeant's test. There are no guarantees that he or she will make the list again, though the officer usually does. This time-consuming and ego-deflating process discourages most officers. Generational tensions between the traditional and new officers are often exacerbated over promotion. Many of the traditional officers have hit the wall and are attempting to promote, but feel they are being discriminated against. They believe that it is easier for the new police, especially minorities and women, to promote, not based on merit, but on political grounds. An example:

> I just made it. On the next list, if I had not made sergeant on this list it would have been all over, because they're handling the orals differently now. [Laughs] Ten points for being female. Fifteen points for being black. Black female they'll give you the keys to the city. You tell me who is going to be on the top of the next list. They, the city, has to promote the minorities, no matter what. So it's a scramble. If they don't do it, then everyone's going to be calling "racism"—"how come you have so-and-so a percent of Blacks and women and whatever, and you don't have the same percentage in management?"

Another sergeant, who was hired in 1968 and had nineteen years on the job at the time of the interview:

> You have officers who tend to be very proactive, who go out and actively seek out suspects and crimes and so forth. You have another type, probably on the other end of the spectrum, the guy that gets by doing as little as possible. "I'll sit here. I'll wait for them to give me a radio call. I'll go to that call and only do as much as I have to, to satisfy the people and then I'm out of here to go wait for another call." That has become the norm. Now. For new people. When I came on, that was not acceptable behavior. You went out, you took care of your area, and you took pride in your recap at the end of the month.

The same officer commented on the changes in the department:

> A lot of it is brought on by the department itself, and not to beat a dead horse, a lot of it goes back to their selection process. For training officers, and affirmative action, and so forth. In the interest of promoting minorities, they are promoting them before they are qualified to train. They don't know themselves. What you don't know, you can't teach—and now it's even into the promotion of the Caucasian officer. The whole emphasis seems to be promoting those who kept a clean package. The best way to keep a clean package is don't do anything. If you're out proactive you're going to end up with paperwork in your package—beefs, and altercations and so forth. The best way to keep your package sparkling clean is don't do anything. If you don't do anything, if you don't make any decisions you can't be wrong, and unfor-

tunately the staff has taken to weighing those packages too heavily
when it comes to selecting training officers. The people who are not
doing anything are passing that on. They're teaching their probation-
ers that the best way to get along is to do as little as you can, and it's
scary.

The limited number of desirable positions, coupled with perceptions
of preferential treatment for minorities, creates even more resentment
and feelings of betrayal and disillusion among traditional officers, most of
whom are white males. This is one of the features that increases their dissatisfaction with the job and with management.

Withdrawal

At this point, many officers seek an "indoor" job. It does not matter
what the job is as long as they can get off the streets. Many officers who
become almost obsessive about getting off the streets are not simply
indulging a whim. They are usually working hurt and in chronic pain. At
this point they may take drugs to control their pain, as in the case of one
officer with eleven years on the job:

> . . . now I just take what the doctor will give me for it. I'm not looking
> to be Mr. Macho anymore. Mr. Macho with no knees, bum shoulder,
> bad back. Every time I 'cuff [handcuff] some Bozo I pray he won't go
> crazy on me. If they cut out on me, I hope [my partner] can retrieve
> 'em if they do that. Drunks do it all the time, that little lunge, bump-
> ing into my shoulder, I know I'm going to be crippled for the next
> week. I'll take the drugs now and they help, but I remember when I
> wouldn't touch even aspirin. [An officer] told me if you're taking aspi-
> rin and you get shot you can bleed to death before they can patch you.
> Your blood won't clot the way it's supposed to, or it gets thinner—it
> isn't like normal blood. You just bleed to death and there's nothing
> they can do because it's so fast. I didn't believe it at first but I heard
> it from [several officers] and figured, if there's anything in it, why
> take the chance. So no aspirin. Even when I was m.t.ed [medically
> treated] I wouldn't take the drugs. But nowadays, if I'm shot, I'm shot.
> If I die, I die. That's a "maybe," but this pain is here. This is here and
> this is now, so thin blood or not . . .

Patrol officers who cannot get off the streets can "cut themselves
some slack" if they are working with a partner who is amenable. One way
is finding what they call "the hole," a place where an officer can drop out
of sight, look busy, but bide his time until the end of watch. Officers cannot
do this as a regular pattern, but it is difficult to spot if done infrequently.
Police who adopt this pattern often choose daywatch where, as one officer
put it:

There are so many of us on the street, relative to the other watches I mean, that you can always take a street you know will be jammed up when you take it, too bad. "Gee, sorry. Got caught in traffic, you know how it is." I'm not talking about something big, but the other calls where it doesn't matter when you get there. Nothing's going to change in the time it takes to get there.

These officers only respond when requested to do so; they may even take their time to get to the call. Their handling of the call can also become a "time sink," a way of using up time. One officer commented that when a supervisor complained about the time he was taking on his calls, he would say he was performing "public relations." This justification would usually be successful with the management cops. It was less successful with street-oriented sergeants.

Attitudes of traditional officers toward sick days change during this period. They begin to use more sick days, partly because they are physically unable to work and partly because they begin to view sick days as "mental health" days. This may be a good strategy for obtaining immediate relief from job pressures, but leads to even more pressure. Many believe that taking too many sick days can hinder promotion. They may set themselves up for more criticism at precisely the time when they are trying to escape job pressure.

Changing Watch, Duty, or Division

Changing watch or duty is another popular strategy. Changing watch is the change that represents the least disruption to officers' lives. It is usually easily accomplished and involves a change in the time they go to work and in their watch colleagues. They may have some adjustment problems, but most officers have experienced similar changes previously, and the change may well be a welcome one. Changing duty can usually be done with a minimum of problems if the officer requesting the change has a great deal of seniority and a good reputation. Some refer to this change as "retiring" to the desired watch. A change of duty involves assignment to special duty or units. Officers seeking this option may encounter problems because often only a limited number of positions are available. In addition, officers who try for these positions to avoid patrol are not considered desirable candidates by the new unit, who would rather have someone who is a hard charger rather than someone on the brink of burnout. While changing duty or watch can provide the impetus for recommitment and immersion in the job, it does not necessarily eliminate feelings of the burnout or the desire to pull back.

Changing divisions requires a period of adjustment: dealing with new people, new supervisors and the flavor of this new division. Different divisions have different personalities: crime statistics, officer profiles, and standards. There is also a need to learn the physical and social geography of the new division: the streets, problem spots, halfway houses, local characters, escape routes, sites of major happenings, drug houses, burglars, gangs, new sets of partners. Most officers look forward to the change of duty, watch or division if they have requested it, but may find that it does not solve the real problem. They may move back to their previous division or be looked upon by management as malcontents.

Many officers close this phase of their careers feeling removed and distanced even from the police community. However, it is rare to find an officer who does not maintain close ties to at least some colleagues, even if his or her withdrawal is quite pronounced. Adding to the tension is the fact that many officers do not have any real support from the department. If they are lucky there is the possibility of deriving support from home, but unfortunately at this stage, this is often not the case.

When officers have to prove themselves for promotion or new duties, watches and divisions, they go through a shorter and less demanding version of the initial proving period they encountered early in their career. However, their way is made easier by the fact that they all have reputations and friends, and are part of the folklore of the department—unless, of course, their reputations are not good. Officers may know they must prove themselves once again, but they resent having to do so. At this point they need some sensitivity from a system that does not even recognize the officers' needs, much less address them.

7

Phase Four
Regrouping

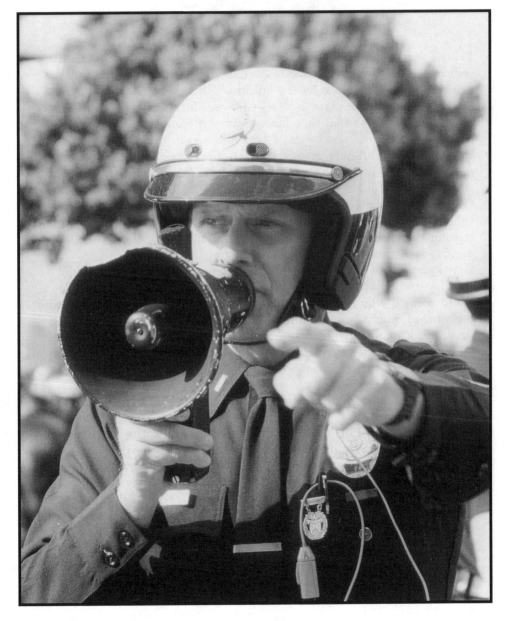

Phase four should see the officer from about the tenth or thirteenth year of service through the end of the career, ideally at twenty years. It can be a period of change for the officers, although rarely as radical as the changes that take place in phase three as officers "hit the wall." Frequently the changes that take place as they regroup are the fruition of changes in their on- and off-duty lives initiated in the previous phase. Changes in their off-duty lives can take the pressure off negative feelings and experiences linked to the on-duty component of their lives. Officers who felt burned out in phase three can find renewal in phase four. Officers who took action to change their lives in phase three can reevaluate those changes and chart their next course, if necessary. Officers who tried unsuccessfully to change their lives can mount another attempt or decide simply to stay where they are and finish the job.

Few officers quit at this point. But some do. An officer with many years on or even an officer with less experience but a previously unblemished record, who has done something for which he or she will be terminated, might be offered the option of resigning "in lieu of" being fired. It is a small and mostly technical way of saving face, but for all the officers who discuss such things—and that is all of them—everyone knows who left "in lieu of," so the salve to the reputation is somewhat lost within the police community.

For those officers who found neither renewal nor any plan to change their lives for the better in phase three, phase four is a period of mellowing. It is rare for officers to sustain the despair and turmoil usually experienced in phase three for much longer. If nothing else they become exhausted. Officers may become resigned to "droning" through the job, but they do not sustain the angst of the earlier period. They decide to, as one officer put it, "just put in my time and do it." Some officers opt for keeping a low profile, doing as little as possible and waiting to retire; sometimes they refer to this as ROD—retired on duty. Others are seized with the desire to seek a last-minute promotion in the hopes that they can retire at a higher rate of pay. One officer described the many strategies he had employed to no avail, and said it was his intention to "bite the bullet, finish the job and get the hell out."

Once officers make the decision just to put in their time, it seems to get easier for them. They relax about their careers, but not in their performance on the job. They remain alert on the streets. Being vigilant is by now totally internalized. In this case what starts as required behavior for the job usually becomes an off-duty behavior as well. The distinctions between alertness on and off duty are reduced because officers believe alertness is essential for any functioning adult. Paying attention encompasses making decisions from the most mundane to those which are critical and have survival value. Officers are constantly amazed at how unobservant most people are, and they consider this to be a clear sign of their vulnerability and extreme foolishness. They talk about other people

having their "heads up their asses" or, more politely, "in a dark place." It expresses the belief that many pitfalls could be avoided if people would only pay attention. Police officers are extremely observant on and off duty.

GETTING THROUGH

Officers tend to be calmly productive on the job during this fourth phase regardless of their mode of getting through, whether this means rededication, promotion and change of watch or duty, or simply being resigned to do the job until one can honorably quit, that is, retire. Those who pull back plan on putting in the time and hope nothing will happen to disrupt their lives. Some officers view the job as "just what I do eight, nine, ten hours a day." For those hours, they know they must remain alert and pay attention to the way in which they do their job. When they are not working they must be vigilant and plan their retirements well.

Officers who feel revitalized or rededicated to the job are in an excellent position. They feel good about what they are doing, they do it very well, they are not likely to make mistakes that can result in physical injury, and they know how to avoid all but extreme "off-the-wall" legal problems. They are the role models for some of the officers who have minimal time on. They are more relaxed in their style of policing and are frequently the preferred partners for officers in the second phase. One such officer observed:

> I like working the specialized units because the guys are older. They've had a lot more time on the job. They're relaxed. They work hard but they know how to have a good time. They laugh. They don't have to prove themselves and drive around at a hundred miles an hour. . . . I found that on patrol a lot, working with guys who are twenty-one or two with two years on the job, they were real dangerous to work with.

A female officer with two years on the job also expressed appreciation for older officers.

> You can't be a good training officer until you have at least eight, ten years on the job. You just don't know enough. I worked with guys who were training officers and they had maybe two years more experience than I did, and they'd want to cook along real fast 'cause they're trying to get their recap and look real good, but I felt maybe they didn't have the experience to back themselves going boom, boom, boom, and making all these decisions. Whereas somebody who's been out there, and has gotten over having to be rough and ready out there, has worked through that phase of it where they

have to kick ass all the time, now they know how to talk to people and train you . . . I've just found that the older guys who have been on fifteen plus years or so were really good training officers. 'Cause they were really nice, they didn't have to prove themselves out there, they could train you and not make you feel like you're a dork . . . I remember this one training officer, it was really nice, when I'd get in the car I felt that no matter what happened, anything, anything that we could encounter, this guy had enough experience to get us out of there. I felt really calm and confident all night.

Those officers still on the streets are now very confident of their abilities and have generally broken in partners with whom they can work with a minimum of friction and danger. When they work with officers with little time on, they work very conservatively. They take more time with officers with less time on than do some of the training officers, who get overburdened with the prospect of doing nothing but training until they promote out of the position.

Officers in the fourth phase begin to enjoy police work in a way that they were not able to previously. The vitality associated with phase two may be in short supply, but phase four officers have a greater sense of perspective and less of a sense of peril. They are more confident in their abilities to "sort it all out." They no longer feel that they are the targets of all ambient menaces as they did in earlier phases. They become more mellow. True, some officers mellow the way old dynamite caps do—that is to say, not at all, but most become more content with their jobs and their own performances. They become more relaxed about being police officers, although they do not relax in their techniques and tactics. They still value reading the streets and acting appropriately and believe that it is that skill which will get them through to retirement.

Officers in the fourth phase know the job, themselves and their limitations well. If they are not feeling up to a rigorous night, they know ways to keep busy and safe, out of harm's way and potentially demanding situations, barring something dramatic and unpredicted. They have become comfortable in their role of police officer and they no longer feel so keenly the frustration of not being able to do the job as they once thought it ought to be done. They don't worry, as much as officers do in phase three, about all that they cannot do: the impossibility of the policing task with all its component parts, the limitations of the police officers themselves and the inadequacies of the criminal justice system. They are less likely to characterize the other systems as foes actively working against the police, as they did in phase three. Now they are more likely to view them as imperfect bureaucracies, just as is the police department itself. They recognize that all of the systems in the city are flawed and subject to the same kinds of folly and mismanagement. In short, they are much more satisfied with their own performance and are much more tolerant of imperfections in the system as well. They are much more easygoing toward themselves and others than was possible in earlier phases. They achieve a balance between productivity and safety, with a modicum of frustration.

They worry less on the job, about the job. They remain careful, but they start talking about the danger involved in the job as not being extraordinary. They talk about the dangers of living, not the dangers of the job. They are less concerned about legal dangers inherent in the job. They do become more anxious about the dangers their families face while they are at work, and encourage their parents and children to relocate out of the city.

Many officers in this fourth (and according to most of them, final) phase of their career begin to wonder if the job is really so bad. They no longer feel they are in great physical jeopardy, and they are at a point where they often genuinely enjoy the work. They believe that, knowing what they now know, they can protect themselves from further hurt. The money is good and gets much better at the twenty-year mark.

There are great financial incentives for staying at least another five years. After all, these officers are relatively young (usually in their early forties) and not really ready for full-time retirement. They begin to think it might make good sense to stay on. Five years doesn't sound like so many when you already have close to twenty years on the job. At twenty-five years, not only do they retire at a higher pension rate (55 percent of their salary instead of 40 percent), but they are also entitled to cost-of-living adjustments immediately (those who retire at twenty years have to wait the additional five years for adjustments). Given the fact of inflation, waiting to retire at a higher percentage of a higher salary with immediate adjustments to help meet the cost of living makes for a pretty compelling package. Officers who opt to work thirty years are entitled to retire with a pension which is 70 percent of their salary—indeed, a great incentive to stay if the officer is so inclined.

The closer some officers get to retirement, the more likely they are to start romanticizing and idealizing their policing experience. On the eve of what turned out to be his unofficial retirement party, one officer expressed the sentiment that, even though the department may have lost some of its former reputation, it was still the best police department in the nation. He spoke at length about the accomplishments of the department in general and the division in particular. The whole conversation sounded like a paid testimonial to the department, the division, and every police officer who had ever put on the uniform. Not seven months earlier the same officer expressed nothing but disdain for the institution he was now lauding. However, it should be noted that some officers may also go in the opposite direction and do whatever they can to distance themselves from policing.

THE VETERANS' PERSPECTIVE

In this phase many officers become sentimental about their jobs. Having spent half of their lifetimes or more as police officers, they want to share their insights. In the past this was a time when the relationship of older officer to newer was clearly regarded as mentor/apprentice or teacher/student. Today many veteran cops would like to have this relationship, to have an opportunity to teach some of the new police officers and pass on what they have learned. One problem is that many traditional police doubt that the new police are well qualified or committed to be police officers. Traditional officers express feelings that the continuity, effectiveness, integrity and reputation of the department are doomed by the infusion of new police who, in the opinion of traditional officers, are not capable of doing the job safely and effectively. Traditional officers seem especially concerned about the future of the department. However, there are a few exceptions to these gloomy predictions: some veteran officers are impressed with an increase in numbers of recruits holding college degrees. They especially enjoy talking to the better educated new police who are more like their own sons and daughters.

Some veteran officers are not impressed by college degrees one way or the other. Some may even be intimidated by them. Some who are anxious to pass on their pearls of wisdom may be utterly dismayed by the new police. Ultimately it is not the presence or absence of degrees, but the amount of experience and commitment the new police bring to the job. According to one officer:

> If you pay close attention, and look at the numbers, at any given time in this division about 40 to 60 percent of patrol has under three or four years on. Those aren't good stats. Pretty frightening. It's going to get real hairy out there. In ten years, it's going to be worse. You won't recognize the department.

On the other hand there are many critics outside the department as well as some within who voice a heartfelt "Amen" to this sentiment. Transformation of the department is a major goal. The department has been rocked by many controversies and will probably continue to draw criticism from many quarters. Some will blame the traditional officers, often seen as dinosaurs, some will blame the new police. In a diverse setting with quite different political and social agendas it is difficult to imagine a department capable of satisfying all concerned.

OFFICERS' CONCERNS

During this phase officers are beset by new kinds of worries. They fear there is nothing else they can do if they are not police officers. They fear they will be lonely without the structure and support of the police community. They fear the unknown—their retirement plans begin to look less enticing as they get closer to the date.

They begin to worry about money, second careers, children in college, relationships in which they have seen very little of their mates for prolonged periods of time. Officers who are divorced begin to think about what it will be like to be off the job without a family. The department does not serve as a substitute for family no matter how many times that is a part of their speeches, but in many instances the police community does function as a kind of extended family. Officers facing retirement are often reluctant to give this up.

Officers again express fears about their physical condition. Now they are not so much worried about job-induced violence. They begin to believe that if they haven't been killed or severely injured by now they probably won't be. However, they are troubled by their diminished physical abilities and fear illness, strokes, getting cancer or Alzheimer's disease. While these concerns may not vary dramatically from their citizen counterparts, they are more often associated with people who are significantly older than these late-thirties–early-forties officers. Because they are already dealing with physical limitations, they fear further physical losses and trauma. Most officers have a large number of things they can no longer do, at least not without pain. The specter of even greater physical limitations impel some of these officers into rigorous physical regimens designed to get them in shape for their retirement. They want to be able to play once they are retired. Some officers are quite successful at this, others learn the extent of their limitations and become fretful over their deteriorating physical condition.

Early in their careers they enjoyed the notion that they can take the city pension and walk away "a young man." By phase four, they are chronologically young, but they seldom feel young. The toll on their bodies, in terms of injuries and other abuses, refutes the image of the youthful retiree. The injuries accumulated in the early phases of their careers come back to haunt them in large and small, expected and unexpected ways. Basic flexibility and mobility are frequent problems, as are bad backs, elbows, knees, wrists, ankles, and feet. Many officers suffer partial hearing loss from exposure to weapons being fired. The department requires each officer who carries a gun to qualify every month by demonstrating his or her competence with their firearms under supervision at the academy. While they are waiting to qualify—which can be forty-five minutes or more—they are exposed to virtually the same noise without ear protection. In addition, if there is ever shooting on the job (a rare occurrence for most officers) there is, of course, no such protection.

Eye injuries are also quite common with police officers, as are broken noses, damaged sinuses, orbits, and eardrums. Dental trauma—loose or broken teeth and broken jaws—are common injuries. Internal injuries to the kidneys, spleen, liver and lungs as a result of altercations, assaults with a variety of weapons, or car collisions can initiate long-term conditions. Often this damage becomes manifest during this phase. Physical pain can be a great impetus to reflections and reevaluation of one's life and goals. This is a period when many officers realize the pain is not going to go away; rather, it is getting worse. Their lives may be a far cry from what they envisioned when they first started planning to retire at "twenty and twenty"—twenty years, and twenty minutes:

> When I was twenty-five, and I'm thirty-seven now, I had been on the job three years and I thought I knew it all. I loved the job, still do, but I see it for what it is now. I don't have any false expectations you might say. At twenty-five I thought, "I'm halfway to fifty and this ain't so bad. I'll be retired at forty-three and I'm going to have it all." I was married then, and I thought we were real happy, but it turned out I was real happy and she was on her way to bigger and better things. . . . She found out being married to a doctor isn't much better than being married to a cop. You're just lonely in a better rent district. But anyway, I didn't know then that she was planning on leaving, and I thought we had it made. We were going to have a place on the lake near where we used to spend our summer vacation—and we had it all planned out. In the summer we'd have the Boy Scouts in . . . and maybe even in the fall too.
>
> When I was a kid scouting about saved me. Now they'd say I came from a "dysfunctional family." At the time we were just called "white trash," and that was pretty accurate. My dad drank all the time, and so did my mom and they'd really go at it. I got to hoping the cops would come just so we'd have some quiet. They'd come, he'd go, she'd cry, go to sleep. It still gets to me when I go to a family disturbance and there are kids there. They get all the grief and there's nothing we can do. Nothing at all we can really do. It tears me up to see that—still does.
>
> Anyway I was talking about the summer camp. We had the outbuildings planned, and where the garden was going to go, and my wife wanted to do pottery. . . . It really was wonderful and when I was twenty-five I was going to do it. Now, I'm a practical man. I don't sleep so well, I have to get up and walk around, read, sometimes I just stay up. I've got a gimp knee, and a real bad back. My feet hurt . . . that's a big deal, your feet hurt, you can't enjoy anything. My stomach is finally settled, but I came this close to having to eat cottage cheese for the rest of my life. Rotator cuff is gone,

even if I had the surgery I can't chop wood. So what I am saying here is that I'm not going to be in any shape to enjoy my retirement. At least not the way I wanted it and planned it. I can't physically do the things I thought I could. Well, I mean I never gave it a thought. You don't think that your body is going to change so much in such a short time. I didn't know I'd be like this, and I still have six years to go. What will it be then? What kind of shape will I be in then? Yeah—just wheel me into the sunlight. . . .

ANTICIPATING RETIREMENT

Even though these officers are only in their early-thirties and have almost a decade of police work before them, they begin in earnest to start their retirement plans. They literally count the days until they can retire.

Retirement looms large in the legends of police officers. During phase one, when they start listening to the veteran officers, they learn the conventional police wisdom regarding retirement. It is tremendously important to them symbolically. The status of retired officer garners great respect from all working police. In addition to bringing elevated status, retirement is also financially very rewarding. Police officers have a more generous retirement program than most workers. Anticipating this exalted state provides them with the vision of a way out that sustains them through many difficulties and hard times on the job. An officer with two divorces and sixteen years on fantasizes about retiring:

> . . . sometimes the only thing that keeps me on the job is knowing that it's finite. It's gonna be over, and I'm gonna be okay, I can get through it . . . I only have [to work] four more [years], and I'm home free. Actually, it's down to three years, five months, if I use my vacation, and sick time. Just knowing that the end is in sight helps me make it through another day of . . . whatever. I kept my pension, all of it. [His ex-wife] took the house, we sold the boat, sold a bunch of stuff, but, I kept the pension . . . just thinking about getting out of here, off the job and out of here, a free man . . . Yeah, that's a nice thought for the day. . . .

Officers remind themselves and others that policing and the military are the only jobs where you can retire after twenty years of service and start a new career. They feel it is a reward they have earned because, by this phase, they have given so much of themselves—or lost so much, in health and social relationships—to the job. They feel that they have given an extraordinary amount, and they want to be compensated. Early retirement is partial compensation. This is another reason so many of the men are adamant about not sharing their pensions with ex-wives.

This is also why ex-wives often feel entitled to share in the pension. Both feel they have paid an extraordinary price for the years of policing.

Officers always enjoy talking about ways of pulling off retirement schemes, but these discussions reach a fever pitch during the fourth phase of their careers. They attend department-sponsored or sanctioned seminars designed to ease them through retirement, as well as public seminars on retirement, real estate and franchise schemes. Their "code seven" (meal break) discussions are filled with exchanges of retirement information: the relative virtues of different deferred compensation plans, tax laws, real estate rulings, and the like. A great deal of the focus at this stage is on retirement even though it may be close to a decade away for some. It is especially easy for them to slip into this preoccupation because there is always a substantial number of officers who are similarly focused. Even young officers with only two or three years on the job will be drawn into these discussions and may implement their own retirement plans. It is interesting to note that female officers rarely discuss their retirement plans, and although there have been cases of ex-husbands being awarded portions of pensions, there are not sufficient numbers of female officers for whom this is an issue to warrant much discussion—either among them, or here.

Discussions of money accompany discussions of retirement. In this phase of their career, off duty is filled with financial schemes, attempts at second careers, the inception of new businesses, and the investigation of possible retirement havens. All of this centers around money, not necessarily because money is the major focus, but because it is assumed to ensure a successful retirement.

Police officers are comfortable talking about money, and all know what each other makes. An officer's salary is no secret, and all officers of the same rank with the same time on make the same amount of money unless they qualify for a bonus. Many officers commented that they know more about each other's finances than their own spouses know about their own finances. I suspect this is true, as officers are sometimes very secretive about discussing their economic status with their spouses, especially in the event of a remarriage.

Officers receive bonus pay for superior marksmanship, bilingual abilities, and college degrees. Again, officers know which other officers are receiving bonus pay. The net result is that their finances are known to anyone with the slightest interest. This lack of economic privacy is one of the features that quickly draws officers into retirement discussions and plans during earlier phases of the job. Young officers are exposed to the strategies of the older, more experienced officers.

Some events that have altered retirement plans include major shifts in the economy; health changes, including the onset of a serious illness or disability or relief from chronic pain through surgery; changes in the occupational status of spouses, children or parents; changes in their family structure, including divorce, remarriage, the responsibility of additional children; the expense of college for grown children. Any of these can dramatically alter their retirement plans.

Although most officers are "working hurt," many officers who might easily qualify for early pensions due to injuries or other medical conditions do not seek them. Some of their reasons appear to be due to machismo. They don't want other officers to think they are "sandbagging" or malingering. Some are embarrassed by their conditions or reluctant to reveal their concerns to others. This is a police version of "big boys [and girls] don't cry." Others are reluctant to set the procedure in motion so late in their careers or feel that they will be treated badly and may not be believed.

It is true that an officer requesting a medical disability pension must undergo rigorous examination by several city doctors. This is because the pay structure for city disability pensions is different from regular pensions. Disability pensions are tax free and, in addition, may yield significantly more money than the normal retirement pension, which is not tax exempt. Partly because of these features, disability pensions are difficult to obtain, involve massive amounts of paperwork, and must be reviewed on a regular basis. Officers who pension off with medical disabilities may be called back to light duty if a subsequent evaluation deems them able to work. One officer compared this with being on call for court all your life. "You never know when they're going to call, but you'd better be ready to go when they do call. How can a person 'retire' on that basis?" In general, unless an officer is totally or severely disabled, he or she will not opt for a medical pension. Officers are especially reluctant to pension off if they are nearing the end of their mandatory period of service. To retire is an honor, one highly prized by the officers.

Some officers begin to get superstitious about retiring because they all know stories of officers who became seriously ill or died shortly before or after retirement. One such account, which immediately entered the folklore of the department, concerned an officer from the principal division under study. The officer worked twenty-seven years, without ever using a sick day. This alone made him exceptional in the eyes of the others. This officer was well liked and highly respected. He was a "policeman's policeman." He had worked the streets admirably, had been promoted to detective, where he distinguished himself with his colleagues and the public with whom he came into contact. He worked a number of different details, but spent most of his time as a detective.

When he announced he was going to leave, many officers were surprised that he did not go three more years to the thirty-year mark. Other officers, who knew him well, were aware that his wife had died a few years previously and that he had expressed the desire to retire and move to a small town in rural North Carolina. When the officer informed the department he was going to retire and that he wanted to "play out" (use) his sick days they refused to allow it. Most retiring officers are permitted to use their sick days, by adding them to accumulated vacation time and regular days off, so they can be paid for that period of time without going into work. This is not formal policy, but it has been semi-traditional for officers retiring at twenty years, and certainly for those retiring after that time.

Because the officer had never used a sick day in his entire career, he had amassed the maximum the department would allow, far too many to be handled in this fashion. Many officers save their sick days just in case they become severely injured and need the time. To the officers, the department's handling of the situation was viewed as an insult to the officer who was about to retire. It was obvious to them the officer must have made many sacrifices never to have missed a day. Even without running his sick days, the officer filled out the paperwork for retirement, set the date, and planned to run out his vacation days, so that he could still technically be carried on the books and paid. The department approved this approach. For all practical purposes, he retired even though he was technically still employed for several months. His colleagues threw the traditional formal retirement party, which was well attended and extremely moving due to the officer's sterling reputation and charismatic presence. After the party, he moved to North Carolina.

Two weeks later he went to the doctor complaining of back pain. He was diagnosed as having terminal cancer throughout his bones, liver and other vital organs. He was hospitalized and given a week or two to live. Officers in the division took up a collection to send some colleagues to visit him in the hospital. He died before he retired. His death had a stunning effect on the officers who knew him, and the story of his life in the department and death at the brink of retirement has had a chilling effect on those who heard his story. Later other officers went to North Carolina for his funeral. They did not approach the department or the police relief league for financial support in these efforts. The officers felt the department had not treated this officer well, but his friends had:

> It always comes down to the same old song. No one else is going to look after you—maybe not "look after" but "care" about you, except maybe your friends. To the department you're just there when it needs you, and when it doesn't—you're on your own. You're replaced. They've got another [the officer's name] and he's young, and he's ready and he can't wait to be a cop for the city.

Police officers learn a great deal from the stories and gossip about each other's lives. As a result of hearing the story of this "twenty-seven-year detective," officers currently on the job and others to follow will do things differently, or at least think about their own lives with this story in mind. As a direct result of the department's action in this case, many more officers now use their sick days spread throughout their last two or three years in the department. Some of the officers from this division express feelings of loss and betrayal, believing that the department "used up" a good man. They are also quick to point out that the officer's pension reverts to the city since he left no heirs: the final ironic end to his twenty-seven years of service.

A daily ritual in roll call is to mention briefly the death of any retired L.A.P.D. police officer. The announcement always follows the same format, beginning with "We regret to announce the death of . . ." The date of the officer's appointment, the date he or she retired, his or her duty, and the divisions he or she worked in follow. Any anecdotal information anyone in the room has to contribute is also part of the memorial—another link in the continuity of the job. Officers cheer when it is obvious from the retirement date that the officer had collected many years of his or her pension—a link with the hopes they cherish for their future.

8

Phase Five
Deciding to Retire

Phase five lasts from the twentieth year of service until the officer chooses to leave, whenever that may be. Officers in this phase tend to be very relaxed about the job. The officers who choose to stay see it as only slightly or no more dangerous than any other line of work. Since they feel they understand the danger and have dealt with it successfully for twenty years, they are not overly concerned about doing it for a longer period. They are very confident of their policing abilities and they feel they are creating a secure retirement. They are real veterans and are regarded as such by other officers. They have found their niches and are comfortable. The officers who are bitter, hurt and unhappy generally blame the job and leave it.

The job can be both scapegoat and salvation for officers. For those who have few or no outside interests and activities, life off the job has little appeal. Fortunately, most officers in the third or fourth phase have realized the importance of doing something other than police work and have taken action to broaden their horizons. For these officers, the fifth and final phase holds few terrors, but perhaps a few surprises.

Retirement may be a goal for people in other occupations, but for police officers retirement is more than a goal—it is something the officers have thought about, talked about, and obsessed over for the last four to sixteen years. For officers in phase five, it is possible at any point to start the paperwork for their retirement. It is up to the individual officer to initiate the process. Some officers start this process amid great pomp and ceremony, others do it quietly. It is impossible to know how many officers come close to starting the process and then change their minds, but most of the officers in my sample thought they would have retired months or even years before they actually did so (this is not true for officers who pensioned off with injuries and disabilities). Since officers are the ones who instigate the process, and can stop it, it is never completely clear whether or not they waver in their decision. The decision is a difficult one for most officers, and I suspect they revise their retirement dates many times.

YEARS ON THE JOB

Officers remaining on the job past the beginning of phase five have opted to extend their career beyond the twenty-year minimum, which in earlier phases is stated by most patrol officers as the maximum amount of time they wish to work as police officers. Many officers who have attained rank or duty that takes them off the streets stay on the job until at least the twenty-five-year mark, and many of these stay thirty years.

The twenty-five-year mark is also significant because as previously mentioned there are great economic incentives for staying. Retirement at twenty-five years nets the officer 55 percent of his or her salary in a pension and an immediate cost-of-living supplement. This translates to thousands of dollars. As one officer with twenty-one years on the job observed:

> It makes no sense at all to leave the job at twenty. If you just hang in there to twenty-five, you almost double your pension. That's what it works out to once you take into account the pay raises, and the cost of living and the extra 15 percent. You end up with double anything you'd take home at twenty.

This represents a shift in attitude. The consensus in phases three and four was "get to twenty, and get out," but once officers attain twenty-year status, the conventional wisdom is that it is foolish to leave before twenty-five if at all possible. Often the longer they stay, the easier it gets.

Officers who plan to stay until twenty-five or thirty years are officers who are usually no longer on the streets. In the recent past, patrol officers might opt to stay on to twenty-five years if they felt they could rely on their colleagues for back-up and general support. They realized that they were not as physically able to do the job as they had been in the past, but relied on their experience, their expertise, and their fellow officers. One officer bemoaned the drain of officers who were trusted and deemed competent by their peers. In his view traditional officers were the only ones on whom one could depend. The officer in question had been a patrol officer for twenty years and eight months at the time of the interview and had changed his retirement plans:

> I'm pulling the pin. I was going to retire at twenty and for all practical purposes that's just what I did, because I'm still on the books, they're still carrying me as working, but I haven't worked since last November. I would have stayed; at first I wanted to stay. Why not? Plenty of job security. The work's not hard, and I'm dialed [competent, comfortable with the demands of the job]. No problem. But you know you expect the assholes on the street to make life hard and that's no problem; they're scum and they've never been any different. Really it's no problem, but it's the department.

> You know they could keep some good policemen if they cared. You
> turn twenty, all right, "Now what would you like to work?" You know,
> it wouldn't kill them to give a little something back. Like, "Okay, you
> gave us twenty and you did a good job, what would you like to do now."
> I'm not talking about something you're not qualified to do; that's
> what's gotten us in this position were in now, but I mean something
> you can do, that you'd like to try. Make it a little easier for the last
> five. You know? If they would just give some sorta sign that it was
> worth it, that they even noticed the job you've done for twenty years.
> But, you know, the bottom line is nobody cares anymore. It's just a
> paycheck anymore. Nobody cares if you do a good job or if you just piss
> away the time, as long as the numbers are up and there are no beefs.

The reference to numbers being up is most likely a reference to the recap
totals of arrests made. It could also refer to the deployment figures, the
number of officers carried on the division's roster as working a certain
division or watch. The total number of officers presumably available for
deployment are drawn from these division rosters. If there appears to be
an insufficient number of officers available to work any given watch,
requests for "T.O.s," unscheduled days off, are not likely to be granted.

Officers stay on the job for a combination of reasons: economic concerns, lack of other skills to be self-supporting, fear of the unknown, iner-
tia, fear of being out of the scene, and family commitments. Arguments
for staying on the job are most often framed in terms of economics, but
this reasoning may be a convenient way of masking other concerns. If an
officer states that he or she "cannot afford" to retire, it curbs discussion.
Although they freely discuss their finances, no one challenges this kind of
statement. They simply accept it on face value. From listening to the
plans officers have made over the years and gaining a sense of their
finances and sometimes quite impressive economic resources, I strongly
suspect that many officers who claim they cannot afford to retire are not
admitting to a completely different reason for staying on the job.

The closer they get to leaving the job, the more acceptable and even
attractive it becomes. A typical comment:

> I've been doing this job all my adult life. I know that I can do this and
> do it well, but the skills I have don't translate to any other job that I
> know of. Let's be realistic. What can I do that's going to pull down the
> kind of money I'm making now? And what about medical? You can't
> be without medical. It just makes good sense to stay.

Another officer with two children in high school observed:

> By the time [his children] are ready for college I want to be able to give
> them that, give them the opportunity to better themselves. My son,
> he gives me a hard time sometimes about being on the job when he
> thinks I could have done something better. I'll stay on the job and he
> can go to school. If it weren't for the job he could kiss that off. The job

is what made our life what it is. We figure if I stay 'til twenty-seven, they can both finish; then it's our time. Without the job, if I left now, no way. There's no job for me out there. Nothing. I'll put in the twenty-seven and then we kick back. Really retire. Full health benefits, good pension, kids squared away. That will make it worth it.

An officer with twenty-three years on the job keeps stating that he is going to retire on his anniversary date every year since reaching the twenty-year mark. He is aware that other officers joke about his "final" departure date. These jokes generally imply that he will be on the job forever. He confesses that he is himself bewildered: "I don't know exactly

what happens, but it happens each time I get short [close to retirement].
I just can't see myself doing anything else. I don't *want* to do anything
else."

LEAVING THE JOB

Officers in this phase of their careers are waiting to see what will
happen next, and they express the fear they might miss something important by leaving the job. Others experience difficulties stemming from the
fact that they have defined themselves as police officers to the exclusion of
other possibilities. They know that they are officers, they are unclear as to
what else they might be. They may not even be fully aware of their options
unless they have nurtured outside interests throughout their time on the
job. Police officers have difficulties retiring if they are only comfortable
around other officers. They also do not want to retire if they believe that
they are in danger when they are removed from the policing endeavor and
the police community—if they are fearful in a world they have come to
know as dangerous. In an interesting reversal, many officers now view
their working shift as the time they are "safe" and time off the job (no partner, radio, or back-up) as time of greater danger and vulnerability. Partially for this reason it is important for retired police officers to be able to
carry their guns—something they are not able to do if they quit the job.
While some retirees never do so, many more do until they have eased into
retirement. In any case, they want to have the option to do so. Retirees also
carry a "retired" badge, a smaller replica of their working badge.

Retirement has several facets for police officers. On the practical
side it means that they can leave the job with a fairly good pension while
they are still relatively young. On the symbolic side it means that they
can leave the job with honor. Part of the mystique of retiring has to do
with doing it on your own terms, choosing the time and deciding to leave.
Retiring is preferable to being pensioned off I.O.D., and many officers who
qualify for a medical pension do not apply for it. However, there is no dis-
honor in leaving the job after becoming ill or injured, and there are some
tremendous economic benefits. Disability pensions are tax-free, whereas
retirement pensions are taxed as regular income. Some officers find it dis-
tasteful to apply for a medical pension. One such officer states:

> I could go the pension route, but fuck 'em. I took the job, and put up
> with the shit—mostly generated by the department itself. I put up
> with it, and I did the job, I finished the job and I can deal with this too.
> I don't have a day without pain. I buy my painkillers in bulk, and they
> don't do any good anymore. I know I'm going to need more surgery, but
> the doctor even says it probably won't make a whole lot of difference
> in the pain. He calls it "discomfort"; I call it pain. I don't want to go
> through the bullshit connected with getting the medical—like they

are doing me a favor. Like I'm trying to get away with something. Like I have to prove to them that,"Hey, I'm really injured." Now I have to prove it to them. They can't check the package and say, "Well, yes, we see that in '65 you were in a coma three days, from a T.A. [traffic accident], and we see you had some broken ribs, broken collarbone. Yes, you did fall, and gee, we see these surgeries, but can you prove you're really hurt, prove you deserve it?" Bullshit. Those paper pushers have never been cops; they don't know anything about how it hurts, where it hurts, and it hurts plenty.

All officers know of other officers who have not applied for a medical pension but really deserved one. Most officers know of a few officers who have applied for a medical pension and were sandbagging—they *did not* deserve one. Thus, some officers never apply for a disability pension because they do not want anyone to think even for a moment that they are sandbagging. Others think that it just makes good sense not to apply. It is also common for officers to wait until they have put in their twenty years and then go for an I.O.D. pension. This, they believe, demonstrates that they have honored their commitment to the job and each other. One such officer had twenty-two years on the job. He said his back hurt for the last twelve of the twenty-two years. He said he decided to go for pension when found he would not be able to work until the twenty-five or thirty-year mark. He stated that he asked for the medical pension since his injuries, all the result of police work, prevent him from being able to work long enough to have a sufficient pension to support his family. He believed the medical pension would yield about the same money he would have earned if he had retired at the thirty-year mark.

Officers who would not consider applying for a medical pension consider it entirely appropriate to run their sick days at the end of their career:

> I don't feel any guilt for taking the days [not going to work and using his sick days as vacation days]; they still come out ahead. I didn't expect to get away with it. I thought someone would be getting in touch with me, but they haven't. If they don't care, I don't care. Well, I do care, but that's the way this department's gone. People don't care. Used to be, you were out sick, or I.O.D., you had a sergeant knocking on your door. I never thought I'd still be here, but if they don't care, hey . . . But . . . I wish they did care. It's really—pretty bad. It's sure changed, the department, has sure changed.

Another officer who was very badly I.O.D. in a car crash described his expectations for reaching retirement:

> I knew I wouldn't see the sunny side of twenty [years on the job]. I knew that, for me, it wasn't to be. Then I'd get a confirmation on that. Something would happen and I'd wonder if that was the thing that was going to get me . . . I kept on working, I kept on, but I was always

watching and waiting for whatever . . . for what it was going to be, and then when the crash came, I said, well, damn, here it is now. They thought so too for awhile. Pretty well wadded up, but I'm doing okay now. And now, . . . it's pretty surprising, . . . since I've made it this far, I'm going for twenty-five. I don't have anything pressing. No real reason not to go for it.

Another officer received a bad back injury when he had twelve years on the job. He had spent the entire day in court and had five minutes to go until end of watch as he was driving from the court to the station house in a marked police car. As he pulled onto a major thoroughfare in the division, he noticed the occupants in the car next to his were smoking what appeared to be marijuana:

It was so bright and I was trying to get my eyes to adjust after being indoors and all and here is this guy just smoking this joint. Really working out on it. No attempt to keep it down. No attempt to hide, and the smoke is all around. I can't believe my eyes. Is this guy for real? I fell in behind, and I thought, I can *not* let this get by. I'm driving next to this guy, in a police car, looking straight at him and he doesn't even pay any attention. This guy is so bold and so blatant. I gotta stop 'em. So they took a short run and I got them stopped, I'm alone in the car, I get them stopped, and back-up. [The back-up unit picked up one of the suspects and the remaining suspect was handcuffed in the back of the officer's car. He went back to the suspect's car to check under the seat] . . . and I'm looking at him as I'm checking under the passenger seat.

I was twisted, leaning in the car when it was hit. I never saw it coming. There was no preparation. Some old Iranian guy, seventy-five or eighty, was taking a shortcut through the gas station and he hit the car head on. It was only at about twenty, so the speed wasn't terrific, but it was like being hit head on. It hit me so hard I think I got knocked out for a minute or so. I was alone then, the other unit had gone, and I'd hit my head on the dash. Hit on the head, and all twisted up. The door jammed me up. I was all twisted up and had a bad compression injury. That was when my back got it. At first I thought I'd been ambushed—I wasn't thinking clearly. While I was driving back to the station I realized that I was driving on the wrong side of the road, so I pulled over and called it in.

I went and got M.T.ed [medically treated] and I convinced the guy to let me stay on. I had two days off and I took three specials, so I spent five days in bed. Then I went back to work. They shouldn't have let me. I was dangerous. I wasn't thinking straight. I had a concussion. If there had been any leadership they would have said, "That's it, you're grounded." I don't know what I was thinking—I've been in trouble from that day forward. Not a pain-free day since.

This injury caused such chronic pain, the officer realized he would never be able to complete his twenty years. He decided, with about twelve years on:

> That twenty was the dream, but I knew that I was in trouble because the pain was so bad. It was even bigger than that, bigger than just the accident. I had been working in a bonus pay grade when the accident happened, and they took that away, so it was a five-and-a-half percent pay cut. So immediately I made an adjustment. After I got hurt I realized that I had to have another plan in case something happened to keep me from being able to finish up. I put together a parallel trail. I got myself the flight instructor rating, and figured that I could get away from police work—we bought the place near the airport, and we had our horses, and I planned on doing the extra flying and instructing. Meanwhile I got on the mounted unit—I got through [major events during the next two years as part of the mounted unit], but after that I was done. I couldn't do it anymore.

The officer left the mounted unit and went back to light duty field positions as the problems with his back continued to increase. He put all his discretionary income, and perhaps a bit more, into the purchase of a home, a plane and the necessary training and air time to qualify as an instructor. He gained his instructor's rating in addition to his pilot's license. Because his home was distant from the station, he flew his plane to work or drove the two hours one way. His back continued to deteriorate. It became to painful for him to drive to work. He considered leaving the job with a medical pension, but he had not put in his twenty years. It soon became evident that he could no longer fly either. His back pain was so severe he could not sit in the plane for prolonged periods. He sold the plane. He and his wife sold the horses. The officer stayed in town and drove home only when he had several days off in a row. He managed to complete his twenty years, but decided to go to twenty-five, so he could retire at a higher rate with added benefits:

> All these people who get I.O.D., and everybody gets hurt, but those officers who get I.O.D. to where they even think of going medical, there's a problem. They're trying to proceed 60 percent tax-free. That's all they ever get, but the problem is that it is not really a pension. You can be sixty-five years old and they can order you back. They can make you come in and go through a city examination any time they want, and you know how all that political stuff changes. They can decide that they don't think you need it any more, that you're okay now, and they can order you back to work. And you have to go. I want to be productive. I want to get to the point to where I can give a good day's work, but I want to be done with policing, and I want a pension that I can plan on.

In some real ways the pressure is off for the officers who have reached this phase of their career. They have options unavailable to officers in earlier phases. For some, just the knowledge that they can leave enables them to stay. They have proven their mettle, they have achieved the goal of the twenty years, and now they can turn to what they want to do.

CELEBRATING RETIREMENT

The traditional police officer who reaches twenty years can retire with his or her pension, but the new police officers do not have this option. If they retire before the thirty-year mark, or before the age of fifty-five, they have to wait until they are fifty-five years old to collect their pension. When a traditional officer retires, this difference is forcibly brought home to the new officer. New officers who observe traditional officers' retirement after twenty years see the traditional officer (who may be in his or her forties) as still being young. On the other hand, the new officers envision themselves as not being young when they reach retirement. At ten years on the job, traditional officers are half-way through their careers, new police are usually only a third of the way from being finished.

There has been a change in the formal and informal parties given to honor the retiree and to mark the occasion for those still in service. In the past these events were well attended. The informal retirement party was a semi-spontaneous celebration held at the end of watch on the last day in which the officer "suited up." As the watch progressed word would be passed that the event would take place at a certain location—almost always one of the local "watering holes" frequented by the watch. At the end of watch anyone who wished would filter in and celebrate the last working day of the retiring officer. Usually these events involved a great deal of drinking, reminiscing and genial esprit de corps. It is a time when officers talk about their own retirement plans and get the details about plans of the retiring officer. There is usually a fair amount of joking. Usually the only people attending are police officers and a few police community people. Spouses and family of the retiring officer usually do not attend. In the past officers who were totally new to the division would be expected to show up at such occasions to honor the retiring officer and to show their commitment to the working watch. It was viewed as a sign of belonging to the "family." All officers were welcome, whether or not they were close friends of the retiring officer.

Celebrations of this sort are now quite different. There are fewer participants, especially among the new police. The new officers who do attend rarely talk about retirement. They talk about leaving or making a lateral transfer to another department. The sense of continuity that used to be a major component of these rituals is now absent.

Family and non-police friends of the officer are invited to the formal retirement party. A notice of the occasion is sent city-wide through department mail, attracting friends and former partners from all over the city. The atmosphere of these celebrations varies with the personalities and tastes of the participants. Again, this is a time when most of the officers, often in the company of their wives, reiterate their retirement plans, grumble about the department, and express the desire to be the one leaving. It is not uncommon for officers to know how many days they have until they "pull the pin."

While always a celebration, these retirement parties include many of the aspects of a wake or funeral. Friends, family and co-workers eulogize the officer—often using the past tense when referring to the officer. The milestones of the officer's life on the job are recounted and commented upon. The departing officer is often given citations and commendations as well as police gifts—shadow boxes containing police related items—guns, medals, insignia and so forth. Like a funeral, the person is feted and his or her passing lamented, with expressions of hope and the sentiment that they have moved on to something better. The notion that they have fought the good fight, and have gone on to their reward is frequently expressed. Clearly for police the retirement marks a similar break in experience. The retiree, like the corpse, is forever removed from active duty.

These events can be quite emotional for all concerned. Joy, fear, relief, anguish, envy, dread, disappointment, satisfaction—the entire gamut of emotions is experienced if not openly expressed. For most officers this ushers in a wonderful stage of their lives, although it usually takes several years to settle in to happy retirement. It is also true that many retirees do not live long after retirement. Those officers who identify themselves primarily as "police," and who have defined their lives by the job, either have to develop other interests very quickly or face a very stressful and difficult period. If they have totally immersed themselves in the police community to the exclusion of all others, their success in other endeavors is unlikely.

Retiring means they have finished a job that many of them did not really believe they would ever finish. This is the final way to demonstrate to fellow officers that the retiree is a "stand-up guy."

> I talked about it all the time, we all did, but I never thought it would happen. I guess, I sort of thought that something would happen, to keep me from getting here. Something would happen to me . . . funny things go through your head, and you think "these other guys, yeah, I can see them making it, but I can't see myself getting through this, making it twenty years, there's just too much of it. . . ." And then other times, "Yeah, sure, I can do this—all I gotta do is keep going, and watch myself." I always kind of thought I'd get taken out in a chase—

or something. When we had the set-ups and the ambushes and such, that was a real hard time. I'd think about—not worry really—but just think about what it would be that would keep me from getting to twenty. And—and now, here I am and after planning it for the last fifteen years on the job, I don't know what I'm gonna do. I've got my plans, but now I'm not sure of what I'll do . . . really.

Officers look forward to the time they can retire and be "fuzz that was," but, when the time comes, it is rarely as emotionally or economically rewarding as anticipated. Officers start out as citizens who are then transformed into police officers during the course of their careers. At the end of their careers, the transition back to being "citizens" is very difficult. Some officers never adjust—they cannot be just citizens, but they no longer wish to be police officers. I think that prior to retirement many officers worry about not being able to fit into the "other" world when they retire. This may also be part of the reason why, when they do retire, they often move far away from the city. This decision is also problematic, however. They move far from the suburbs, which are already quite removed from the city. This means that with retirement they remove themselves from their closest friends and the community that has sustained them for the last twenty years. It is an all-or-nothing situation. Choosing retirement means that officers cut many of the ties that bind them to the police community as they have experienced it for half of their lifetimes. This makes the decision to retire more difficult for officers, even though they have been actively planning for it for at least a decade.

Some of the officers who plan to or have already retired to distant rural areas encourage other officers to buy property in the same area. Thus there will often be small enclaves of retired officers from this department living in clusters throughout the western and northwestern United States. The neighborhoods created on the outskirts of the city are often reconstituted in these rural areas, minus the firefighters. As one officer put it:

> When I pull the pin, it's time to get outta Dodge. Kenny, the fireman next door, now he can stay here as long as he wants, everybody loves a fireman. They're the all-time good guys, we're only the good guys when they need us, *exactly* when they need us, not any other time. Not when they're driving a little under [the influence of alcohol], or their kids are loaded, or they're pulling some other violation. Then *we're* the bad guys.

Even in leaving the job, their plans are shaped by their often uneasy relationships with the people they serve, the citizens.

Ultimately, most officers look back on their police careers with pride. They take great pleasure in reminiscing about the job and their companions. Most express the sentiment that being on the job was one of the best things that ever happened to them.

9

Reflections of a Traditional Officer

The narrative that you are about to read is told by an officer whom I have known and interviewed over a period of several years, starting in 1976—one year into his career. This particular officer has always been "an easy interview": articulate, well organized, straightforward and passionate. His easy humor is refreshing. He is a popular officer who has received many commendations initiated by citizens as well as supervisors. In addition, he is highly respected by management and street cops. Despite his considerable discomfort due to the repercussions from previous injuries, he basically sat and spoke for over four hours, responding to my request to describe the important factors in his life and in relation to his job as an officer with the Los Angeles Police Department. He started talking and said whatever he deemed important. It is mostly a "stream-of-consciousness" narration rather than the result of an interview comprised of a series of questions needing answers. The transcription reflects very little editing; some names and issues that have no relevancy have been removed.

The officer, whom I shall call "Fred," is representative of many traditional officers, but it would be a serious mistake to assume that he speaks for all, or even a majority of them on every point. There are very few informants who are exactly the norm—whose lives follow a precise pattern established from an analysis of data. Many come close, while others vary dramatically from the majority's perceptions, beliefs and actions. Some of the views of this particular officer are almost idiosyncratic—they are his alone. He is, after all, a remarkable man. His life experiences and perceptions are greatly influenced by his religious convictions. This officer is generally light-hearted and blessed with a quick wit and infectious humor. These qualities are not so evident in Fred's comments, because he was speaking at a time when he was particularly distressed. The tone of his remarks is tilted toward the negative as he was in pain, discouraged, a bit morose and uncertain about his future. Following his retirement from the L.A.P.D., he had taken a position with another, smaller police force close to his home. He believed that with the retirement pension from the L.A.P.D. and his salary from the new job he would be able to send both of his children to the college of their choice, spend more time with his wife, to whom he is devoted, and be able to pursue his lifetime passion, golf. Soon after taking the position with the other department, old injuries that had been somewhat dormant started acting up. They now threaten his ability to perform and keep the new job. He was forced to give up many of his favorite pastimes, including golf. He is quite discouraged, but tries to maintain a positive outlook.

It is my hope that the feelings and attitudes expressed in this narrative (presented almost in its entirety), will manifest the essence of the human who does the job of policing, illustrate how rich an "authentic voice" can be in ethnography, and give readers the opportunity to contextualize the information discussed in the previous chapters.

FRED'S WORLD: A LIVING ILLUSTRATION

I'm forty-six years old; I was raised with two brothers in a suburb of Washington, D.C. I did just enough academically to get promoted to the next grade, no more, I had no interest in school. I was a colossally marginal performer in school all my life. As far as my schooling time was concerned it was a waste of time. Probably the best thing for me was that I was good reader. I'm essentially self-educated. There wasn't much going on during school, but I'm a voracious reader, and so I've been able to cut through to the heart of whatever's being written about. That's been real valuable for me.

If I have a regret in my life, it's that I pissed away my education time. I'm happy with myself, I'm quite content. There is not much that I would change, but if I could change one thing, I would go back and put effort into school. But . . . I really seriously hated school. I really did. I didn't like being confined to the classroom, I didn't like the structure of it. I was bored. All I wanted to do was to go with my friends, or go to the golf course and caddie, or hunt for balls, or play in the creek, or whatever I was doing back in those days.

The four years that I was in high school, I think my G.P.A. was about 1.2, and that was back when they were giving A's for gym. So if it weren't for gym class, I'd probably still be in high school.

When I graduated, the family wound up in California by some histrionics with my dad's job. I don't remember what it was about. I went around trying to find work anywhere, and couldn't get it. I got rejected every place. Vietnam was in progress, and they didn't want to hire me 'cause they sensed that I would get drafted, and it was probably a valid assumption. The only job that I could find, based upon my piss-poor educational performance, and the fact that I couldn't find a job, was to go join the Army, which I did. I had an aptitude for communications. I was a high-speed Morse Code intercept operator. They gave me a test and they said,

"Wow, you're really good at this, and, you know, if you sign up for a four-year enlistment you'll probably wind up someplace in Europe. The likelihood that you'd go to Vietnam is next to nothin.'" The lying bastards—about eight months later, I was in Vietnam. That was probably the *most* educational experience I ever had—the thing that shaped me as person, as far as how I feel about what's important, what's a hardship, what's necessary. That did it for me. And, although I don't want my sons to ever have to go to war, I kind of wish that they could see one from the inside out, because it would give them a good perspective on life in general.

I wound up working for six months in a, what we would call a "rear echelon mother fucker job" in a place called Phu Bai. And then I got tired of being in that intelligence bunker twelve hours a day, so I signed out to go as a crew member on an intelligence-gathering airplane, and I flew about a hundred missions over South Vietnam, and doing the communications intelligence thing. When my time was up, I came home.

I got on with my life. Tried to find a job. There was some stuff going on as far as veterans' preferences and all that stuff, and they were trying to get all the guys coming back employed. The first job of any consequence that I landed was the assistant pro at the Coronado Country Club in El Paso, which was where Fort Bliss was. I applied for it, and was offered it, and at the last minute, I chickened out. I went instead to Georgia to help some guy start a golf school. My primary motivation for going to Georgia wasn't the golf school, it was to get in the pants of his daughter, who was knock-down beautiful. I went to Georgia, and the golf school was kind of a flop.

I left Georgia, and my nearest point of refuge was Baton Rouge, Louisiana, where my mother was. My parents got divorced right after I got back. That was an interesting period there, because my dad and I had our coming-of-age thing when I got back. I got back from Vietnam, and I'm driving Mom somewhere, and she breaks down and she starts crying, "Dad's been cheating on me and we're getting a divorce," and this is all news to me, and I guess they wanted to keep it from me when I was overseas. So she's cryin', "and it's been goin' on since you were a little boy, and now he's gonna leave me, and he's gonna marry this other woman," and all that stuff, and I was pretty seriously pissed off about it.

When my dad came home from work I was layin' for him, and I confronted him. He backed away from me, he cowered away from me. That was the time in my life that I knew that we were on equal footing after that. It was kind of like Little Bull versus Big Bull, and Big Bull realizes he can't win the fight, type of deal. It wasn't a physical altercation, but I stepped toward him, and I drew back. I was kind of maladjusted anyway, I had been away from home, you know, in a war, for cryin' out loud, so violence was a resolution for everything. So I reared back like I was gonna slug him, and he backed up, and then I could tell it was, kind of like a pointless exercise. So we kind of came to some understanding. I helped negotiate the divorce terms, and then I went on about my business.

I lived in a back room in Mom's little house, and I managed a shoe store for a while, like an assistant manager 'cause I couldn't find work anywhere—and I was a mechanic's helper at a taxicab place, and just going from little job to little job that never did have any meaning—I tried to sell insurance, that was a disaster; I was just trying to scramble around, trying to find anything that would work, and wound up being a cop.

An ad comes out in the paper, "the City of Baton Rouge is looking for police officers," and they gave a veteran's preference of X amount of points for being a cop—you know, being a Vietnam veteran, you get points in the process. I went down and applied, and got accepted and went through the academy and all that stuff, graduated from the academy, and the very first thing that happened to me as a cop after I graduated from the academy was to chase a traffic violator. I'm in a car with the other cop, and this guy runs a red light, and we go all over trying to catch him. The guy ducks through a couple of back streets, and we wound up on the lawn in front of my mother's house, where I was living. That was the very first thing I did, was to write a ticket to a guy on the front lawn of my house. I stayed there for eighteen months. It was a poverty-level wage. There was no advancement situation there. If you stayed around long enough, they made you a sergeant, if you were there long enough after that, they made you a lieutenant. It's still that way. But there wasn't really any control that I had over it, other than go to work day after day and do the same crap, until I had enough time to do something else.

I believe it was about this time they had all this Black Panther stuff going on in Los Angeles, and campus demonstrations, and they had the SLA [Symbionese Liberation Army] shoot-out. L.A.P.D. had this ball-busting reputation, and my dad is here in town, in L.A., living, and he calls me up, he's trying to recruit me, "you really should come out here and do this," and so I'm listening and I'm listening hard.

Well, in the interim the guy's daughter, from the golf school called me up, "My dad's flipped out, he hit me, and all that stuff, and I'm leaving home," she's probably eighteen or nineteen years old, and she says, "Can I come to Baton Rouge?" I said, "Yeah, come on," so she came, and we set up housekeeping, and ten days later we got married, which was a really stupid thing to do. A couple weeks after we were married, she tells me, "Oh, by the way, if I get pregnant I'm going to get an abortion, because I want to play tournament golf, and I don't want it to get in the way." I said, "Well, it would have been nice if you had told me this before we got married." We really didn't think this thing out; it's kind of a glandular thing. She was so beautiful, [and] she wanted me. I'm maladjusted because I just got back from the war, and I hadn't really had any attention or affection, like boy-girl-friend in my whole adult life, 'cause I was stuck over there doing that.

So I was like, Yeah! Let's get naked! That's kind of where that went.

Then, she did get pregnant, because she was sloppy about takin' her birth control pills, and she did get an abortion, and I sent her packin'. She went back to Georgia to be with her family. . . that has always been a big heartbreak, to this day in my life, that I had a son, apparently, that was aborted.

So, she's back in Georgia, I'm in Baton Rouge, I'm tired of being on the police department there, 'cause I'm bored. My dad says, "Come on out." I say, "I'm having this problem with [my wife]." My dad says, "Hey, if there's anything to the marriage, when you come here she'll follow you." I said, "Okay." So I follow my dad's advice. I sold all my shit, bought a little car, packed it, drove to Los Angeles. Applied to the police department, and by January of 1975 I was in the academy, and by the time I graduated from the academy, she was back with me in Los Angeles. We set up house-keeping in West L.A., and she got pregnant again, she got an abortion again, and that was it for me. We were married for four years, and out of the whole period of time, I think we were together maybe twelve or thirteen months. Because she was out on the tour playing golf, she was out doing exhibitions in Japan for months at a time, and we were apart a lot, and then when we did get together, it was just dumb. It was just a mistake. We just went our separate ways. I filed for divorce, we got a divorce, sort of a no-fault deal, you go your way and I'll go mine.

We got divorced in January of 1977, and by June of 1977, I was married again, to my present wife, Lannie. I have two sons, a National Honor Society high school senior who's got an Air Force ROTC scholarship, going to UC-San Diego, and his little brother is a scholar, athlete, in high school. They're good boys, mannerly, gentlemanly, respectful, attentive, alert, decent kids, that America needs more of. I'm real proud of them, and most of what's good about them is owing to the devoted attention of their mom over all these years, and that's the damn truth.

My kids are seventeen and fifteen, I've been married for just a little bit under twenty years. Personally, in the interim, the only thing that really happened of any consequence is I went to college. It's kind of funny, when I decided that I wanted to go to school, and when I had to pay the bills, I wound up on the dean's list. I stayed long enough to get an associate of arts degree. Then my kids were in school, and I've been paying tuition for them, so all the tuition money went to them instead of me. I probably will go and get some kind of a four-year degree. Right now it's not feasible. I've got tuition to pay for the kids, so it'll probably be a while.

I'm proud of my academic performance, because it's something where I set my mind to it and studied real hard and worked real hard and made the dean's list, and the A's were easy to come by with a real focused attention that I didn't have when I was in high school. So, it's not like I'm academically underprivileged or anything. I could do it once I set my mind to it.

As far as my career with L.A.P.D. is concerned, it is probably the biggest formulation of me as a person. My identity was that organization, was that group of people. That's who I am. Who I was. Who I am, I guess.

I have been places and done things that almost everybody on this planet will never go and do. I have been involved in so many different things, and so many different aspects of a career, that people make movies about it, or they make television shows about it, or they write about it. People write books about the stuff that I did or the stuff that my peers did. Half of the shows on television or the movies are about cops. People are fascinated by it when cops are doing something on the side of the road. Everybody has to stop and look. Everybody wants to be there. Everybody wants to press up against that yellow crime-scene tape and have a look.

I've been inside the ropes, all that time, inside the investigation, in the know, knowing what's really's going on, who's doing it, how it's done, how it got to be that way, what the outcomes were. All the personal conversations, and all the little personal contacts, that people in their heart of hearts wish that they could have had, I did, and my peers did. Inside the tape. Riots, earthquakes, famines, floods, stabbings, shootings, vehicle pursuits, explosions, chemical spills, foot chases, fistfights, gunfights, whatever. Things that people fantasize about, and stare at, and wonder about, I don't have to wonder about it because I've done all of that, in great measure. That's been a privilege. I consider myself to be very fortunate to have had those experiences.

Anything good that I have acquired materially in my life has come from being associated with L.A.P.D.—that and the fact that my wife has kind of a nesting instinct. When I got married to her, I didn't have a pot to piss in, and now I have pots all over the place, and I'm pissed off all the time. I have a house, I have some money in the bank, I have a pension, they're gonna have to send me a check for the rest of my life, and the rest of my wife's life. That's hard-earned money. Those are the practical aspects of it. As far as the fact that I look back, and I've spent my life on something important, that other people would have given their eye teeth to be able to be a part of for just a week at a time, I've done it for thousands and thousands of days. And I'm proud of that.

I'm also proud of the people that I've been associated with. I have seen such *extraordinary* sacrifice, *extraordinary* courage, on a daily basis, day in and day out, around the clock, for all that time. People have no appreciation for it whatsoever. If people could just sit in a cop's shirt pocket, in 77th or Southwest or Hollywood, for a day and find out what gets done, and what gets said, and see the risks that cops take, for people that they don't know, just because they have a sense of duty. Just because it needs doing. They have this vocation, they have this devotion, that they take these risks. There's always the Medal of Valor ceremonies, and you see all the Top Cop stuff that's on TV and all of that. But it's really the day-to-day, routine courage that is shown by these people that is so remarkable. It has been a privilege to be around it and a part of it. I do not consider myself to be courageous, in any sense of the word. I've done some particularly risky things, because I wanted to, because I was pissed off, and I wanted to catch somebody, or something like that. I never, I can honestly say that I never was actually frightened the whole time.

My big fear was not physical harm. It may have something to do with the fact that I had a service background, and combat service, I don't know. I just never got worried, I never got physically scared for my well-being a single time in all that twenty years. I would just go around, make a calculated assessment about what needed doing, figure out a way to get it done, so it came out my way, and just go do it. I came out fine. I don't have any regrets as far as that goes. So I don't consider myself particularly courageous. The people that are courageous are the ones that are scared to death, and go do it anyway, the ones that are really mortified about having to do something, and then choke that mortification down, and go do whatever needs doing. Those are the ones that are courageous.

I take that back. The one time I did get scared in my life, I got stuck in a house full of smoke, and couldn't find my way out. Scared the living shit out of me. There's no way that I would ever want to be a fireman. No possible way. Those guys really earn their daily bread. It was just a kind of a smoldering fire that filled the house with smoke. We were trying to find people in there, we broke the window out, we crawled in, I'm crawling around trying to find anybody that might be in the house. I couldn't figure out how to get out, couldn't breathe; and so I'm laying in a strange environment, and not knowing how to get back the way I came, and there's broken glass all over the floor, because I'm the asshole that knocked the window out. I didn't care for that experience one bit.

The rest of the time, the only fear that I had was that I wanted the stuff I did to turn out right. I did have a fear of incompetence, I had a fear of making a mistake that would turn a case bad. Asking the wrong question, or not asking the right question at the right time, or leaving a piece of evidence behind, or something where my competence would be in question. This could have been a great case, but I fucked it up, 'cause I didn't do this—that was my big fear. I didn't have any fear of physical harm, I just wanted to make sure that the stuff I did was right.

The biggest heartbreak that I had during the whole time was when Russ Kuster was killed. Russ was a twenty-five-year detective at Hollywood; he was the homicide coordinator and somebody that everybody liked. If there was anything that I wanted to do in my career that I didn't get to do, it was to work Hollywood Homicide under Kuster. Right before it would have happened, he was killed in a gunfight in a restaurant in

Hollywood. Of all of the things that happened to me in my career, and I've had some significant heartbreaks, and significant troubled periods in my life, that was the one that really busted my chops.

We used to have these binge drinking golf tournaments, where everybody would get together and just, go out and be stupid . . . and just drink and just be reckless and crazy and trashy. I went to one of these things, and I think it might have been a Kuster Memorial, as a matter of fact, a couple of years after he died. And one of the guys slipped me some kind of a drink. I think I asked for a vodka tonic or something like that, and he slipped me some double or triple, and I just got so thoroughly, comprehensively smashed that I had to be driven home. Everybody was passing drinks around, and we were toasting all the dead guys that we knew. You know, "Here's to So-and-So," and "Here's to So-and-So," and "Here's to So-and-So," and on and on . . . so many, just so many good people. So I left just really melancholy, and really just drunk as a skunk. Lannie was with me up there. . . . We got home, and it must have been maybe one o'clock or two o'clock in the morning, and she had the bad judgment to ask, "Who were these people," this guy, that guy, this guy, that guy, and when she got to Kuster, I started crying. I couldn't stop. I was just snot-slingin' drunk, sittin' in the bathroom, and I sobbed, and I just convulsed in violent weeping that went on all night. Lannie was real scared, I could tell by the look on her face, I could *not* stop. She was putting cold towels on me, she was splashing water in my face, it woke up the kids, and I've never been through anything like that in my life. It was just terrible. When I was done, even after I was sobered up and hung over, I was still crying over that. After that, it was over, and I could pretty much talk about it, and talk about him, without breaking down. But it was a. . . . Boy, that just broke my heart. As far as personal impact on me, that was the biggest hurt I suffered during all of that time.

Police Olympic Road Racing

I did have some big, really big achievements in that period of time as well. In 1995, my very good friend and I conceived a piece of madness—the World Championship Motorcycle Race. We put our heads together, and put it on, with the help of private sponsorship, some personal ingenuity, and the devotion of a big network of friends. We put it on as a family, and as a group of friends, particularly between my wife and me. That was probably the biggest learning experience of our lives, as far as taking risks was concerned. To make a long story short, we sent out a teletype in the Interpol Network, and it went all over the world, to like 126 countries, and it said, "We want to put on a World Championship Motorcycle Race, does anybody want to come?" Well, we got some answers back from all over the globe, and then we said, "Okay, well, we're gonna do it"—and we started working on it, and we had no idea what we were doing. Well, what'll we do next? We need a racetrack, so we went out and found one. Gee, we need motorcycles, found those. We need this, we need that. Fundraising and publicity and correspondence and diplomatic customs red tape, and all kind of stuff going on, and we just shot from the hip, and did it with a network of volunteers.

Not very many people know about the inner workings of that. But in the course of putting on the first race, a lot of the sponsor commitments that we had, and expectations for money that we had coming in to finance this thing, a lot of the companies backed out. It got to the point, about ninety days before the first race was supposed to go off, we had no money. We had all these bills piling up, and all these expenses, where we were going out of pocket to try and pay the postage and phone bills and Xeroxing, and all kinds of stuff going on, and the money that the sponsors had promised wasn't coming in. We had to make a decision, my wife and I; we sat down, and said, "What're we gonna do? What *are* we gonna do?"

People all over the world had been saying to us, "Yeah, we got a team," Norway's got a team, France has a team, we've bought motorcycles, we've got the team together, we got the team riders, we've got sponsorship, we've got the plane tickets, all these plans are made, and, you know, we've got the blessing of the king and queen of Denmark, or whatever the heck it was. So we had to decide: We either have to send out a telegram to stop this before it goes any farther, or we have to go through with it. I want to talk about the level of devotion of my wife. We're sitting there stressed. We have to make some kind of decision, and we've gotta make a decision tonight. I asked her, "What do you want to do? We're risking losing the house, we can't borrow any more money, the credit cards are maxed out, what do you want to do?" She looked me right in the eye and said, "Let's go racing." So that was a big turning point, as far as going up to the edge, and either backing away, and saying, "No thank you," or jumping over the edge and just taking a risk. After taking that risk, after jumping over that edge, we don't have any more edges. We don't feel like we have limitations, so as far as our ability to grow or succeed or do anything, we're not intimidated. After jumping over the edge, and then making it succeed because we had to. We had that race and two others. They were colossal successes. So as far as personal growth is concerned, none of that would have happened without the connection from L.A.P.D. It was an L.A.P.D. event, Los Angeles, Hollywood is here; everybody from all over the world wanted to come to Los Angeles; they wanted to go to Hollywood; they wanted to do the California West Coast thing. I don't think those races would have come off if I was calling them from St. Louis.

Police Funerals—Walk of Fame

For the first ten or twelve years of my career, I never went to a cop's funeral. I didn't care who it was, I didn't want to be around it, I didn't want to have to face it. I didn't want to deal with it. So—just a boxcar load worth of guys got killed over the years, and I never went to anybody's funeral. Then I started going, because I felt like I was kind of chicken shit, and kind of neglectful, avoiding that aspect of police work. I decided that I was going to go to the funerals, and pay my respects to these guys, because I started to have some understanding of the sacrifice that they made, and the impact that it had on their families. I saw that most people had no clue as to what these people were doing on their behalf, and they didn't care then, and they still don't care. You know what I said? I said, "I need to acknowledge that, I need to be a part of that." So I started going to funerals. In 1992 there was deputy killed. Nelson Yamamoto, an L.A. County Sheriff's Deputy. Yamamoto was killed in a gunfight, and I don't remember exactly where the funeral was, but at the time that he was buried, they didn't know who did it. I think the suspect got away at first. I think he subsequently got arrested. Anyway, I'm out there and I've got all my L.A.P.D. stuff on, and I'm milling around with about four thousand other guys that are just showing up from everywhere. There was a captain from L.A.P.D., and he came up to me and said, "What do you think you could do as far as getting the L.A.P.D. people put together in some kind of a formation? Having all of these thousands of people just milling around with no direction," he says, "is not doing the deputy's memory any good, and it just really looks like a gaggle of people around here that need some direction. Do you think you could put something together?" So I stood out in front of, I don't know, probably six or seven hundred guys from L.A.P.D., and I started barking out commands, put them in platoon formation, rank and file, and got them all straightened up and standing at parade rest, and then the other people started to just kind of follow suit, and they just put themselves in rank and file, and all you could see was just regimental strength of uniformed coppers, as far as the eye could see in both directions. I couldn't even see each end of the formation. Darryl Gates came up to me and complimented me, and Sherman Block came up and complimented me, and that was fine. Then the deputy's family came up and complimented me, and thanked me, and I was really gratified by that.

Shortly after that, two Compton officers were killed, and I went to that funeral, and somebody came up to me and said, "You were that guy at the other thing, and would you do here what you did there?" So then there's another massive regimental strength funeral for these Compton officers. Compton had never had an officer killed, as rough a place as Compton was, in its whole history of its police department, they never had anybody killed, and they were just beside themselves. They didn't know how to handle a funeral, they didn't know what to do, step by step, they had never had to face it before. They asked me to help at the church, and then when everybody was taken care of at the church, they put me in a car, and asked me to go to the cemetery, and organize at the cemetery as well. I did that. Whenever I bump into a Compton officer anywhere, "Hey, you're the funeral guy . . . thank you."

So I started getting a thing about the courage of these officers, and the sacrifices that they made. In the attending these funerals, I got into the pageantry of it. Into the doing of it, as something that needed doing. To me now it's something people need to rub their noses in. In the blood of this sacrifice that these people make. They [civilians] hide behind their little cocktails and watch the evening news, and they have no clue. When one of their family members gets killed, then they've got some idea. But when somebody gets killed on their behalf, trying to protect their family members. . . . They just don't care. So I just got hung up doing that.

In the midst of that, I had an idea about putting a memorial in front of the Hollywood Station. That was really driven by Russ Kuster's death. The end result of that was that there's a replica of the Hollywood Walk of Fame, the black terrazzo floor with the pink star on it. I researched all of the officers that had suffered a violent death in Hollywood. I went to robbery/homicide to do research, I researched the *Los Angeles Times*, and the Historical Society, I found all of the officers that had been assigned to Hollywood that had died violently, over all that time. I got their relatives together from all over the place. "Hey, you were seven years old when your dad was killed in 1936. I'm glad you're still alive. We're gonna do a memorial, would you please come?" I mean, it was a big, big deal. And that, as far as personal gratification of anything I did at L.A.P.D., getting that memorial installed was my biggest personal accomplishment. Because a hundred years from now, when I'm dead, that will be there, because I decided that that was something that I wanted to do. I was able to that, because of my success in the past with the Police Olympics, and putting on the events and the funerals. All of the things that came up with that just kind of rolled up into a package. I go there now and I look at it with a great sense of satisfaction, when all of those people are properly memorialized. I'm personally very proud of that.

I was walking up on the Walk of Fame, and it was at some movie premiere, I got some duty assignment at some movie premiere, I'm walking along that sidewalk that's been there forever. There's people back there from the thirties and forties, and people that I never heard of before. And I'm going, "Gee whiz, you know, it seemed like, if we can memorialize all these hundreds from the movie industry, back in the 1930s and '40s, it would seem like we ought to be able to do something decent for our cops that were killed here, keeping this place up and running, so all these movies could be made, and all these people could be famous."

It was timely, it fell together well. It was kind of bulletproof. It had a tremendous amount of public support, and the money rolled in for that, corporations and movie companies, and you know, Paramount, Universal, Disney, places like that, they were all cutting big checks for it. So it fell into place quite nicely. It's been a big success. When people see me now, I'm not only the funeral guy, but I'm also the Memorial Walk guy. So I did leave behind *a little something* of what I got out of it. I got much more out of being on the Los Angeles Police Department than I gave. Before I left I wanted to do something special, not to show that I was there, or that I had been there, but I just wanted to make a contribution to the organization that would be lasting. That would give some sense of the gratification that I have for having been there. That memorial was a big part of it.

Working South Central

Coppers spend their lives sacrificing for other people. That's what they do. There's a certain calling; some people are called to teach, some people are called to be lawyers, and some people are called to the religious life. I don't think people have any clue about the amount or level of sacrifice that all these officers make every day, that's all devoted to the welfare of other people. These guys, and the women now, in the later years, who are killed putting their lives at risk for people that they don't know, and particularly in the minority areas of the city, in the Black areas, and now in the Hispanic areas that are mixing in South L.A. There are guys that have been down there thirty years, busting their ass, and wrecking their own lives personally, and wrecking their health, trying to salvage some sense of peace and security in a section of town and for a group of people that everyone thinks they hate. Which is bullshit. People don't have any idea. Some copper's down there, has been working 77th for fifteen years, and gets in some shooting, and it's questionable because the gun was a cap gun, or some kind of crap like that, and there's all these activist groups down there, saying that this guy's a hate-monger and he killed someone because he was Black.

What he really did was spent fifteen years down at 77th, risking his life every day and sacrificing to protect all these Black faces that, to him, have no names. People that he never knew, probably never will know. Now there's a great many people down there who understand that, and appreciate that, but there's also a bunch that believe that race is the basis for everything. So when things don't go right, it's because of their blackness and the officer's whiteness, and the "racist" department, and all of that. That is just so much bullshit, I can't tell you. There are guys that have been down there, working 77th, Southwest, Southeast, Willowbrook, all of their adult working lives. When somebody's got a problem, and always it's somebody of color that has the problem—that's who's living there— the victims, the criminals, everybody. It's always that same detective that handles it, it's always that same officer that comes out and tries to get it right. Now, it would seem to me that if coppers are all a bunch of racist assholes, like they're depicted in the press, or by some of these activist groups, why would they stay down there and do that? There isn't really very much down there to like about it, because it's violent. The violence is oppressive. It wears them down, but they continue to go back, day after day, to find the guys that did it, get them in custody, to heal the wounds, to do the best they can to maintain some order and some level of peace, so that people can raise their families without worrying about their kids getting killed in front of a 7-Eleven. It's just cruel. It's a cruel lie, the way coppers are depicted.

I've been down there, I've worked South Homicide. South Homicide wore me out. Eighteen months was all I could take. There are guys that have been down there working it for ten years. They've probably been through three or four hundred cases. I've seen how hard they work, I've seen them collapse at their desk, with angina or fatigue; one of the guys had a stroke—thirty-eight years old. They're down there, busting their ass, trying to exercise some kind of control, and some kind of influence of right or wrong over what's going on. They're not down there because they hate people, they care about people. They're down there because they are devoted. They're down there because they're trying to do the right thing. They have a duty to be there, *and* the desire to be there. People need to have an understanding of that.

There is a preoccupation and a conception that cops are racists, and that's just nonsense. The only racists that I've seen down there are the ones [citizens] that are preoccupied with it, that keep bringing "race" up as the rationale or the basis for all decisions. Life-and-death decisions. The officer shot this guy *because* he was Black. Like it's gonna matter. You know, there's a White guy here, and a Black guy here, and I think I'll shoot the Black one. For crying out loud. What are they thinking? That's always bugged me. All the little behind-the-scenes kindnesses that the officers do on a daily basis, particularly the ones that work down in the South end. I've seen them bring books, I've seen them bring baskets of food, I've seem them take money out of their pockets, I've seen them go back and make visits to people. Small things, meaningful things, the comfort that they try to give people in the midst of all of this. I've seen the bullshit that they take on the people's behalf. Why would a detective work seventy-two hours straight, without going home, and collapse on his desk with a stroke, trying to solve a murder case, for people he hated? Why would he do that? If he hated Black people, or hated brown people, or hated anybody, when the bell rang at 3:30, he'd pack his crap up and go home, because he doesn't care. Well, I'm here to tell you, nobody does that.

Everybody works too hard, and everybody stays too long, because they have a devotion to duty and a love for people that permeates even the abuse that they have to suffer, by people that should know better. Running around condemning officers whenever some Black kid gets killed—not when they're killed by the carload by their own Black gang-bangers, but anyone else. They are the most small-minded, short-sighted people on the planet, as far as I'm concerned. They have an agenda—to keep themselves in the headlines. They have no understanding or no interest in what the real truth is. They should be ashamed because the level of ignorance that they display is amazing. They wouldn't know a racist if they saw one in the mirror, because it's what they do every day, and they miss it. They do, for the most part. I'm not talking about the people in general, in the general population of South Los Angeles. But the activist groups have an agenda, their own issues and their own self-promotion—and they are the racists of the planet, as far as I'm concerned.

Rodney King, O.J. Simpson and Racism

Everybody instantly thinks about Rodney King. They say, "Rodney King got his ass kicked because he was Black, because if there was a white guy that was driving his car, he's not gonna get treated the same way." That's bullshit. There was a perverted public perception of what occurred. If you asked people across the world if they knew that Rodney King got up off the ground and tackled Lawrence Powell, they would say no, that that never happened because it was never shown. I think that there were eighty-one seconds of videotape and the fifteen seconds of the end was the beating. His behavior which precipitated the beating—aside from the chase—aside from never doing what he was told to do—is they had him on the ground and he charged headlong into Lawrence Powell and tackled him like a linebacker and knocked him on his ass and was fighting with him. Then Powell got disengaged and then King righteously got his ass kicked. He had it coming; he deserved it. His blackness had nothing to do with it.

Another Black/White thing—O. J. Simpson is guilty as sin, in front of everybody and it's an overwhelmingly Black jury that turns him loose. And that was not racist? They say these cops got together and conspired to plant all this evidence on a national hero, because he was Black. That is the most asinine thing, and people buy into it. Talk about a level of ignorance, people sitting around saying, "I don't think O.J. did it, I think they planted all that evidence. These incompetent cops, who can't get anything right, these bumblers somehow managed to plant all this evidence in all these different places, and keep it all coordinated, and everyone's keeping the secret."

When it comes to racism, on the department, there's more of it on the part of Black officers than Whites. Oh, yeah, there are racist cops. But race is more of an issue, for reasons that are kind of obvious, with minorities. It's a problem because of our preoccupation with it. Now on L.A.P.D., they have a Black Officer's Association, they have a Black Command Officers' Association, they have a Female Officers' Association, they have a Hispanic Officers' Association, a Hispanic Command Officers Association, a Gay and Lesbian Officers' Association, and probably a couple of other ones that I don't even know about, all of which are vying for predominance. They're competing with each other for center stage, I guess. That's part of what drove me away from the L.A.P.D.

I had some financial concerns after the earthquake, and some realities that I had to deal with, as far as getting some money to stay afloat financially. The biggest thing about me leaving was financial necessity. When I look back, it was tremendously uncomfortable and stultifying to work there, because you had all these competing groups. There was nothing that you could do or say that somebody wouldn't take exception to. You know, the biggest concern was not your welfare on the street, but that you would do or say something, in and around the police station, that somebody would take umbrage to and complain to the captain, and you would wind up with a 181 [a written complaint against an officer] for being sexist, racist, or whatever. I'm not saying that that stuff didn't go on, I'm not saying that there aren't some people that are maliciously racist or sexist, I'm not saying that that stuff didn't go on. But I'm saying that it's getting to the point that nobody felt comfortable doing or saying anything. To the point where guys that have known each other for twenty years and wanted to have a casual conversation used to pull each other into some alcove and whisper, because they were afraid that anything that they would say might be overheard and used to "beef someone" [as a complaint against the person].

When there are so many words that you are not allowed to use, things that you're not allowed to say in anybody's company at any time, ever. Somebody got suspended for saying "gal." *Gal*. Talking to somebody: "What happened? Oh, this ol' gal got slugged over the head." Some female was walking by said, "'Gal' is a sexist term." Filed a 181. Officer took seven days off—for saying "gal" in the hall. Not on the streets, in the station—in conversation with another officer—not the officer who made the complaint.

I found the environment stultifying, and un-American, really. Because people did not have the right to say anything, they were so fearful of making any kind of politically incorrect, insensitive statement. And it was so easy to do. Well, this might offend this group, and that might offend that group. So what do you do? I just might as well walk around with my hands in my pockets, and stare at the floor, and not say a thing. If I don't say anything ever, and I don't do anything controversial, then nobody can make any accusations against me. It was, at the time, and is now, choking the life out of that organization. It has lost a lot of its spirit and a lot of its camaraderie, because it's preoccupied with a lot of this factionalized bullshit, instead of what they have in common. They have their law enforcement in common, they have L.A.P.D. in common, they have their Americanism in common. Instead of emphasizing that which they have in common, they emphasize that which they *do not* have in common, and they use that lack of commonality to compete and divide themselves into all these little factions. It's choking the life out of the organization. That was one of the things I absolutely do not miss.

The other thing that really bothered me, and made me have no regrets about leaving, was the O.J. Simpson case. I saw detectives that I've known all my career, they're the best guys on the planet. Confident, straightforward, really, really good guys, wouldn't hurt a fly, the guys that have spent all their life making the sacrifices that I talked about earlier. And they wind up getting vilified in the press. Then the Butcher of Brentwood gets off, based upon a perception created by Johnny Cochran that they're a bunch of racists, evidence planting, and all that kind of crap. When the jury bought into it, and acquitted him, . . . it was . . . unbelievable. The level of ignorance that it required, or the level of manipulation that it required, to me was insulting. I said, "What am I sacrificing for these people for, and what am I risking for these people? Why am I risking my life? Why am I making all of these sacrifices for people who hold the law in such little regard? Who hold victims in such little regard, that they want their football hero to be a free man, in the face of all this damning evidence?"

So—and I've never felt this way before—when I heard that verdict come out, I said, "That is *it*, no more risks, no more sacrifices. They deserve what they're willing to settle for. If this is what they want, then they deserve to have it." When I realized I was not willing to take any more risks, or make any more sacrifices, I knew it was time for me to go, and I started looking for another job. That was actually the thing that pushed me over the edge. The two things that pushed me over—well, the three things, the earthquake, and I had to have the pension money and a salary to stay afloat financially, that was number one. Number two was all these agenda-driven organizations in the department that were choking the life out of it. Number three was the Simpson verdict. When I heard myself say, "No more risks and no more sacrifices," I knew it was time to go. I was completely disconnected, not when the verdict came out, but when I said that to myself and I meant it, I knew it was time to go.

Affirmative Action

All the to-do about race, gender, ethnicity. To me, it's evolutionary. You're powerless to do anything about it. . . . The world is compressed— it's so small—all of this mixture of people and cultures is inevitable. The problem I have with affirmative action is the hypocrisy. The hypocrisy of it is what's bothered people the most. It certainly did bother me. It bothers me now. And Proposition 209 [a measure passed by voters that eliminates the use of race and ethnicity as a consideration in hiring practices]; well, if you're going to operate by the letter of the law and say none of these things matter, then why would we put a program together where *all* of these things matter? To the point where they're so dwelt upon, that they become the focal point of our hiring and firing.

When I came on the job in 1975, everybody was a veteran, they were all men, almost all of them were White, and in the middle of this affirma- tive action stuff that was going on, when it first got started, I don't know, it might have been 1980 or 1982, something like that, I'm not exactly sure. I walked into the roll call room at Southwest, and it just hit me like a pile driver—I looked, and all these people, the night watch roll call in the Southwest was about 90 percent White men. In the midst of a neigh- borhood which was 90 percent Black—the contrast registered. "Okay, all right, now I get it. Now I understand what people are talking about. All right, now I see why they view this as an army of occupation. They all have military experience, none of them live here, they're all of a different race, they don't look like us, they don't talk like us, they don't have the same opinions or feelings that we do. They come in here, and they run roughshod over us, and then they take off and go back home to West Cov- ina, or wherever." I don't know whether it was just the day of the week when all the White guys were there and none of the Black ones were, I have no idea. But I walked in, and it was 90 percent blonde-haired, blue- eyed ex-Marines for the most part. You know what? They've got a point. Okay? And that point becomes more and more well taken when you look at the fact that there's a big Korean population, a big Orthodox Jewish population, a big Hindustani population, and none of the officers can relate—couldn't even say, "Hello," "Good-bye," or "Thank you."

So it seems to me, now, in looking back on it, that having a police department that could mirror the community that it serves, so at least the people could communicate and have some basic understanding, is an inherently good thing. But don't put out this big smokescreen affirmative action. I mean, bullshit. Look, we need to hire fifty Koreans right now, and get them through the academy, so we can transfer them around the South area, so we can have translators for the people. Let's just not bullshit about it. Let's, for the next four academy classes, let's not hire anybody except for male and female Blacks, because we don't have enough representation on the department to respond to the people there—Let's just not make it a big, fluffy bullshit deal, which affirmative action is. All right?

Let's just say what the needs are. We need to create a department that reflects the city. We don't have enough women, we don't have enough Black officers, we don't have enough gays, we don't have any Orthodox Jews. We've got to go out and recruit them. All right. Well, they would, I think, if you went out and said, "It's not about affirmative action. It's about the opposite of that. It's about race and it's about gender. We don't have enough of this race, we don't have enough of this gender. Let's just go get them, swear them in, and put them out there." So we can have some communication and interchange, without this big affirmative action lie, about the fact that, all else being equal in the selection process, that the appointment is going to go to the person in the protected class. That was immediately subject to abuse, and that abuse was blatant hypocrisy, and the officers had to live with that hypocrisy.

Take the promotional thing—there's a guy that's been a supervising detective for eighteen years, here's a female that's been a supervising detective for two years. This guy has worked everywhere, robbery, homicide, all over the place; this girl's worked the blotter desk at Van Nuys for the last eighteen months, and she gets appointed, because, since all things being equal, the appointment goes to the protected class. Well, that was insulting to people. If they had just come out and said, "Look, we don't have enough female detectives even to do our routine sex crime stuff, which they had traditionally always done, or, women have never done auto theft, or never done homicide, or never done robbery, and, so now we're going to have a cadre of females that are on the job right now, and involve them in everything that goes on in the department, so we're going to make some female robbery detectives." I think that would have gone over much better, if they had been more straightforward about it. In looking at it, provided that the people are competent enough to handle the job, let's just find what we need. What does IBM do when they need something? They just go out and find whomever it is that they need, and give them a job. Well, why does it have to be different?

You want to be a cop? Yes. Fine. You know what? We don't have enough Koreans, and we don't have any Korean women. Would you please come and give this a try? We'll help you get the job. I don't think it's avoidable. I don't think affirmative action is merit-based. It's not merit-based, it's based on race and gender, and they ought to just do whatever they need to do, and stop the hypocrisy. I think it would be a calming influence on everybody, and there wouldn't be any need for all those six or seven organizations, vying for predominance, if they just went in and did what needed doing. Just say, "You know what? Our census in the department is way down, we don't have nearly enough Blacks, and we've gone out and tried specifically to recruit them, and we just can't find enough. All right?

But we still need police. Okay, so, until we're able to find enough, we're just going to have to hire a few white guys. Live with it." Come on.

The Career

My career with L.A.P.D. was twenty-one years and seventeen days. But who's counting? There would have to be—in twenty-one years there would have to have been at least twelve transfers—transfers or promotions. I have a very low threshold for boredom, so I always had the understanding that when I got bored or I had worn out my welcome, there was always someplace else to go. So when my feet hit the floor and I said, "You know what, I'd rather be somewhere else," I'd start looking and transfer somewhere else. I'd move to a different environment, a different job, and it was interesting for me—that's probably the only reason I stayed for twenty years is I didn't have to do the same job for twenty years. I always knew that when I really got really stuck, that I could promote.

So, let's see if I can remember them all. There was training division recruit, then I went to West L.A. and I did my probation in West L.A. I transferred to Venice for a very short time. I went to Public Order Intelligence Division for a very short time. When I got out of there, I went back to West L.A. I stayed in West L.A. for about eighteen months. Then I went from West L.A. to Communications (that's six). From Communications I went to Southwest (that's seven). From Southwest I went to Juvenile (eight). From Juvenile I went to Hollywood (that's nine). From Hollywood I went to Wilshire. From Wilshire I went to 77th. From 77th I went back to Hollywood. From Hollywood I went to South Homicide. From South Homicide I came back to Hollywood, and from Hollywood I went to the Field Command Post Unit. From Hollywood I went to the academy, and from the academy I went to the Field Command Post Unit—sixteen transfers in twenty-one years. Some of them were very short-lived because I was there for a short time and promoted. So I would say in general the transfers that meant anything, probably about ten.

In the middle of the Second Police Olympic Race, at the end of the race I was told that I was promoted to sergeant and transferred to Wilshire.

Injuries

I can't say that I was unlucky. I was just kind of a bull in a china shop, stupid a couple of times, and because of that I wound up getting myself hurt. When other guys would have stepped back and taken a second look, I decided on a course of action and carried through. I had tackled a guy, an ADW [assault with a deadly weapon] suspect. I tackled him and chased him in the parking lot of a gas station and I suffered some significant injuries to both arms. That lasted for sixteen years. I had four surgeries and I was in chronic distress for sixteen years. There were certain things that I couldn't do with my left hand and I worked around, found a way to operate, but it was a significant handicap. It was painful. I couldn't manipulate my hand in a certain way without really getting shocked at the level of the pain. They never did quite get it right. The city sent me to doctors of their choice, and then finally I wound up bumping into, by accident, a surgeon from [a major medical clinic that specializes in sports medicine], the one that does the athletes, the PGA tour, he says, "If there's anything I can do for you ever, let me know." I said, "Well, you know what, maybe you could connect me up with your hand guy, because I'm having trouble with my hand, I've been having trouble with it for years. I've been operated on before. It's terrible, it hurts." He says, "Well, I am their hand guy. I'm the number-one hand guy at [the clinic]." So he's sitting in his car poking around on my hand, he said, "I can fix it." So anyway, long story short, they reopened the workers' comp case and sent me down to [the clinic] and they fixed it. So that part of it's done—after sixteen years of unnecessary distress, that part's done.

When I first injured my hand I had been on the job less than a year. I was all torn up, I had scars all over me, I was bleeding, my uniform was torn, and I went up to UCLA, and the emergency room doctor says, "You have some significant trauma here and it's gonna take a very long time for it to heal up and stuff." So I said, "Okay, fine. I can live with it. Bumps and bruises, I've had them before. I'm twenty-four years old; it's nothing." So after about seven or eight months, it seemed like it wasn't getting any better so I went back to UCLA and I said, "Okay, he told me to wait a long time. I think I've waited long enough. I'm in a lot of pain." So they sent it to the city. The city gives me an examination and said, "Well, I don't know what the diagnosis is but it's definitely not duty-related. See you later." So I wound up having to hire a lawyer to get them to acquiesce to the fact that it was related to this tackling thing. They treated me. I had surgery. They fixed my elbow and then they worked on my hand, but they didn't fix it. I went back two or three times. At the end of one of the things they gave me a lifetime medical, which means that in the event that this thing flares up in the future I would be able to get treated, which is all I really wanted in the first place. I had no other agenda than to not have my body hurt.

So I went back a couple of years later in Torrance and said, "Oh God, I'm having so much trouble with it." So I talked to the medical examiner and they denied the claim again and I said, "Well, you know what, I got lifetime medical on this. I just want to go get treated for it." "No, it's denied." I wound up going back to the same workers' comp commissioner that heard the first case and he actually remembered me because he thought I had been subjected to a bit of neglect at the hands of the city. He said, "What're you doing back here?" I said, "Well, I wanted to get some treatment done on my hand and they said 'no.'" He said, "Well, didn't you get lifetime medical?" I said "yes." So he just bangs the gavel and says, "Mr. City Attorney," and the guy stands up and he says, "I gave lifetime medical on this guy back on this claim for x and x months ago." Essentially he said, "If he ever comes back to me again and says that he didn't get what he wants for these injuries, I will wreck you," or words to that effect. So after that I didn't have any trouble. In the wake of that, it's a few years later. I'm just living with it because they've tried so many times to fix it and it's not working. I gave up. Then I bumped into this guy and he was poking around and he says, "Hey, I can fix it." Anyway, I went and he fixed it and, you know, I'm fine with that.

I did have some stress-related illness—gastrointestinal distress, heart palpitations, insomnia, migraines and all of that stuff. I dealt with that. That was more or less the period of my life when I made decisions about my attitude and my conduct. I knew I was going to change in order to help mitigate how bad I was feeling. I didn't want to go down there and say, "Hey, I'm wracked with stress illness." That would have ended my career. I just kept my mouth shut and I wound up being a counselor for stress cases and also teaching a stress management class at the police academy.

Late in my career, about the nineteenth year, I awoke one morning with a paralyzed left leg. The underlying cause was probably the work I was doing, driving big rig trucks for this unit that I was running, and it was aggravated by the wearing of a gunbelt. To this day, I have a tremendous amount of trouble with it. I contacted L.A.P.D. again about trying to get a medical pension because I'm not sure if I could keep my present job because I'm having so much trouble. They said that there was still an open workers' comp case on it so they've been busy trying to diagnose it. I've had MRIs and upper and lower GIs and bone scans and every other possible diagnostic test. Right now I'm waiting for the results of that to find out what's going on because I'm in significant around-the-clock distress. I have to wear a foam rubber pad beneath my gunbelt just to be able to get back and forth from the locker room to the car. It's pretty difficult right now. I'm forty-six, and maybe I shouldn't be pushing a black-and-white [driving a police car] around at my age.

Deadly Force

Officers don't use their guns as often as people think. I know more officers that have gotten shot than have ever shot anyone. Most injuries are not that kind. It's the Flying Wallendas [a spectacular and risky flying leap in an attempt to catch a suspect], it's the auto accidents, getting kicked in the back, being tackled during foot pursuit, tripping over the fireplug.

I've never shot my gun other than for qualification or training. The number of times where I could have justifiably shot somebody and gone to bed with a clear conscience is probably about fifty times over the years. I never did because I never found it necessary. This may go back to that lack of fear thing or that lack of feeling threatened. I never had that fear of my life, him or me, gotta do it or he's gonna do me—never had it. It never occurred. So I think—I would hope—for the people that have actually shot, and they are an incredible minority, a fraction of 1 percent, who have ever fired their guns and even a smaller number who have ever hit anything they were shooting at. I would hope that it would have been a him-or-me scenario. Even if you had someone who works SIS [Special Investigation Section], who has been involved in several legal shootings, the number of lethal encounters that they've had probably outnumber the lethal shootings they've had by at least a hundred to one. Knowing nothing about SIS, I have some friends there, and I know that they have these sensational shootings that hit the paper three or four times a year. For every one of those, they probably make more than one hundred apprehensions without firing a shot, and that's the part that misses the news because it lacks that sensationalism that people thrive on, but that is a fact of life. It's the duty they've drawn—they are tailing identified armed and dangerous felons every place they go. The fact that they can get them in custody without blasting first is an act of God.

Growth of the Department—Growing Pains

The biggest complaint right now, because the department is growing at such a rapid rate, is they've got guys with eighteen months experience thrown in with recruits. We're talking about recruits out of the academy, being thrown in the cars with nobody else to train them other than these eighteen-month wonders. They have so many new people on and so few officers that have experience to train them that they're just taking essentially children and throwing them in the cars together. You just go out and hope they get it right and they're operating on the abject hope that things will go okay because the officers have so little training across the board right now. What traditionally happens is—you get out of the academy and you work with somebody for three or four years and you go up somewhere else. You work Detectives, or you get promoted. You get an administrative job. You get a back room job.

The guys that are actually doing the work on the streets are the hard-core lifer street cops or the youngsters that are coming on that haven't been able to graduate to something else to get away from it. Working patrol, it's not really something people want to spend their whole life doing, for the most part. You either have the oldest, most hard-core guys there—a cadre of maybe 10 percent of a watch would be the guys that love working the streets, been doing it for fifteen or eighteen years—or officers with fewer than five years on whose options are limited or who have never promoted or haven't been able to find that back room job. So you've got a bunch of just really baby-faced youngsters out there running around just trying to get it right. It's not the best scenario—it's just demographics because the department is growing so fast.

I don't know, when you interviewed me back in 1980 or something, I said probably one of the biggest disgraces was the fact the department was so small and continued to shrink in the face of a rising population. I said one day in a political panic, they're gonna start hiring people by the busload to try to fix it, all in a two-year period. I said that then and now they've done it and they're payin' the price for it now. When you push it through, it's just like a wartime draft. They could have been hiring all along, quality officers, good people, people who respected the job and were willing to put it on the line because it is a job that needed doing and they were willing to do it the way it should be done. Ideally, if they could do it like they wanted, they'd be hiring fewer people at a slower rate with better background investigations and more training.

Now all they want to do is fill the spots, and it's all political. For the past thirty years the department's been significantly undermanned by thousands. Now we're going to fix it. Now, after thirty years of neglect, we're gonna make it right. We don't have room to put 'em. The station's not big enough; the locker rooms aren't big enough; we don't have enough cars; we don't have enough secretarial support; the jails aren't big enough; we don't have enough pencils, or forms or any of that. But we're gonna fix it. That's what they've done. They've gone into a fire sale of hiring—and they've taken the detectives' cars and painted them to look like black-and-whites to give people the illusion that there are more officers on the street than there actually are.

Now, the insult of insults—response time is a big deal if you're a police manager. From the time the call gets out until the time an officer gets there, for some reason in police managerial circles, it's a big deal. So the lower that number is—like the average response time is seven minutes or six minutes—it just seems to be a big police managerial thing. So in order to make that response time calls for service number lower, they're still giving the officers calls five and six at a time, but their instructions are to go to the place, leave them a business card saying, "Hi, my name is Officer so-and-so. I know you called about your burglary report. I'm here. Stop the clock. I'll be back." Go to the next one, leave a business card—go to the next one, leave a business card.

They've created the perception that the service is better, but they have literally made the service worse by making an extra trip out there, and it slows things down. These are people with a master's degree in public administration who sat there and thought this up, and it is—*it's offen-*

sive, it's filthy—and it's just to create the perception things are better. If you're this person who had their car stolen, the officer comes by at 2:30 in the afternoon, drops a business card, comes back at 9:00 that night and says, "Okay, I'm back to do this," you're not doing anybody any favors by living that lie. So there are some things being done to make it look better than it is instead of dealing with reality. The way things actually are— they create a false level of security, or false level of service, and it's offensive to me. It's asinine.

Response time is just something that they can measure. It serves no purpose. The primary thing that they should be concerned with as far as an officer's performance, or as far as performance of the police department in general, is the absence of turmoil. That's page 1 of Criminal Justice 101. Your goal as a law officer is the absence of public turmoil. If you're not doing—if you're doing anything that takes away from that goal, if you're wasting time with any administrative program or any function that takes away from reducing public turmoil—you're not doing your job. I don't care if you're the chief of police or some kid that just graduated from the academy. Your job is to maintain the peace, keep order, create or maintain the absence of public turmoil. All these little side trips, painting the cars, dropping business cards off and this other eyewash crap that they do, wastes time and energy.

His Children and the Job

[This is in response to my query as to how he would feel if his sons decided to be police officers.] That's an interesting question. Mark never would, so I wouldn't concern myself with it, but Luke may one day, and it's hard for me to answer because there's a generational evolution, and I wouldn't in one sense want him to go to it because it's not the L.A.P.D. that I knew, but the L.A.P.D. that I knew is something that's completely out of his frame of reference, and what he walks into in this generation is probably something that he would be comfortable with. For my own purpose and for my own sense of security as a parent, I wouldn't want him to do it because of the level of violence, and I know that he's just a good-hearted guy that wouldn't want to hurt a fly. Everything that would go on would be a curiosity. He's fascinated by police. He watches all the cop programs. He asks me questions about it. Because I know that he doesn't have a violent bone in his body—I would be afraid for him to be out in it. I'm a decent guy too but I have the absolute inherent ability to become lethal at the drop of a hat, and have no reservation whatsoever. I could be the most cold-blooded lethal person on the face of this earth if the circumstances warranted it. I can say that without any reservation right now. I could kill somebody right now if they needed killing without a whisper of reservation. I don't believe that Luke could do that. I don't want him to grow into a person who could do that because he is such a decent, kind-hearted, well-mannered kid.

Guns, Killing and John Wayne

All of my adult life, I've been a policeman or a soldier, and I've been one right from high school through Vietnam and right from Vietnam into police work. There are just things that appear to be necessary at any given time. I never killed anybody when I was in Vietnam. I never fired my gun with L.A.P.D. But I can tell you right now without any reservation that if I were confronted and had to that, I could do it without batting an eye. It's kinda strange when you tell people that after a twenty-year police career, I was never scared. I was never scared in Vietnam—not once. No. Flying over hostile territory, feathering engines, battery explosions, breaking, running out of gas—never scared one time. Crash-landings, mortar barrages, that stuff, nothing actually scared me. It was exhilarating, it was exciting. Of course I was eighteen at that time. Then in the course of my police career—I never hit anybody because I wanted to. I never wrestled with anybody because I felt like I needed to get in there and mix it up. I never shot anybody. I never shot *at* anybody—but I am a distinguished expert shooter. I have been for years and years.

I did a shooting scenario yesterday in my present employment. I went through thirteen scenarios. I had two misses and about fifty-five or sixty lethal hits out of the scenarios that were going on on this movie screen. So my ability to do it, I have no reservations about, technically being able to hit what I shoot at, being calm in the process, and being comfortable with the fact that it was made necessary by whatever this other person was doing. It would *never* be made necessary by something that I did.

If I did something careless or reckless that precipitated a shooting that I could have avoided—if I did something tactically stupid, that would probably bother me. If I have gotten to the point where this person is dictating the circumstances and because of their inappropriate behavior they have to be killed, well tough shit. They made that choice when they chose to do what they're doing.

When I said it was educational for me and all of that stuff, in Vietnam and being a policeman and all that, I would like my son to be able to live peacefully. He loves animals. I'd love to see him be a veterinarian. If the kids didn't go into police work, it would just thrill me to death. If they did, I would support them, but personally, to me, my kids are much more valuable as a social commodity, and as my sons: something that I cherish—my sons. They are much more valuable than anything that they would die for out on the street.

It's kind of funny. I was watching a movie—I've seen it a couple of times, I don't remember the name of it. It's a cowboy movie. John Wayne is talking about the difference between somebody who's a good shot and somebody who's a good gunslinger, the good gunslinger is the one who is willing to stand there and take the risk while he unloads the lethal shot. Somebody that can stand there and be a good target shooter all day long might not have the willingness to stand there flat-footed and trade shots with somebody. I don't want my boys to have to deal with that. I could do it. I could stand right now in the middle of a gunfight without ducking and it's probably stupid and reckless, but that's just the way I am. I just don't have that fear. I don't want my sons to be in a situation where they even have to make that choice. I would like them to be peaceful, educated, productive gentlemen. That's all I'm after.

Family Dynamics

I have an understanding with Lannie—she's older than I am by a year and a half. She was raised in a traditional family in Pennsylvania. Her father died when she was very young, four years old. There was a lot of love and effort in her family, but it was very fragmented because her mom worked in Ohio at the telephone company and she could only come back to see Lannie and her brother on the weekends. Lannie grew up in the basement of a partially completed house because her father died during the construction of the house, the only bathtub that she knew for a period of time was the washtub in the basement. She had a very difficult upbringing, but her family, she and her mother, are very, very close. So her devotion to the family and the well-being of everybody is right up front. She fusses over all of the details of that family life that she missed when she was growing up. She is fiercely devoted to me and to the boys. She does work mornings, four mornings a week, half-days, around kids, doing a computer lab at the school.

I think we were drawn [to each other] because I was raised in a typical fifties family. I had two brothers, grew up in Maryland. Mom was there, Dad was there from the time we were growing up. It wasn't exactly Ward and June Cleaver, but it was a close approximation of whatever was going on for the Boomers back in those days. That's how I believe that families ought to be raised.

Lannie came up to me after we were married for about a year with this glowing look on her face and she says, "It's time for me to have a child." "What the hell does that mean?" "My body is telling me it's time to have a child. Sit down and we'll talk about this." I said, "Okay, I love you and I would love to have kids"—probably four was my estimation. I said, "I'll be happy to [raise a family] with the understanding that you're home for them until they're in school. Then if you want to have free time, or if you want to work, then it's done between the hours when they're away at school. You're here when they're here, when they get up in the morning and when they get home from school." I said, "I'm a cop. My watch changes. My hours change. My divisions change, and I cannot guarantee you that I'm going to be there. So you have to be—this is the way it's gotta be. As far as our family is concerned, if we're going to raise them, the kids have to be raised with parental attention," because I see in the midst of my work all the degradation and all the crap that goes on, and it is absolutely rooted in the erosion of the family.

I don't have to have a Ph.D. or any of that crap to tell you that. I'm telling you from practical experience, the erosion of the nuclear family is what's causing all this turmoil in this country in general and worldwide too. In America in particular, it's the drive for commerce that never stops. Material goods. More stuff. If you go elsewhere, other parts of the world, commerce has its place and when you're not at work, you're home with your family. The phone isn't ringing off the wall and you don't have Internet coming through the computer all the time, and a pager and all of that stuff. You go to work, and when work's over, you come home and it's home time.

We had this discussion, and she agreed that that was the right thing to do and that that's the way she was going to live her life. We sat down and we talked it out. So when Mark was born, she came up to me about twelve to fourteen months later, "It's time for me to have another child." Okay, fine. Bliss. Boy, when women want to get pregnant, your life is good. So then after Luke was born, I wanted to have another one. She said, "Well, you know, you need to think about this, because every child from conception to first grade takes a seven-year chunk out of my life." I didn't think about it in those terms, but obviously she had. So that would mean that by the time another one was born, it would be too many years before she could actually go out and get a job. She said she didn't want to do that: "Two's enough and when the boys are in school, I'm ready. That kind of parenting time is over." She felt she was going to be ready to go on and do something for herself in the way of work, so she wasn't so completely tied to the house. That's how that evolved.

The only reason I have educated, articulate gentlemen living in my house is by the influence of their mother, because I was gone working all over the place all of the time, around the clock. All kinds of assignments, and I was always able to come home to a stable household. She always got up when I was working Homicide and the phone went off in the middle of the night and she got up while I got a shower, and she cooked for me so I would have something to eat before I left. She was there with the anesthetic when I got back after I'd been gone for three days. She'd be there with a cocktail. I'd drink a cocktail, I'd hit the rack, and she'd leave me alone for the next day and a half until I was slept out and had to go back.

When I needed to go back, she had all the clothes laid out for me, ironed, ready to go. She was all through my life, and is now, the only thing that allowed me to function at the level that I'm able to function. *She is the greatest.* The great love of all time. I'm here to tell you I could have accomplished nothing without her support over the years. So that's how it was done—it was done that way because it's the right thing and it's the way we wanted to live our lives.

The turmoil that I see now is tied to the transitory nature of people's commitments to one another, and the fact that what they want is more important than the welfare of the kids. It's "you know what, I don't like you, I'm out of here. Well what about the kids? Well, fine, I'll take them on the weekends. See ya." That's the single biggest problem that we have in the United States today is that lack of commitment between people.

The Influence of Women: Women's Roles

I might be talking out of school on this, but I'm forty-six years old and I've seen and done enough that my opinions deserve to be heard, and I really don't care who likes it. So if there is a social problem right now in the United States or in the world in general, it's a lack of good "womaning" skill. It's lack of good "wifery" and lack of good motherhood, because the only thing that civilizes society in general is women. Women civilize men. Women civilize life in general. Women civilize children. If you don't believe it, what would the world be like with its all-out violent competition between men, between tribes, between neighborhoods, between companies? What would it be like without the civilizing influence of women? If you try to imagine what a world without women would be like, the turmoil, the inherent violence that men have, the twenty-four-hour sex drive that men have, the competitive attitude that men have. God has a plan that men go out and kill the meat and the women prepare the meat and raise the kids. That's part of the way it is. I'm not saying that it's wrong for women to go out and have careers. But if you're gonna have a career, then have a career. If you're gonna have a family, then have a family. If you try to mix the career and the family to such a degree that more energy is put into the career than the family, you will pay a price—you will wind up with maladjusted kids, you will wind up divorced. You will be part of the problem rather than part of the solution, and there is nothing of greater value in a society anyplace in the world than when the woman is doing her evolutionary job.

There are times you say, well, God, I don't like it. I don't like being a wife. I don't like being a mother. I don't like being the man's helpmate or any of that stuff. Well, I'll tell you what, there are many times in my life when I am sick to death of having to be the one that has to stand up under it all, that has to be the one that has to go out and stay at the job and bring home the money and protect the family, and do all that. That stuff wears [me] out. I believe that men have a role, and I believe that women have a role. My role—I'm tired of my role. I would love, love to stop—and I would love to work around the house. I would love being around my boys all day. I'd love those things, I'd love to have a garden, I'd love to landscape, I'd love to read. But I can't stop. If I stopped for thirty days, everything I've worked for my entire adult life is in jeopardy and in sixty days it would go completely under. So since I've been eighteen, I've been on the wheel running for the cheese, and if I stop, then somebody else who wants the cheese more than I do will run over my back and take the cheese, and I am stuck. My role is to keep that from happening.

I don't like being a man all the time. I don't like being a hard ass all the time. I don't like being a disciplinarian all the time. I don't like having to fix all the shit that needs fixing. I don't like the competition that has to go on all the time. I don't like not being able to relax for a period of time for fear of what would happen because of my lack of attention. If you're a woman and you're on the other side of that, and you get tired of being a wife, get tired of being a mom, and you don't like to have to cook, and you don't like to have to clean and do the laundry and all that stuff, it's a role that needs playing whether or not you like it. When you try to reverse the role or try to abdicate the role, or try to adulterate it in some way, it weakens, and when that weakness gets into your family environment, it degenerates. That's just something that I personally believe that you can't do. If Lannie had said to me, "I want to be a career woman," and I said, "Fine, if you and I will be a career couple together. I'll have mine, you'll have yours, and we'll meet in the middle. We'll accomplish these things, but we can't have children under these circumstances," she would likely have agreed.

Career Choices and the Nuclear Family

I know that the world needs more ladies and gentlemen and it needs more nuclear families. If you look around you see so much turmoil and so much of that is traced to the lie that you're not a complete woman unless you've had a career and babies and a marriage and . . . God knows what. . . . The rearing of children into ladies and gentlemen is the most denigrated skill right now, and it's the thing that's most important. When you hear that it's more important for women to have a career or it's less important or less fulfilling, or less necessary, for women to be good wives and mothers, and that the "wifing" and mothering is subordinate to a career—that is all being driven by commerce. People who are selling things, people who are selling dresses and office furniture and—for the selling of the image and the making of a buck, and they don't really give a dead rat's ass about whether children grow up as ladies and gentlemen or whether Mommy's home or Daddy's home when they get home from school. They really don't care.

The nuclear family is the essence of a stable society, if you wonder, gee, why has it gotten so bad in the last twenty-five years—because the nuclear family has eroded over the last twenty-five years. We're now paying the price, because we have a bunch of young adults that have been passed back and forth from one home to another and half the people that get married get divorced, and it just seems to be okay to do, and it's not. I wish everyone a powerful and fulfilling love like the one I have had with my wife and a success like I have had with my family, but I cannot take any credit for my situation—it is all owing to the devotion of Lannie.

Female Officers, Violence and the Early Days of Fred's Career

I was one of the ones that didn't want to see it—women on patrol, and I'm still not really comfortable with it because I'm just a traditional guy, if that last little interlude didn't really bring that out—but the fact is that back when this was evolving early on, we thought there was gonna be all kinds of violence, the women were gonna get their ass kicked. There was gonna be this and that. *None* of that stuff occurred. The society evolved along with the police department, and women seem to be functioning quite well. They seem to be much more of an asset than a liability. Police work in general used to be much more violent.

When I was early on with L.A.P.D., two guys in a car from L.A.P.D. could get out of a car on a street corner and thirty people would get up against the wall and put their hands on the wall and stand there in silence out of fear of what would occur if they didn't. That part of it has gone away. I don't know now if, you know, if two officers came up in a car right now and told thirty people to get up against the wall, they would probably be laughed at, but that's literally the way it was.

When I was twenty-four years old, and out of the academy, I'd go to a situation and my training officer would say, "There's a big dispute going on and I'm trying to communicate with them and they're not listening." He looks at me and says, "Take that guy over there. Pick the biggest one. Take that guy over there and choke him out." You'd just walk over there and put a bar on the guy and choke him out [put a choke hold on him]. Then when he's laying on the ground unconscious and I roll him over and handcuff him, all the other people on the street would all of a sudden just stop and start behaving and start listening and that's the way it was done back in those days. This was 1975–76. The first instruction that I got out of the academy from my training officer, "If we get in a pursuit, the guy we're chasing gets choked down. If you don't choke him, I'm choking you."

That's the way it was. If you've got a pursuit, get the driver, pull him out of the car, choke him out, cuff him up. That's the way it was done.

It was probably right at the time because of the interaction that we had with the Black Panthers and all that stuff. I mean people needed to be essentially afraid of police, because there were very few of us, number one. We were horribly outnumbered, so if we didn't act like a busload when we got there, we were in trouble. That was back when we had, like, 6,500 police in Los Angeles. You had to be a bad son of a bitch in order to keep order in some places in the city. People had to essentially be afraid of you—because there were so few of us. The only reason that order was kept was because people were essentially afraid of what you would do if they didn't do as indicated.

Now that females are on the job, and now that the job has evolved to where there are more officers and it's a little calmer, the war is over. You don't have as many veterans as you did. Things are a little bit easier-going, a little bit less confrontational. When you have somebody's sister or mother in the car with you, getting out there and doing that macho man thing is just not the thing to do, because you're eventually responsible for what you start. What you start, you have to finish. So if you're a combat veteran and the guy next to you is a Marine, and he's a combat veteran, well you know what the hell's going on and if you go start something, you know you're gonna finish. Well, if that's not an equation anymore, then you have to figure out another way to go around.

So when I talk about women generally civilizing things, women have civilized police work in Los Angeles to a great degree over the years, and I can't say that it was unwarranted. It was probably something that needed to happen. Along with the women being hired on, there are just more people now, and so you're less pressured. It's like two officers don't have to act like ten now, two officers can be three or four, and it's much easier and it's just much calmer than it used to be.

The Thin Blue Line

The things that I'm talking about were things that you needed to do when you had to maintain control or order. Because if people in general knew what a thin line there was with the 1965 L.A. riots, and what a thin line there was when that happened again, how unable we were to maintain order with the few numbers that we had, they wouldn't believe it. They wouldn't be able to sleep nights. It's not like we would walk up to a bunch of people and just start slapping them around. We would come up to a corner of people where there was some kind of a problem and we were outnumbered by thirty to two with no expectation that anybody was going to be there to back us up, and there was a lot of bluffing going on back in those days. There's something going on, there's been a shooting, there's been a cutting, or there's something going on, three or four out of these thirty people are involved, and we've gotta find out which three or four it is without being hurt, and we'd get out of the car and say "Everybody up against the wall"—yeah, we really did say that—and nobody argued. They got up against the wall—and nobody would talk to us—we got them up against the wall and we would search everybody and interview and do whatever we had to do, and we would get it figured out. I'm not saying we went around roughshod slapping people around. We didn't. We exercised the proper amount of force necessary to control the situation. It was different in those days than it is today. That's just a fact of life. I lived it. It was much more reckless, much more dangerous in those days, and that's owing to the neglect of the city fathers, perhaps a department that was three thousand officers too small. We wound up with that responsibility on our back, to maintain order without getting indicted or killed. The things that were done were necessary; they're just *not* necessary today based upon the size of the police department. We don't have to be ten guys when we get out of the car.

Of course there wasn't the gang problem then that there is now. Back then, it was the Crips and the Bloods, and now there are so many street gangs and so many competing street gangs that it's much more dangerous now than it was back in those days. So the things that you would do back in those days, where you would see a bunch of people standing around the corner and know that three or four of those people are packing, a couple of those people are probably on parole, and a couple of those people are probably holding dope, and the car that's parked around the corner is probably stolen, and you will just jump out and go mix it up with those people. You just don't do that anymore because of the fact that there is so much weaponry out there and so many street gangs out there, it's just not the thing to do.

There are a lot of things that I see now, lots of things that I've seen over the past few years, I'd look at well, gee, if this were 1976, I'd be right in the middle of that. There are a lot of things that you just let go. If you can get around the corner and get on the radio and talk to a couple of guys and say, "Look, we've got this and that. [Now Fred uses gestures to indicate the deployment of back-up units to ensure that escape routes are covered and that back-up is provided for the officers initiating contact with the suspects.] I want to take two of you guys, come over here, and two of you guys come over here, and I'm gonna go over there and do this. If it degenerates, we'll at least have enough people to cope with it." Back in the early, early days, you would just kinda jump in the middle of it and do it. So it was more dangerous back then because if the people knew how few of us there were, or how much power that they would have over us, that group of thirty people lining that wall could tell us to go piss up a rope. It was incredibly dangerous what we were doing, but it was the only game

in town. That was all there was, and the communications were considerably less sophisticated.

Women on the Force Revisited

When I say that women civilize things in general and now that
women are involved in police work, it's just much more civilized. It's less
confrontational, it's less macho, less manly. Since women are half the population, it's probably not a bad thing.

But there was a lot of resistance to it coming out of the department.
I graduated from the academy and was out of the academy about six
months and was part of a pilot program. They brought recent graduates
back to the academy to perform acts of physical agility and daring to
establish a baseline and show the police commission that women couldn't
do the job. I was part of that. Go back in there and take that thing and
drag it over here, climb that hill, lift this and that, drag this dummy.
These are basic aspects of the job. You're doing them at this rate; women
can't do them. Therefore, women are not suitable to do this—that was
what they were trying to prove.

The mayor, Bradley, and the city council and the chief of police and
the city attorney, et al., were fighting the Blanchon Blake lawsuit by
establishing a set of standards to show that women were not physically
able to do the job. I was part of it. I lived it. They brought me back out of
the field to help establish those standards. The sole purpose of that was
to prove that women could not do the job. They lost the lawsuit and then
overnight they said, "Okay, women can do the stuff and we gotta have
them." Then they said, "Well no we really don't need these standards,
officers can perform at a lower rate." In my mind, well, which was it? That
transition was kinda difficult for me. When women actually came on the
job, I was part of proving you couldn't be here, and here you are, and I was
real bothered by that for a period.

I'm still a little bit uncomfortable with it, but all of the predicted
things that were gonna happen, the bad things that were gonna happen—there's gonna be more fights, women will get their ass kicked, and
all this—none of that stuff happened. Is it a fact that less confrontational
police work is being done? Yeah, definitely so. It's also true that some
things that need immediate attention out there just aren't getting immediate attention anymore.

There are things out there that in the old days it would be done, but
then if you talk to people that were on the job back in the 1950s and talk
about me in the 1970s, they say, "Back in the '50s we wouldn't have done
this, we would have done that." My time has passed. My era has passed.
We're in a new era now. I'm a dinosaur as far as law enforcement is concerned. I understand that. I don't expect people to behave now the way I

did back then. I don't resent the fact that it's different now than it was because it was different for the other generation when [they] came on. It was different in the '20s, it was different in the '40s, it was different in the '60s—this is just social evolution marching to wherever the hell it's going. Anybody that resists it or resents it—well, there's no way to stop it.

10
Making a Difference

All jobs have a formative effect on the lives of the people performing them, but the job of policing appears to have an extraordinary influence. Officers are transformed into a series of very different people with distinctive concerns and issues as they pass through the phases of the job. As occupational socialization goes, the experience of the police career is intense, all pervasive, and constantly reinforced. Part of this is due to the effects of isolation—self-imposed and otherwise, but it is likewise influenced by the job itself and the public nature of the job. Dealing with life-and-death issues and situations profoundly intensifies the process. The necessity for making decisions that may have dire consequences for other people's lives is a truly awesome responsibility. Clearly police officers are not alone in this, but just as physicians and firefighters, police are subject to the necessity of making split-second decisions, often under adverse conditions. The personal transformations of officers as they pass through the phases of their careers result in people who experience and define the world in a very different way than most of us.

One aspect of the job that profoundly distinguishes it from other occupations is danger. Police officers are continually reminded in numerous ways that their job is dangerous, that they must pay attention, and that they must do the job *the* right way. As we have seen, there are a number of right ways, which the officer learns through both formal and informal socialization.

In formal training conducted by the department, officers learn a legal, a procedural, a political, and a safe "right" way. From their colleagues they learn variations of all these—adapted to the practical demands of the street. Police view the priorities of the department as being shaped by a legal, economic, and political agenda. In the informal training conducted by their colleagues, however, they believe the emphasis is on the officer's well-being. Police rely on each other for help, support, understanding and protection from the dangers inherent in the job. Veteran officers view the job pragmatically: "You do what you do to get you home after watch. That's the way you do police work. By the book, by guess, and by God whatever it takes. That's what you do." Among themselves, officers recite the unofficial police maxim: "A good policeman never

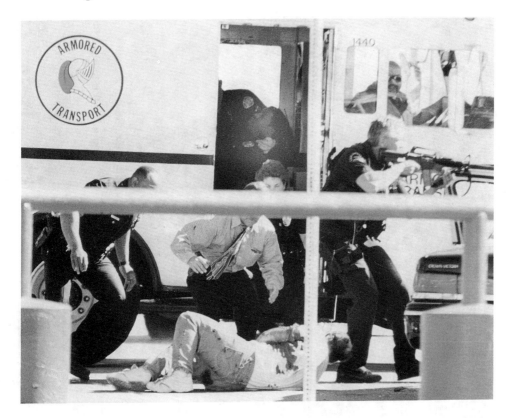

goes hungry, never gets wet, always goes home." The significant element is going home. The job is, after all, only a job—there is supposed to be more to life than the job. The key is to perform the job well *and* go home.

The perceptions of danger involved with the job pose challenges to this objective of going home. For officers, perceptions of danger, feelings of solidarity and issues of morale are intermixed. Understanding this relationship is helpful in any attempt to understand the relationship of officers to the department.

The importance of police solidarity, camaraderie, and clannishness permeate all phases of the career. These work in combination to create strong bonds between officers; solidarity has to do with structural and emotional interconnectedness, camaraderie refers to feelings of friendship and esprit de corps, while clannishness refers to the kind of defensive and exclusive feelings shared by police. Ultimately, officers turn to other officers because of their shared perceptions of the world. To the degree that these perceptions have become more diversified, solidarity is reduced. As a result, in the view of traditional officers, the dangers of the job have increased markedly. Policing has always been known to be dangerous, but

officers learned to deal with danger together, as they passed through the phases of their career.

The introduction to the job of policing emphasized its physical dangers and, during the first two phases, officers worked at striking a balance between learning to do the job in a stand-up fashion and trying to avoid getting hurt in the process. In the third phase, officers generally are hurt. Residual physical injuries acquired during their early years on the job, combined with the psychological hurts of disillusionment with both the department and the criminal justice system, are elements in hitting the wall. Still, the camaraderie between fellow officers remains a source of succor for them, particularly for those estranged from their families and non-police friends. Traditionally, during the third and fourth phases, they figure out how to come to terms with their discomfort with the department; they regroup and renew social contacts both inside and outside the job. They find a way to finish their twenty-year career. They relax. They mellow.

Trust in their fellow officers is essential. This trust makes it possible for them to continue their careers, even when they know they are not as physically capable of dealing with some of the emergencies encountered on the job. In the past, officers in this phase of their careers were not overly concerned, because they felt they could rely on the younger officers. In the past, traditional police believed their partners perceived the world the same way they did, were motivated by the same ideals and concerns, and would respond as they did. In a dangerous job and a dangerous world, police surrounded themselves with colleagues who had proven themselves. This greatly reduced the dangers of the job.

With the influx of new police, this is less the case. Now, in the eyes of traditional police, the job has become more unpredictable and much more dangerous. They distrust the department, and their faith in their fellow officers is greatly eroded. Phase five—staying on the job beyond the mandatory twenty years—is less likely to be considered a viable option. The camaraderie nurtured from the earliest phases continues among age mates—whether traditional or new police—but no longer permeates the entire department. Both groups have observed and noted a significant difference in the degrees of solidarity between and within the two groups.

The amount of time officers choose to spend in each other's company is considered to be a measure of solidarity, camaraderie and clannishness. New police socialize much less with other officers off the job. One new officer commented:

> I can count on one hand the number of times after work I've gone out with the people I work with. I never had the desire to meet, or just hang around and meet with them. Basically I've been with them for eight hours already so there's no sense in hanging around with them any longer. I'm ready to go home and just relax and do the things I've always enjoyed doing, even before I was on the job. Why would I want to spend more time with them?

As more traditional officers leave the job, the core off-duty socializing group shrinks, reducing opportunities for off-duty gatherings and the boost to police bonding they provide. On and off duty, new police officers lose access to all those years of expertise and experience—this makes the job more dangerous for them. They also face the additional danger of performing the job without the safety net of peer support and solidarity.

One new African-American officer reflects on an incident that illustrates the current lack of camaraderie:

> Now there is something missing. A lack of camaraderie in the new recruits, maybe that's because they come from so many different walks of life. An officer was in charge of raising the flag, and for some reason he ran to answer the phone, and some of the other officers took exception to this and said, "Hey, you know man, you could have let someone else get the phone, you don't let the flag touch the ground, you should have finished raising the flag," and his response was, "Hey man, it

isn't my country." Well, what more can I say about that? Things like
that say you're not really one of us. The camaraderie seems to be gone.
I just don't see it like I used to. Now it's a group of individuals. I'm
worried that our department might be coming to be based on a group
of individuals rather than officers working toward a common goal.

Because there is less solidarity and camaraderie new officers tend to
function more as individuals and they are less likely to be sustained by
their fellow officers. Because they function more as individuals rather
than a unit, sentiments of solidarity and camaraderie are not nurtured. It
appears to be a self-perpetuating system which does not bode well for
future bonding, and it has a profound effect on the morale of the department.

Currently, officers are baffled and disheartened by the continued
and accelerating fragmentation of the workgroup. Traditional officers
and new police who have been on for ten years or so, for whom this represents a radical reversal of the prior norms of camaraderie, are particularly distressed. There has been a marked increase in the proliferation of
groups for whom identity as police officers is at the least tempered, and
often overshadowed, by their membership in groups identified by sexual
orientation, race, ethnicity or sex. This is underscored by a proliferation
of complaints filed with management, not by citizens against officers, but
by officers against their colleagues. In police circles this is almost
unheard of, and in the L.A.P.D. it is a major factor in the breakdown of solidarity. Usually such issues, whether real or imagined, have been handled
by the people involved—sometimes addressed directly and resolved,
sometimes simply ignored. Currently, our society is far more confrontational than in the past, and this trend extends to the L.A.P.D. rank and
file. Undoubtedly some of these complaints are justified, but some are not
and the resulting loss of cohesion in the working watch is potentially
disastrous. Supervisors are now spending so much time following up on
the internal complaints—officer vs. officer—they do not have time to hit
the streets and supervise the policing activities. Many officers refer to this
as the thing they like least about going to work these days.

Perhaps one of the most significant issues to arise during the course
of this study has been the steady erosion of morale largely exacerbated by
the infamous and often-repeated image of the Rodney King beating. Officers were stunned, shocked and shamed. The vast majority were truly
incredulous. Officers who had performed their jobs honorably for decades
felt compromised and discredited. Officers with little time on questioned
their career choice. They felt disappointment and anger that, once again,
all officers were tainted by the actions of a few. They were surprised by
the willingness of citizens to assume that the actions viewed on the tape
were representative of most officers. They were depressed and demoral-
ized. One new, African-American officer commented:

After Rodney King a whole lot of people pulled back. Didn't make stops. Would not make a traffic stop. A call was different, but not traffic stops. Didn't follow up the kinds of things you would normally move on. I think part of it was fear of lawsuits, the other part was frustration, "Well if I'm not going to be backed, I'm not going to do it. They're going to pay me the same amount of money so why should I stick my neck out. If they want officers to be proactive then you back us, otherwise just drive down the street and wave and let the bad guys get away." Some people felt that way. For the city, I think, as far as the use of force, and being proactive, it's going to go down. It's like a roller coaster ride. Another ten years from now it will be totally different, another fifteen years and it will be totally different again. Generally it's what society thinks we should be doing.

The combination of the Rodney King beating, the trials of the officers involved, the subsequent riot/rebellion, the appointing of a new police chief—an African American—from outside the department, and the O.J. Simpson trial had two major consequences for police officers: (1) morale was demolished, and (2) the department became polarized and fragmented. Indeed, this process was not unique to the police department—the entire city suffered similarly.

Race became an issue as it had never been before the events involving King and Simpson. These incidents did not create race as an issue, but they did bring it to the foreground. Police solidarity became a casualty of these events and gave way to a fragmenting of the force. In the past police solidarity had prevailed to bond officers, cutting across all other subgroups—including those whose members were linked by race.

On the issues of race, sex and gender another male African-American officer had these observations:

I don't think most officers have a problem with race, at least they wouldn't consider it a problem, but probably a good 30 to 40 percent of officers may look at your color first and make assumptions about the part of town you live in and such. As a matter of fact, the percentage is probably higher among Black officers in forming opinions about White officers and other minorities. It goes both ways. But I think my life on the department would have been more different if I had come on the department as a female rather than a male. More of a difference than coming on White instead of Black. If I'm a female, and I'm out there, there's a chance that I might get into a physical altercation and my chances of losing are greater. Females are better at talking things out and not getting into trouble in the first place, but I think of myself as a reasonable officer and I can usually talk things out and not get into trouble so I don't factor that in. The only factor is that physically I couldn't get out, get safe, so I guess I would need to promote to get out of the field, or just go to a position that doesn't involve the field. The men do tend to stay in the field longer than the female officers.

In the past what was often viewed as the difference between a policing style which emphasized negotiation and a more aggressive style are now categorized as female and male styles of policing. Of course, this generalization is far too simplistic—officers now, as in the past, develop a style that works for them. As we have seen, the phases of the job also affect, to some extent, the styles of policing. Clearly race, ethnicity, and issues surrounding sex and gender have become more prominent as considerations than they once were, not just because there is more diversity in the department, but also because they reflect societal concerns and issues as well.

Recent legal rulings illustrate challenges that the L.A.P.D. currently faces. A federal judge ruled against the L.A.P.D. in a reverse discrimination case. The plaintiff in the case, a white male, claimed that he had been discriminated against when a promotion was given to an African-American officer who was less qualified for the job. This ruling has opened the door to a class action suit filed on behalf of other majority officers who feel similarly discriminated against. At the same time the department has

been trying to negotiate a settlement with minority officers who claim that women and minorities are still victims of discrimination in promotional policies. The net result is that now the L.A.P.D. finds itself in the position of attempting to reconcile diametrically opposed court-mandated judgments: one dealing with reverse discrimination and the other dealing with discrimination against women and minorities. In a classic understatement, one City Hall insider was quoted as saying, "The L.A.P.D. is in a pickle. It can't please anyone these days." Not only is the department unable to please outsiders, it also appears unable to please its own members. This is reflected in its inability to create and maintain solidarity among its ranks.

Differences between experiences of new and traditional police serve to emphasize generational differences in some cases. While it is true that the new police have had less input from the veteran officers, new and traditional police have worked together long enough to value each other. In some cases this means that both groups have had to confront and overcome their own biases. In the case of traditional officers this often means if not embracing then at least valuing the insights and perceptions of the communities brought in by new police, and for new officers to be able to value the assessments and input from experienced veterans. Not all veterans are know-it-all-dinosaurs and not all new police are know-nothing-dilettantes. It all comes down to doing the job well. Officers who cannot perform well are not respected; officers who can, are.

New and traditional officers of varied sex, race, ethnicity, and socioeconomic backgrounds bring different strengths to the job. It is beneficial for officers to have more ties to the citizens they police. It is beneficial for officers to be less insulated in their attitudes and their contacts. It may well prove to usher in a new era of policing for the L.A.P.D. that does not live up to the dire predictions of some of the officers who cannot conceive of the department as being able to do the job in any way other than the way they were taught.

Very recently police morale has improved slightly, largely due to two factors. First, a dramatic shoot-out in which two would-be bank robbers in full body armor, with automatic weapons, randomly sprayed the area with machine gun fire, effectively terrorizing a whole neighborhood. Against markedly superior weaponry, and with weapons ineffective against the body armor, the police prevailed. Because the shoot-out was televised live, citizens became swept up in the real event and started rooting for the underdog, the L.A.P.D., long before the outcome was certain. One officer stated, "It's nice to be seen as the good guys again. To feel like they're rooting for us." Another commented, "It's just the upswing—today we are heroes, tomorrow who knows. But it's fine with me. It feels real good. Yeah, this feels real good." The other factor, which had much farther reaching and significant consequences involved the appointment of a new police chief—again an African American. However, this time he was an officer who was promoted from within the ranks of the L.A.P.D., which made all the difference in the world to the officers. The job of chief of police is a political appointment, intended to send messages to various constituents. Therefore, it is significant that the new chief is an African American. It is significant that he has been with the L.A.P.D. for over thirty years. It is significant that he favors a more proactive policing style. It remains to be seen how this will impact the department, but many are hopeful.

This twenty-one-year study has gone beyond the more obvious aspects of the job, to the other side, to the part that is less well known and more difficult for officers to express, revealing many of the negatives. Yet, clearly there is another even more compelling side of the job. Police officers, for all that may appear to be a steady medley of complaint, injury and disillusion, love their job. They often comment on the job as being the best thing that has happened to them in their lives. It *is* exciting, and it does provide an opportunity to make a difference—for the better—in the lives of other human beings. They see themselves as doing an important and honorable job. They believe in and are committed to their job. The values of caring, commitment and standing for something they believe in are recurring motifs in police descriptions of the job. One officer said:

> You know how good it feels when you can help someone just find an address, or locate a service they need? Just a small thing like that? Well, magnify that a thousand times, we get to do that every day, and there isn't anything that feels that good. You really can make a difference in just the day-to-day small stuff to the really important life-changing stuff. Every day. It's a great job.

References

Agar, Michael H. 1980. *The Professional Stranger.* San Diego: Academic Press.

Alpert, Geoffrey P. and Roger G. Dunham. 1997. *Policing Urban America*, Third Edition. Prospect Heights, IL: Waveland Press.

Baker, Mark. 1985. *Cops: Their Lives in Their Own Words.* New York: Simon and Schuster.

Banton, Michael. 1964. *The Policeman in the Community.* New York: Basic Books.

Barker, Joan. 1991. "Danger, Duty and Daily Life: Phases in the Career of Urban Patrol Officers." Ph.D dissertation, University of California, Los Angeles.

_____. 1993. "Shades of Blue: Female and Male Perspectives on Policing." In *The Other Fifty Percent: Multicultural Perspectives on Gender Relations.* Mari Womack, and Judith Marti, eds., pp. 349–60. Prospect Heights, IL: Waveland Press.

Bent, Alan Edward. 1974. *The Politics of Law Enforcement.* Lexington: Lexington Books.

Berger, Peter L. and Thomas Luckmann. 1966. *The Social Construction of Reality.* New York: Doubleday and Company.

Bittner, Egon. 1980. "The Functions of Police in Modern Society." In *The Functions of the Modern Society.* Cambridge, MA: Olegeschlager, Gunn, & Hann.

_____. 1983. "Legality and Workmanship: Introduction to Control in the Police Organization." In *Control in the Police Organization*, M. Punch, ed., pp. 1–11. Cambridge: The MIT Press.

_____. 1990. *Aspects of Police Work.* Boston: Northeastern University Press.

Black, Donald. 1980. *The Manners and Customs of the Police.* New York: Academic Press.

Blumer, Herbert. 1969. *Symbolic Interactionism: Perspective and Method.* Englewood Cliffs, NJ: Prentice Hall.

Bohannan, Paul and Dirk van der Elst. 1998. *Asking and Listening: Ethnography as Personal Adaptation.* Prospect Heights, IL: Waveland Press.

Bordua, David J., ed. 1967. *The Police: Six Sociological Essays.* New York: John Wiley and Sons.

Buckner, Hubbard T. 1967. "The Police: The Culture of a Social Control Agency." Ph.D dissertation, University of California, Berkeley.

Davis, Kenneth C. 1975. *Police Discretion.* St. Paul: West.

Easterday, Lois, Diana Papademas, Laura Schorr, and Catherine Valentine. 1977. "The Making of a Female Researcher: Role Problems in Field Work." *Urban Life*, 6(3): 333–48.

Edgerton, Robert B. 1985. *Rules, Exceptions, and Social Order.* Los Angeles: University of California Press.

Emerson, Robert M., ed. 1983. *Contemporary Field Research*. Boston: Little Brown and Company.

Fogelson, Robert M. 1977. *Big-City Police*. Cambridge: Harvard University Press.

Goffman, Erving. 1959. *Presentation of Self in Everyday Life*. New York: Doubleday.

Goldschmidt, Walter. 1990. *The Human Career: The Self in the Symbolic World*. Cambridge: Basil Blackwell.

Harris, Richard N. 1973. *The Police Academy: An Inside View*. New York: John Wiley and Sons.

Keiser, R. Lincoln. 1969. *The Vice Lords: Warriors of the Streets*. New York: Holt, Rinehart and Winston.

Klockars, Carl B. 1980. "The Dirty Harry Problem." *The Annals*, 452 (November): 33–47. In *Moral Issues In Police Work*, Frederick A. Elliston and Michael Feldberg, eds. Totowa, NJ: Rowman and Allanheld, Publishers.

_____. 1983. *Thinking About Police*. New York: McGraw Hill.

_____. 1985 *The Idea of the Police*. Beverly Hills: Sage Publications.

La Fave, Wayne R. 1965. *Arrest: The Decision to Take a Suspect into Custody*. Boston: Little Brown and Company.

Lee, Richard Borshay. 1969. "Eating Christmas in the Kalahari." Originally published as "A Naturalist at Large: Eating Christmas in the Kalahari." *Natural History*, 78(10). In *Conformity and Conflict*. James P. Spradley and David W. McCurdy, eds. Boston: Little Brown and Company.

Manning, Peter K. 1998. *Police Work: The Social Organization of Policing*, Second Edition. Prospect Heights, IL: Waveland Press.

Manning, Peter K. and John Van Maanen, eds. 1978. *Policing: A View from the Street*. Santa Monica, CA: Goodyear Press.

Mead, George Herbert. 1934. *Mind, Self and Society*. Chicago: University of Chicago Press.

McNamara, John Harold. 1967. "Role Learning for Police Recruits; Some Problems in the Process of Preparation for the Uncertainties of Police Work." Ph.D. dissertation, University of California, Los Angeles.

Muir, William Ker, Jr. 1970. "The Development of Policemen." In *The Police Community*. Jack Goldsmith and Sharon S. Goldsmith, eds., pp. 197–224. Pacific Palisades, CA: Palisades Publications.

_____. 1977. *Police: Streetcorner Politicians*. Chicago: The University of Chicago Press.

Niederhoffer, Arthur. 1963. "A Study of Police Cynicism." Ph.D dissertation, New York University, New York, Sociology.

_____. 1967. *Behind the Shield: The Police in Urban Society*. New York: Doubleday and Company.

Niederhoffer, Arthur and Abraham S. Blumberg, eds. 1970. *The Ambivalent Force: Perspectives on the Police*. San Francisco: Rinehart Press.

Quinney, Richard ed. 1974. *Criminal Justice in America: A Critical Understanding*. Boston: Little Brown and Company.

Reiss, Albert J., Jr. 1971. *The Police and the Public*. New Haven: Yale University Press.

Reuss-Ianni, Elizabeth. 1983. *Two Cultures of Policing: Street Cops and Management Cops*. New Brunswick, NJ: Transaction Books.

Richardson, James F. 1974. *Urban Police in the United States.* Port Washington: National University Publications, Kennikat Press.

Rubinstein, Jonathan. 1973. *City Police.* New York: Farrar, Straus, and Giroux.

Skolnick, Jerome. 1966. *Justice Without Trial.* New York: John Wiley and Sons.

Skolnick, Jerome and Thomas C. Gray, eds. 1975. *Police in America.* Boston: Little Brown and Company.

Spradley, James P. 1980. *Participant Observation.* San Francisco: Holt, Rinehart and Winston.

Spradley, James and David McCurdy. 1997. *Conformity and Conflict.* Reading, MA: Addison-Wesley Longman.

Stratton, John G. 1984. *Police Passages.* Manhattan Beach, CA: Glennon Publishing Company.

Van Maanen, John. 1973. "Observations on the Making of Policemen." *Human Organization,* 32(4): 407–18.

_____. 1974, "Kinsmen in Repose: Occupational Perspectives of Patrolmen." In *A View from the Street.* Peter K. Manning and John Van Maanen, eds., pp. 115–28. Santa Monica, CA: Goodyear Publishing.

_____. 1975, "Police Socialization: A Longitudinal Examination of Job Attitudes in an Urban Police Department." *Administrative Science Quarterly,* 20 (June): 207–28.

_____. 1977. *Organizational Careers: Some New Perspectives.* New York: John Wiley and Sons.

_____. 1984. "Making Rank: Becoming an American Police Sergeant." *Urban Life,* 13(2–3): 155–76.

Viano, Emilio C., and Jeffrey H. Reiman, eds. 1975. *The Police in Society.* Lexington, MA: Lexington Books.

Wambaugh, Joseph. 1970. *The New Centurions.* Boston: Little Brown and Company.

_____. 1972. *The Blue Knight.* Boston: Little Brown and Company.

_____. 1973. *The Onion Field.* Boston: Little Brown and Company.

Wilson, James Q. 1963. "Police Authority in a Free Society." *Journal of Criminal Law,* 54:175–76.

_____. 1968. *Varieties of Police Behavior: The Management of Law and Order in Eight Communities.* Cambridge: Harvard University Press.

Wilson, James Q. and George Kelling. 1982. "Broken Windows," *Atlantic Monthly* (March). In Roger G. Dunham and Geoffrey P. Alpert, *Critical Issues in Policing: Contemporary Readings,* Third Edition, pp. 438–50. Prospect Heights, IL: Waveland Press.

Womack, Mari and Joan Barker. 1993. "Adventures in the Field and in the Locker Room." In *The Other Fifty Percent: Multicultural Perspectives on Gender Relations.* Mari Womack and Judith Marti, eds, pp. 99–111. Prospect Heights, IL: Waveland Press.

Study Guide

prepared by Dorothy H. Bracey
John Jay College of Criminal Justice

Anthropologists traditionally have studied small communities that are either geographically isolated or else culturally distinct from the people around them. In this book, Joan Barker uses the concepts and methods of anthropology to study the Los Angeles Police Department, an "occupational subculture." She has spent twenty years studying how recruits learn to assume the identity of "police officer" and how their values and behaviors change over the course of their career.

A subculture is a group whose members share much of the surrounding culture but also have some beliefs, symbols, values, and behaviors unique to the group. Identify some other subcultures in the United States. How much of its culture has to be unique before a group can qualify as a subculture?

Individuals change, but so do institutions and cultures. One of the main differences between "living" cultures—studied by social and cultural anthropologists—and "dead" cultures—studied by archeologists and historians—is that the former are constantly changing in response to internal and external forces. Changes in the L.A.P.D. provide an important context for this book.

Page xi

"Socialization" is the term social scientists use to describe the process by which individuals learn the culture of the groups to which they belong. Socialization starts in infancy, as babies are gradually transformed into adult members of their culture, but socialization does not stop at adulthood. Changes in status and group membership, as well as in the culture itself, call for more socialization. Have you gone through a socialization process recently? Can you predict socialization processes waiting for you in the next few years?

Page xii

Both police and anthropologists use the term "informant" to describe someone who gives them information. Police informants share information about criminal activity, while anthropological informants help anthropologists understand the cultures they are studying. What are some of the factors involved in choosing informants and evaluating the information they give? Are these factors similar for police and anthropologists?

Page 5

Prior to 1980, female police officers performed tasks that were associated with the female role of the time—tasks involving work with women and children or some version of clerical and secretarial work. Most cultures have a sexual division of labor, but the nature of that division varies widely. For example, among the Pueblo Indians weaving is considered men's work while the nearby Navajos reserve weaving for women. Have you encountered a sexual division of labor in other cultures you have studied? Can you describe it in the contemporary United States? How has it changed as the United States has gone from an agricultural to an industrial to a post-industrial economy? What other factors, such as war or depression, influence the sexual division of labor? What other types of division of labor can you identify?

Page 5

Police departments often resemble military organizations; both feature ranks, uniforms, and a hierarchical chain of command. But police work is essentially different from the work of the military. Soldiers work as units and are under the close supervision of their superiors; orders can be given to them at any moment. Police, on the other hand, usually work alone or in pairs, removed from the immediate supervision of their sergeants; they are constantly exercising discretion and judgment. Soldiers fight an enemy; police protect their fellow citizens. As you read the book, look for examples of the tension produced by imposing a paramilitary organization on an organization that mostly performs nonmilitary functions.

Page 15

A woman in a business suit would look out of place in an athletic field filled by teenagers in blue jeans and T-shirts, but she probably would not attract the attention of the police. What particular aspects of "looking out of place" would the police be looking for? What cultural beliefs does that reflect?

Page 16

In U.S. police departments, members of management have reached their positions by moving up from the lower ranks. In some other countries, higher-ranking police officers are hired directly into management, often upon graduation from college or from similar positions in some other line of work. With what other hierarchical organizations are you familiar? How are the ranks filled in those organizations?

Page 20

Most of the cultures traditionally studied by anthropologists are homogeneous; i.e., members share the same beliefs, attitudes, and values. Barker is reminding us that Los Angeles is heterogeneous: it is composed of individuals and groups who think and behave in many different ways. How does this affect the work of the police? Barker suggests that Los Angeles is a cultural "salad bowl." What does she mean by this? Other people have suggested "stew" or "mosaic" as metaphors for our heterogeneous society. Do the different metaphors suggest different things about our culture?

Page 21

The fact that many parts of a culture are implicit means that members of a culture may not be conscious of things that influence their words and behavior. It may be easier for an outsider—such as an anthropologist—to identify those things than it is for an insider. Sometimes members of a culture disagree with the anthropologist's understanding of the implicit aspects of their culture. What could be some of the causes of such a disagreement?

Page 23

Barker describes two phases of her own socialization. As the daughter of a conventional white family, she was taught to trust and rely upon the police. Later on, she became a member of groups with beliefs and behavior that differed from those of the larger society and she came to perceive the police who defended mainstream values as the opposition. There will be two more phases—as an anthropologist and as the wife of a police officer. Can you identify such phases in your own socialization?

Page 24

At one time, anthropologists felt that they—as social scientists—had to be neutral toward the cultures they studied, i.e., they had to be free of emotional involvement or value judgments. Later generations have wondered if this is desirable or even possible. Anthropologists tend to study one culture rather than another because something about that culture appeals to them; after all, why choose to spend long periods of one's life immersed in a culture that leaves one emotionally cold? Barker describes how she became "hooked" on studying the police after her first contact in a bar. As fieldwork goes on and the anthropologist comes to understand the values, beliefs, and perceptions that guide previously mysterious behavior, it is natural to become more sympathetic. Fieldwork also means coming to know individuals; those who were once mere statuses—chief, elder, basketmaker, cop—become flesh-and-blood people, people who are sometimes irritating and frustrating, but often welcoming and endearing, people who are struggling as best they can with the problems that life has presented to them. At other times, fieldwork may invoke negative responses. For example, it is probably harder to remain neutral after actually seeing female genital mutilation than after reading about it; to remain objective in these circumstances may require a detachment that is less than human. Does sympathy in these circumstances necessarily result in bias or can it enhance fieldwork? What can a fieldworker do to ensure that emotional involvement or bias is not slanting his or her work?

Page 23–24

Although all fieldworkers are exposed to the problems of objectivity in one form or another, Barker is in an unusual position—during the course of her research, she married one of her informants. Is this just one more source of potential bias or is it qualitatively different from the factors discussed above? What are the pluses and minuses of studying a group of which you are a member or to which you are related?

Page 26

How do anthropologists know if the people they meet are "representative" of the group being studied? What does "representative" mean? Is it the same as "typical"? Of what groups are you representative or typical? Any? Discuss this with a group of your classmates.

Page 27

Socialization is an ongoing process. Not only do newcomers to the group have to learn its values, beliefs, and behaviors, this knowledge has to be reinforced in older members. The informal scenes that Barker refers to here are a common way of doing both.

Page 28

"Cynicism, "suspicion" and "clannishness"—are these words descriptions or value judgments? Is it unusual for a group to react negatively when an outsider tries to penetrate it? What other words might Barker have used here?

Page 29

Have you encountered any groups that seemed to be homogeneous until you got to know its members as individuals?

Page 31

Many police officers changed their attitudes when Barker went from being an interested observer to being a researcher. What is the difference between the two? Why would the police officers react negatively toward the change?

Page 33

When was the last time that you asked or were asked an inappropriate question? What made it inappropriate?

Page 34

What do you think of Barker's discussion of the implications of her gender in her fieldwork?

Page 34

Discuss the phenomenon of "groupies." Do you think that there are "police groupies"? Why or why not? What other occupations might attract groupies?

Page 38

At the end of this page, Barker describes her own socialization into aspects of the police culture. She feels that this experience makes it easier for her to understand the transformation that takes place in the lives of police officers. This is called "experiential learning" and has been considered an important advantage of "participant observation," the fieldwork method that calls for researchers to take part in the lives of the people they study. Compare it to learning through interviews, survey, or simple observation. What are its disadvantages?

Page 41

What image of police officers do you have in your own mind right now? Write it out as fully as you can and put the paper away. Take it out again when you have finished this book and see if your image has changed.

Page 44

Barker talks about the role of the police uniform in creating an impression of homogeneity and obscuring individual personalities. The police uniform also represents authority and the right to use force. Clothes have important symbolic meaning in many cultures. The headdress of the Commanche chief and the turquoise jewelry of the Navajo herder, the long robe of the Chinese scholar and the silver-buttoned suit of the Mexican mariachi all convey messages to the observer in addition to any utilitarian benefit they may have. What other occupations require clothes with symbolic meaning? Do the clothes you are wearing right now say anything about you as an individual or as a group member?

Page 45

The second quote is an excellent description of *socialization*. The officer understands it to mean that one must not only learn to behave appropriately, but also to see and think appropriately.

Page 51

Quotas are one way in which management can exert control over patrol officers, even though most of a patrol shift is spent out of the sight of management. Watch for other examples of such control.

Page 53

What does the author mean when she says that danger plays a "metaphorical role" in officers' expression of frustration?

Page 54

Think of other instances of people in different ranks or statuses viewing the same situation differently.

Page 60

An "age grade" is a group of people who enter a new status together and who progress together through all the subsequent stages. Other members of the culture may rank individuals and decide how much deference to show them according to their age grade. Look for signs of age grading as Barker describes the phases of the police career. Do other cultures you have studied make use of age grading? What about institutions or subcultures within your own culture?

Page 67

A ceremony or event that marks a person's change from one status to another is called a "rite of passage." Often such rites include tests of one sort or another; passing the test proves that the initiate is worthy of the new status. The rigorous physical training of the traditional police resembles such a rite. Because the new police do not have to pass these tests, the traditional officers are free to wonder if they really deserve the change of status from recruit to police officer.

Many rites of passage do not include tests; weddings and funerals in our culture are examples. List other examples of rites of passage that do or do not include tests.

Page 90

Are there other occupations that call for "command presence"? Have you noticed it in other cultures you have studied? Can people who are not large or tall display command presence in other ways?

Page 72

What else encourages police to rely primarily on each other? What other groups in U.S. society rely primarily on each other and distrust outsiders? What factors encourage this? Do all groups distrust nonmembers under some circumstances?

Pages 76–77

The graduation ceremony from the academy is a rite of passage, marking the change from recruit to police officer. Your high school graduation was a rite of passage also. What do they have in common?

Page 77

"Fictive kinship" is the custom of calling nonrelatives by kinship terms and acting as if an actual kinship relationship exists. In some cultures, fictive kinship is a formal institution, not to be undertaken lightly. If a woman calls me "daughter," her husband becomes my father and her children my brothers and sisters; we all have the rights and obligations of true relatives. In our culture, godparenthood is the closest we come to such formal relationships, but there are other circumstances in which we use kinship terms to indicate a relationship stronger than friendship or collegiality. It is in this sense that the police talk about "the family" or "brotherhood." Can you think of other examples?

Page 78

Police prefer to work according to known statistical probabilities; for example, a traffic stop involving a young male is more likely to be dangerous than a traffic stop involving an elderly female. But the law, based on the U.S. concept that each person must be treated as an individual and not as a member of a group, demands that each be treated the same way. Police feel frustrated by the conflict between the larger culture's values and the teachings of the police culture. These conflicts between mainstream culture and its subcultures are what makes life in a heterogeneous society more complex than in a homogeneous one.

Page 81

In most cultures, the proper action is the expected action. In fact, it may be possible to say that one of the functions of culture is to decrease unpredictable actions among its members. Perhaps most people feel that life presents them with enough surprises—pleasant and unpleasant—so that predictability on the part of one's colleagues is a welcome energy-saver.

Pages 81–82

All cultures use stories as a way of teaching. Fables, parables, legends, fairy tales, anecdotes, narratives, plays, movies, sitcoms, and soap operas are all ways of conveying morals and experience. Knowing the same stories strengthens the bonds of group members and not knowing the stories makes one aware of being an outsider. Share some experiences you have had with stories.

Page 82

A "jacket" is a term police use for "reputation." Language is another way in which cultures and subcultures draw their boundaries. Many subcultures have a slang or argot consisting of words known to them and, they assume, unknown to outsiders. Even when outsiders do know the words, it is considered bad form to use them until one has become a member of the group.

Page 85

Labor unions and other groups have fought hard to ensure employees paid leave to recover from illness and injury. The values of the police subculture dictate that its members not take advantage of this benefit. Are you beginning to understand the nature of a subculture?

Page 105

Geography is of great interest to anthropologists. Where and with whom people live tells us a great deal about them. Medieval European cities often had areas composed solely of members of one occupation; they might also have areas mandated for minorities, such as Jewish ghettos. Barker describes a process by which young police officers, scattered over a large area, move so that they live outside the city they police and in communities populated largely by police officers and others in similar occupations. What other groups make an effort to live in homogeneous communities? Do police live in police communities because they want to or because they are forced to? How can you tell?

Page 106–7

What is a "community of sentiment"?

Page 108

"Terms of address" are the words we use when we talk to another person. We may refer to someone as "my father" or "the old man" but address him as "Dad," "Pop," or "Pa." When we use a term of address not used by the community at large, we assert a special relationship. When members of a group use such terms for each other, they are claiming special relationships within the group.

Page 111

When a young person is attached to an older member of the group for the purpose of learning, the younger one is often called an apprentice. This is another way in which culture is transmitted from one generation to the next. What are others?

Page 132

A stigma is a mark of disgrace, a stain on one's character.

Page 133

Always "being there" for a fellow officer is one of the values that distinguish the police subculture. What other values of this subculture have you discovered?

Page 147

We have noted some of the ways in which culture is passed from one generation to the next. Formal education is another method, but it is often distrusted, especially by those members of a culture who have not been exposed to it. How is formal education different from apprenticeship, learning from role models, or listening to stories?

Page 154

All cultures have some way of marking the death of their members. In addition to the funerals mentioned elsewhere, the L.A.P.D. uses roll call to remember the dead. These are also rites of passage. How do they resemble the others you have discussed?

Page 156

People who embody the values and approved behavior of their cultures as they grow older become elders, people who no longer have anything to prove. Elders contain the wisdom of their culture and often exert a moderating force on the rashness of the young. They provide perspective. How does this apply to the L.A.P.D.? Does the concept of age grades have any relevance?

Page 164

Here we have another rite of passage—one marking the change from active status to retirement. There are two parts to the ritual; can you identify them? What are the differences? Both parts are occasions to show respect for the retiring officer and to laud the retiree as a role model for younger members of the force. There are also opportunities for other types of learning. Note the comparison to funerals—what are their similarities?

Pages 166–68

Barker talks about the difficulties of retirees. She suggests that for many officers the process of socialization—of turning citizens into police—is so successful that the retirement process of turning police back into civilians is unsuccessful. Could you design a more powerful "un-socialization" method? Why doesn't the L.A.P.D. have such a method?

Page 168

Fred's story is what anthropologists refer to as a "life history." This takes the form of an individual telling the story of his life in his own words. The resulting document often seems rambling and has moments of stream of consciousness, for the informant is encouraged to talk about memories, feelings, and emotions as well as facts and events.

Choosing an informant for a life history raises the issues of "typical" or "representative" that we discussed earlier. Remember that the anthropologist does not simply choose the person who strikes him or her as the most suitable. Many people will not want to devote the time and effort necessary for such an endeavor, nor will they want to share their intimate thoughts and emotions. What would make a person volunteer or agree to provide a life history for the anthropologist? What must we be aware of as we read such a document?

Page 173

Fred talks movingly about the sense of pride he has in the job and in his colleagues. From what you have read, do you think this pride is shared by all members of the L.A.P.D. and that it is constant throughout an officer's career?

Pages 177–78

Fred obviously takes satisfaction in his role in providing ritual and pageantry for police funerals and in the police memorial. What functions do these things fill in the institutional culture and why do they figure so importantly in Fred's memories of his career?

Page 179

How is policing in a heterogeneous society affected by attitudes in the larger culture?

Page 180

What have you learned about police work in a heterogeneous society that helps you to understand the perception that police are racists?

Page 181

How does this compare with what the author says about phases four and five?

Page 182

Comment on Fred's use of the term "un-American" in this context.

Page 189

When Fred talks about lack of training, he is also talking about lack of socialization. How do they differ from each other and why is Fred bothered by the latter?

Page 194

Like most North Americans, when Fred uses the word "family" he is talking about the nuclear family—husband, wife, and their children. Have you learned about any other kinds of families? Would the "erosion of the nuclear family" have different effects in other types of kinship systems? What provisions for childcare and economic support do other systems provide? Why does the United States rely so heavily on the nuclear family as the economic and child-raising unit? Is this changing? If so, how?

Page 195

Fred perceives the ideal nuclear family as one with a rigid sexual division of labor and roles strictly defined by gender. He suggests that he would have been equally happy as part of a childless two-career family. Do you believe him?

Page 201

Fred appears resigned to social change, in part because so many of the bad things he anticipated did not happen. Ask some people of your grandparents' generation for stories of social change and try to tell if they are optimistic, pessimistic, or resigned.

Page 204

Anthropologists sometimes talk about the "ideal" culture—the way things should be done—versus the "real" culture—the way they actually are done. In the police department, training involves learning the ideal culture, while socialization involves learning the real one as well. Have you had experiences with differences between the real and ideal culture? Is teaching about the ideal culture mere hypocrisy or does it serve some other function?

Page 208

The author deplores the lack of bonding and solidarity among new officers. Can you think of any positive aspects of their attitudes toward the job and toward each other?